READING
CONNECTIONS

SKILLS AND STRATEGIES FOR PURPOSEFUL READING

HIGH INTERMEDIATE

ANNE EDIGER and CHERYL PAVLIK

D1410027

OXFORD

Oxford University Press
198 Madison Avenue
New York, NY 10016 USA

Great Clarendon Street
Oxford OX2 6DP England

Oxford New York

Athens Auckland Bangkok Bogota Buenos Aires
Calcutta Cape Town Chennai Dar es Salaam
Delhi Florence Hong Kong Istanbul Karachi
Kuala Lumpur Madrid Melbourne Mexico City
Mumbai Nairobi Paris São Paulo Singapore
Taipei Tokyo Toronto Warsaw

and associated companies in
Berlin Ibadan

OXFORD is a trademark of Oxford University Press.

ISBN 0-19-435826-7

Editorial Manager: Susan Lanzano
Senior Acquisitions Editor: Janet Aitchison
Editor: Robin N. Longshaw
Production Editor: Janice L. Baillie
Editorial Assistants: Katharine Chandler and Justin Hartung
Design Manager: Lynne M. Torrey
Designer: Mark C. Kellogg
Interior Book Design: Shelley Himmelstein, Inc.
Art Buyer: Stacy Godlesky

Library of Congress Cataloging-in-Publication Data
Ediger, Anne.
    Reading connections: skills and strategies for purposeful
    reading:high intermediate/
    Anne Ediger and Cheryl Pavlik.
        p.cm.
    Originally published: 1999.
    Includes bibliographical references.
    ISBN-019-435826-7
    1. English language--Textbooks for foreign speakers. 2.
    Readers. I. Pavlik, Cheryl,1949-II. Title.

PE1128 .E348 2000b
428.6'4--dc21
                                        00-051661

Printing (last digit): 10 9 8 7 6 5 4 3

Printed in Hong Kong.

Acknowledgments

Illustrations and realia by Alan Barnett, Inc., Uldis Klavins, Moth
Designs, Nina Wallace

Cover design by Mark C. Kellogg
Cover photo: Brian Pieters/Masterfile

*The publishers would like to thank the following for their
permission to reproduce photographs:* Wolfgang Kaehler, Corbis;
Kazu Studio Ltd., Adam Smith, FPG International; H. Armstrong
Roberts; James Schnepe, Liaison International; Chris Lee; K.
Chiang, R. Dahlquist, R. Llewellyn, Museo Del Prado, National
Gallery, Oslo, Norway, K. Zikomo/Superstock; Philip Bailey, Paul
Barton, Peter Beck, Tibor Bognar, Thomas H. Brakefield,
DiMaggio/Kalish, Brownie Harris, Thomas H. Ives, Don Mason,
Roy Morsch, Tom and Dee Ann McCarthy, Evan Myles, Gabe
Palmer/Mugshots, Claudia Parks, Jose Pelaez, Grafton Marshall
Smith, Torleif Svensson, Dan Tardif/The Stock Market; Karina
Lopez/Warner Books

*The publishers would also like to thank the following companies
for their permission to reproduce advertisements:* The American
Cancer Society; Eurail; Gardenburger; Maxell Corporation of
America; Radisson Hotels International, Inc.; Toyota (Lake shot
courtesy of Uniphoto West); Volkswagen of America, Inc.

Acknowledgments

We would like to thank all those at Oxford University Press who made this book possible, especially Janet Aitchison, Acquisitions Editor, and Robin Longshaw, our editor. We are also indebted to Justin Hartung and Katharine Chandler for their help with the often arduous permissions process.

Our heartfelt thanks also go out to Julie Landau and Susan Lanzano, who provided invaluable help and support during the conceptualization of the project.

We would also like to acknowledge our reviewers for their valuable comments and suggestions in developing this series. In particular, we wish to thank:

Roberta Alexander (San Diego City College)

Patricia Brenner

Linda Britton

Andy Cavanaugh (Maryland English Institute)

Gaye Childress (University of North Texas)

Byung-Eun Cho (Sung Kong Hoe University, Seoul, Korea)

Dr. Chung-tien Chou (National Taiwan Normal University, Taipei City, Taiwan)

Teresa Bruner Cox (Soai University, Osaka)

Kathy Flynn (Glendale Community College, California)

Cathy Garcia-Hill (Suffolk Community College, New York)

Jeffrey Grill

Lori Harrilla

Margaret Haynes (Delta College, Iowa)

Patty Heiser (University of Washington)

Cindy Hewitt (University of Tampa)

Carolyn Heacock (University of Kansas)

Pamela Kennedy (Holyoke Community College, Massachusetts)

Chuong Bae Kim (Korea University)

Julia Klein (Tunghai University, Taichung, Taiwan)

Javier E. Macuaga (Athenée Français, Tokyo)

Jean Martone (University of Washington)

Blanca Moss (El Paso Community College)

Denise Mussman (University of Missouri at St. Louis)

Elizabeth Neblett (Union County College, New Jersey)

Eugene Parulis (Community College of Vermont/World Learning, Inc.)

Peg Sarosy (San Francisco State University)

Kathy Sherak (San Francisco State University)

Barbara Smith-Palinkas

Stephanie Snider (Suffolk Community College, New York)

Amy Stotts-Ali (Tunghai University, Taichung, Taiwan)

Christine Tierney (Houston Community College, Texas)

Julie Un (Massasoit Community College, Massachusetts)

This book is dedicated to the memory of my father, Ferdinand Ediger, the first EFL teacher I ever knew. He was my first model as a teacher and my greatest model for life.

—AE

I would like to dedicate this book to my students of the past 25 years, who have taught me more about language learning than any book I've ever read, or any course that I have ever taken.

—CP

CONTENTS

INTRODUCTION

TO THE TEACHER

SERIES OVERVIEW

Reading Connections is a two-volume Intermediate to High-Intermediate ESL reading series that teaches students active reading skills. It is for people studying to enter a college or university in an English-speaking country, for those studying to further their careers, as well as for those who simply want to be able to communicate more effectively.

Each of the two books in the series contains a Preview Unit, which introduces students to basic concepts in reading more effectively, and four main units, each of which focuses on a different high-interest theme. Within each unit, an authentic purpose for reading is first set up, and then a variety of readings and exercises provide information and develop skills that will help students accomplish this purpose. In each unit, students integrate and synthesize the information from the readings and apply it to their task.

Although the series is intended primarily for ESL reading courses, it may also be used in courses where writing is taught as well. Many of the Unit Tasks may be either oral or written activities, and the series may be viewed as the core component in a reading-to-write approach to the teaching of academic literacy skills. Additional suggestions for each of these options is provided below under Classroom Strategies.

READING FOR A PURPOSE: A RATIONALE

When people read in the real world (in academic, business, or other contexts), a large part of the time they do not read simply for the sake of reading (although they do this when they read for pleasure). Most of the time they are required to use their reading skills in order to accomplish some purpose. For example, people use different reading styles when they want to:

- find out a departure time and cost by scanning a timetable or brochure
- prepare to take a test or write a research paper in a college or university class by reading large amounts of material
- set up a new computer or other piece of electronic equipment by reading the manual
- write (or present orally) a business proposal for a course of action in some area of their jobs by reading, analyzing, and synthesizing company materials

In these kinds of reading, readers typically start out with an issue, a topic, an argument, or a hypothesis that is tied to their purpose, be it making a presentation, making a decision, confirming or rejecting a hypothesis, presenting research findings, or analyzing and then producing a better product. In order to find the necessary information, readers generally search through a variety of material (or it is presented to them by a supervisor as company documents, or by an instructor as lectures and textbook readings).

Usually, in the process of searching for this information, readers collect a number of texts and skim them quickly for anything related to their purpose in each text. Sometimes readers find that a text is broadly related but irrelevant to the specific need at hand; sometimes the material is only partly relevant; and sometimes it is exactly on the topic. However, until they skim reading material, readers may not know how useful it is. Occasionally, readers must go back and forth, searching for something that is relevant. Sometimes the material they find is very difficult to understand, and they must decide if it is worth wading through the tough, unfamiliar content, possibly even skipping sections, in the quest for the small bits of truly useful information. Generally, the result is that far more material is read than is actually useful for their task. Thus, readers must constantly ask themselves if the information is relevant or helpful to their purpose.

In academic reading, a reader needs to use a variety of strategies and skills. These include skimming material, scanning for useful information, and making inferences. As a result, not all of the information available is read or utilized equally. Readers must constantly monitor their comprehension of what they read and evaluate how they need to read it, as well as which strategy to use when reading.

Thus, rather than focusing on reading for the purpose of learning grammar, vocabulary, and idioms in English, or even for practicing different reading skills, this book approaches reading as it is done in the real world. It provides learners with a specific purpose and a collection of readings that will help them accomplish it. This purpose then guides them toward reading for true meaning and understanding. Along the way, they are given many opportunities to develop reading sub-skills as support for meaning-making—so that they will be able to follow signaling words; make inferences; deal with words they don't understand; alternate between skimming, scanning, and other techniques; or appropriately use prediction.

In this series, students are also taught to be critical, active, and independent readers. This means helping students become more aware of what happens when they read, including understanding that reading is not a passive process—information does not merely flow in one direction from the page to the reader's brain. Students are taught to interact with text and to bring their own questions, ideas, and analyses to their reading, as well as learning strategies for understanding more and reading faster. In addition, after skills and strategies are taught, the amount of assistance is gradually decreased, encouraging students to try to use the skills on their own. This teaches students (and the teacher) to gradually perform the skills without assistance, so that they will continue applying these skills even after their reading course is finished.

In many cases, students will find this approach quite new. It is important to explain why this approach is being taken, and to assure them that this way of reading works.

HOW THE SERIES IS ORGANIZED

To simulate the sort of reading required in content-area courses and real life environments, this book is organized into four broad themes (one in each unit) with six to eight related readings on each topic. Each collection of readings approximates what students might find in a textbook on a single subject area, in a collection of articles, or in a group of other documents. There are several reasons for including a large number of readings:

• They resemble authentic reading tasks encountered by students in content-based courses at the college/university level and in business.

• The numerous articles/readings on a single topic help students gradually develop topic-related and sub-technical vocabulary and other related language skills necessary for handling the oral and written discussion of an issue.

• They provide a substantial body of informational content that must be understood, weighed, and synthesized, just as real tasks require. In addition, different students can select somewhat different material on which to focus. Students must utilize their critical thinking skills to justify their choices.

• They bring together reading material from a variety of genres, in order to help students become familiar with the different writing styles and patterns, typical language usage, methods of organization, formats, and presentation of information that characterize each of these genres. Because the readings come from a variety of genres, they will not all have the same format or even difficulty level (though they have been roughly tuned to the same level); students need to learn and use strategies to deal with the specific problems that each reading presents along the way.

CLASSROOM STRATEGIES

Unit Format

Each of the units has the following general format:

Introduction to the Unit
 Looking Ahead in the Unit
 The Unit Task

Part A: Focus on Skills
 Reading 1
 Reading 2 (Note: Unit 1 includes Reading 3
 in this section as well)

Part B: Focus on Reading for a Purpose
 The Unit Task
 Pre-Step: Identify the Information You Need
 Reading 3
 Reading 4
 Reading 5
 Reading 6

Part C: Doing the Unit Task
 Building Your Vocabulary: Summary

Part D: Expansion Activities
 Applying Your Knowledge
 The Electronic Link
 For More Information
 Essay Questions
 Evaluating Your Progress
 Setting Your Reading Goals

Unit Features

The Unit Task Each unit in the book covers a different theme and thus may stand alone. However, it is recommended that the units be covered in the order presented. This is because individual skills are taught in detail at the point where they are first introduced, and then they reappear with minimal explanation for additional practice (or as margin questions) in later readings.

Each unit (except for Unit 1, which introduces the concept) begins by establishing a purpose for reading that students will use to decide how they read, to determine the usefulness (or irrelevance) of what they are reading. After each reading, students are guided toward finding the key information that they will need to identify in a particular passage.

The students' attention is focused on the purpose for reading in three specific ways: 1) presentation of the Unit Task; 2) the exercises before and after each reading that check understanding of key concepts and focus on these crucial points; and 3) activities/exercises that require the reader to determine which of the information in each reading (if any) is relevant, and then that ask the student to do something (e.g., synthesize, conclude, decide, analyze, or apply) with the relevant information.

With several of the strategies/skills (e.g., Previewing, Finding Important Ideas), the student is given a great deal of assistance in earlier units, but then explicit instruction on those strategies is decreased. Since the material is geared toward building knowledge, reading, and language skills over the course of a unit and over the course of the book, teaching the units in sequence will ensure that students receive the maximum benefit from their use. However, it may be helpful to know where each strategy is first introduced (see the table of contents).

Skill Development With each passage, the students' attention is focused on comprehending so that they can accomplish their purpose. Lower-level and more specific reading skills and strategies are taught in context through each reading's Focus on Skills section. These help learners develop the sub-skills that underlie and facilitate the accomplishment of the larger goal, including various strategies for handling unknown vocabulary, skimming and scanning, predicting, making inferences, understanding organization, identifying cohesive ties and transition words, and activating background knowledge. Since the accomplishment of the larger purpose or task is of primary importance, the development of the sub-skills should be viewed as the *means* that facilitate this, not as the *end goal* of students' learning to read in English. In each exercise, the skill development is oriented toward understanding the broader content.

Exercises Accompanying Each Reading Each of the six readings in each unit has this basic format:

Pre-reading (Readings 1 & 2)
Preview/Read Closely (Readings 3–6)
The Reading
Checking Your Comprehension
Making Inferences (not in all readings)
Topics for Discussion
Reading Strategies
Strategies for Unknown Vocabulary
Note Useful Information
Building Your Vocabulary
Writing Your Ideas
Making Connections (not in all readings)

The Treatment of Unknown Vocabulary The handling of unknown vocabulary is one of the most troublesome aspects of reading for second or foreign language readers. Typically, nonfluent readers want to look up every unknown word; otherwise, they often feel they are unable to understand any of what they are reading. Unfortunately, this constant use of a dictionary detracts from the meaningful comprehension of what is read, and forces students into a word-by-word reading style quite contrary to the type of academic reading they will need in the future. Thus, the development of strategies for reading and synthesizing large amounts of text has been given prominent focus in this series.

There is also now much evidence from reading research that the development of new vocabulary is best accomplished through *extensive* (as opposed to *intensive*) reading and through extended contact with the written language. Thus, while the development of specific vocabulary is given a relatively small role in this book, a great deal of attention is paid to more broadly applicable vocabulary development skills. These include looking for patterns among related words, analyzing word parts, and identifying related word forms and word families. At the same time, students and teachers are encouraged to use any and all techniques available to them to learn new vocabulary, and students are encouraged to share with their classmates their own strategies. Since different students tend to need to learn different vocabulary,

each student is encouraged to develop his or her own list of new vocabulary, and each unit includes suggestions for identifying, practicing, and remembering these new words.

Suggestions for Teaching

The Unit Task Except for Unit 1 (where it comes after Reading 3), each unit begins by presenting a Unit Task that the students will accomplish. Because it sets up the overall purpose for reading in each unit, the Unit Task should be focused on carefully in class at the beginning (except in Unit 1). As the class progresses through the unit from reading to reading, it is also important to bring the class' attention back to this task/purpose repeatedly. An important role of the teacher here is to help students learn how to identify which information will be useful for accomplishing their purpose.

There are several options for performing each Unit Task. The class may debate an issue (in a formal or informal oral debate), be asked to reach a consensus through discussion, make oral presentations, or write a paper presenting their analysis/synthesis. Also, students may be asked to do the task individually, in pairs, or in small groups.

After being given the Unit Task, students are asked to predict the kinds of information they will need to find in order to accomplish the task, and where they think they will find it. Instead of thinking in terms of "right" or "wrong," teachers are encouraged to guide students toward "reasonable" and away from "unreasonable" predictions. Then, after completing the readings, students should go back and review the predictions they originally made to see if they have any new insights on which information will be useful for the task. This is a good time to discuss where and why their predictions may have been made. The ultimate goal of these exercises is to teach students to create and revise their own predictions.

Previewing (Pre-Reading) Exercises Before reading a text, students are asked to answer a series of questions designed to prepare them for the reading and to improve their understanding.

Some of the important skills include:
- identifying the general topic of a reading
- determining what general knowledge they already have on this topic
- learning what the format of a text can tell them about how information will be presented or organized in the text
- understanding how a particular genre or source of a reading can influence their understanding

However, instead of providing previewing questions, this text teaches students how to preview texts by themselves. The teacher's goal should be to teach students the skills of pre-reading and predicting so that they will be able to do them on their own after their reading course is finished. After teaching students to preview at the beginning of the book, they are encouraged to do it on their own as they progress through the units. By the last unit students are only given brief reminders about what they need to do before reading.

Margin Questions The margin questions accompanying most of the readings are not used the first time a passage is read. Instead, students should first try to read a passage on their own at least once, and then, go through the passage again, making use of the questions in the margins. The margin questions are thus intended to serve several purposes. First, they focus the students' attention on key content issues that each particular reading presents. Second, they recycle skills and strategies. Third, they model for students how they should be reading and provide clues and hints on how to do this. Students should be urged to read each passage several times (as needed).

Checking Your Comprehension The exercises and activities in this section are not intended to be a comprehensive nor detailed check of a student's comprehension of a reading. Instead, they are in most cases a general comprehension check, focused on the key ideas in a reading. True comprehension of the parts of the reading that contribute useful information toward accomplishing the Unit Task will actually come later, when students synthesize what they have read.

Topics for Discussion These are optional questions that push students to express their own ideas on issues raised in the readings. They are not intended to be comprehension questions, but "thinking questions" that grow naturally out of a reading and which require students to make use of vocabulary and information presented in the reading while engaging in critical thinking about what they have read. These may also be used as topics for written journal entries or compositions (either after or instead of oral discussions).

Reading Strategies After most of the readings, several reading-strategy teaching points and related practice exercises are provided. These exercises teach students key skills and strategies for making sense of what they read and for finding the information they need for the task. These strategies range from identifying important ideas, learning how examples support generalizations, or understanding how texts are organized, to learning to make inferences. When they focus students' attention on main ideas, these exercises avoid a common misconception that all readings have a single main idea, teaching students rather that in any passage, different kinds of information are of relative importance, and that they need to identify the difference. Students are also taught that the information that an author may consider to be important may not be the information that they will find most useful for their purpose. Thus, these two different ways of identifying "important" information need to be distinguished and understood separately.

Strategies for Unknown Vocabulary After most readings, there are several exercises that help students deal with unknown words they encounter. These exercises encourage students to develop strategies that they can use *as* they are reading. These are intended to help students obtain meaning from what they read. In each case, they focus the students' attention on strategies that will be useful for that particular reading. Teachers should encourage students to think about and share with the class any other strategies they find useful for dealing with unknown words.

Building Your Vocabulary In this section, students are encouraged to build their own lists of vocabulary items that they want or need to learn (their personal vocabulary list), using the readings as a source of new words. Since each student's list will be slightly different, the teacher should check up on each student to see if he or she is indeed keeping up an up-to-date list and learning it. For this purpose, teachers may wish to develop different exercises or methods of assessment, including the following:

• Based upon a list that each student provides to the teacher, the teacher (or other students) makes up a number of sentences to be used as a quiz on those words.

• The class may (as a group) write sentences using words from all of their lists, and the teacher puts the sentences into a "sentence bank" from which quizzes are later made up.

• Groups of students may be asked to use their words in summaries of individual readings (or to answer some of the questions in the Writing Your Ideas section of each unit).

• The teacher may from time to time ask individual students to share with the class what strategies they use to remember specific new words. These may include various mnemonic devices, individual strategies (e.g., "The word sounds like ___ in my native language"), or other learning techniques a student may have used.

Writing Your Ideas These topics are provided as additional, optional activities that ask students to put their ideas into written form. These are good places for students to practice using some of their new vocabulary from their personal vocabulary lists. While these are presented in the form of written activities, they may also be used for oral discussions or as informal journal entry topics. Some of them may also lend themselves to paired writing activities, in which two students first discuss their responses orally, then write their ideas down collaboratively.

Making Connections These activities ask students to bring together or to compare the ideas from several of the readings they have done. In some cases, they even require students to go back to previous units to make these comparisons. These are also ways for students to recycle vocabulary.

Applying Your Knowledge: Expansion Activities, The Electronic Link, and Essay Questions These activities may be assigned as homework, with the students' findings later presented to the class, or they may be assigned as a follow-up activity to be performed by the whole class. They provide additional oral, written, and extensive reading activities to supplement those in the unit. The Electronic Link activities may also be used to supplement the thematic information of the units. Looking for and reading information on the Internet is an excellent way to motivate students and to provide them with extensive reading opportunities (particularly in programs or countries where additional printed reading materials are difficult to obtain). An interesting takeoff on this idea would be to establish an e-mail exchange with another class using *Reading Connections* as their text, to have students share their final Unit Task reports or findings.

Evaluating Your Progress These self-check activities focus students' attention on the specific skills that were presented in each unit, and ask students to rate their progress. This fits in with the overall aim of this book to teach students to take note of their own reading strategies, and to become more aware of how (and how well) they are reading. By collecting information on the areas that students are still having trouble on, teachers can determine which areas the class needs more practice in, and devise ways to practice them.

Additional Readings An appendix of additional readings has been provided to accompany each unit. These readings may be used in a variety of ways, including as additional resources for:

• assessing students' grasp of reading strategies, strategies for unknown vocabulary, or other skills learned in that unit by having students apply them to a related, but "new" text

• providing even more information for the Unit Task

• additional extensive reading on the same topic

• use with teachers' own exercises for more practice for specific strategies or skills

Class Work versus Homework

Because many of the activities in this text ask students to try to read in ways that may be new to them, teachers are advised to model in class the way such activities should be performed. Although some teachers feel that class time should not be spent on reading silently, it is precisely here that teachers can benefit from observing first-hand how their students are reading. Students will also benefit greatly from having their instructors model for them through a think-aloud procedure what is going on in the teacher's mind as he or she reads new material in English.

Certain activities should be done in class so that the teacher can be sure that the students start out in the right direction; likewise, steps in a process can be discussed, and students can compare their predictions and answers with other students. In particular, teachers are encouraged to introduce each new unit and Unit Task in class. Other activities that are recommended for in-class work include:

Predicting the Information You Will Need

Pre-reading & Previewing Exercises

Topics for Discussion

Reading Strategies and Strategies for
    Unknown Vocabulary (introduction)

Making Connections

A number of the exercise types lend themselves very well to being done as homework activities. These include:

Checking Your Comprehension

Exercises on Reading Strategies and Strategies
    for Unknown Vocabulary

Building Your Vocabulary

Writing Your Ideas

Applying Your Knowledge: Expansion Activities,
    The Electronic Link, Essay Questions

Using This Book in Different Classes

In reading classes This book can serve as the core text in a reading course, with speaking and writing activities based upon it. If a class meets only for an hour at a time, using this text by itself may be sufficient. If a class meets for several hours, the content of this book can be expanded by involving the entire class in some of the Expansion Activities suggested at the end of each unit.

In writing or combined reading/writing classes Many writing courses require students to read material that they are then required to critique or react to in writing. Because of the numerous writing activities built into each reading and each unit, and because of the high-interest readings included here, this text lends itself especially well to such an approach. Although specific, step-by-step writing instruction is not provided in this book, many of the activities ask the student to reflect on written text from both an author's and a reader's viewpoint. In other words, many of the reading and vocabulary strategy exercises focus students' attention on common writing issues such as text organization, main ideas, types of support for arguments, use of examples, use of transition words, common collocations, and so on. Specific writing instruction can easily be added, either through the use of an accompanying writing text, or by supplementing this text with individual writing activities and exercises compiled or developed by the teacher.

TO THE STUDENT

When you are reading for different purposes, you often collect information from a number of books, articles, and other sources. Often these books or articles cover topics that are broader than you need. Therefore, a large part of the job is to discover the articles, or the parts of articles and books that are the most relevant to the topic. You need to learn to find this information as quickly and easily as possible.

This textbook will introduce you to various skills and strategies that will help you select relevant materials for your topic and accomplish a specific purpose. Along the way, you will also learn skills and strategies for selecting materials, synthesizing information (putting it together from different sources), and presenting your work according to the stated purpose.

HOW YOU CAN BECOME A BETTER READER

Here are several things you can do to help yourself become a better reader in English:

• *Think Before You Read* Think carefully before you read. Don't just start reading. Before you begin, look at what you are reading and try to guess what it is going to be about.

• *Find the General Topic of the Reading* Think about what you already know about this topic. What have you heard about this subject before? Are there any pictures with the text? What are they about? Are any of the objects in the pictures familiar to you? Can you imagine something about this subject in your mind? Bring this information to the front of your mind as you read. Then compare the information in what you are reading to what you already know about the topic.

• *Think about Your Purpose in Reading* Use this purpose to decide if the information is useful, if you need to read more, or if you need to change the way you are reading. Don't worry if all of the information is not related or useful to your purpose. Don't worry about skipping some parts of the reading if they are not related to the purpose.

• *Don't Worry About Understanding the Exact Meaning of Every Word* Try to get a general idea of the meaning, using any techniques you can. Take a chance and try to be satisfied with a little bit of fuzziness in your understanding of new words. Later, think again about these words and ask yourself if you understand the meaning a little more clearly after reading a text.

• *Read a Passage More Than Once* Sometimes you will notice something the second time that you didn't see the first time. Each time you read, look for more information.

• *Ask Yourself Questions While You Read* Then look for the answers to these questions in the reading. If you can't find the answers, look again, or change your question, and *then* read again.

• *Question the Author While You Read* In other words, ask questions in your mind as you are reading. Do you agree with the author? Are you surprised by the information? Do you believe what the author is saying? (Remember: Just because it's in print, it isn't necessarily true.)

• *Try to Read as Much as You Can* Find a newspaper, a magazine, or a book about something that you are interested in. Read it whenever you have some free time, such as when you are on a bus, or waiting for someone. Try to focus on understanding the main ideas, even if you don't understand all of the small details. Don't worry if you don't understand some of the words. Try to use your dictionary as little as possible—or only for the most important words. The most important thing is that you read something you are interested in, and that you continue reading and reading.

Getting Started

Reading for a purpose

When you read, there is always a reason, that is, a *purpose* for reading. Whether you are reading a street sign, a textbook, or an advertisement, you are reading for a particular purpose.

1. **Think about the materials below. Why do you read them? Complete the chart. Then discuss your answers with your classmates.**

READING MATERIAL	PURPOSE(S)
1. a telephone book	*to find a business' phone number*
2. a novel	
3. a newspaper or magazine	
4. a recipe	
5. a poem	
6. a dictionary	
7. a personal letter	
8. a movie review	

PREVIEW UNIT

This book will help you improve your reading skills by teaching you how to read a variety of reading materials for specific purposes. In particular, the goal is to help you become better readers in preparation for academic, business, or other settings that often require you to read and understand large amounts of material.

2. **When you are not reading for pleasure, you often begin with a specific purpose that you need to accomplish. Some purposes are listed below. Now look at the list. How often do you read for these specific purposes? Rank them from 1 (most often) to 6 (least often).**

   _____ 1. to make an oral presentation for a business meeting

   _____ 2. to summarize information

   _____ 3. to make a decision about a purchase

   _____ 4. to confirm or reject a hypothesis

   _____ 5. to write a research paper

   _____ 6. to take an essay exam

Discuss with your classmates some of your own reasons for reading.

Reading Strategies

Good readers use different strategies depending on their purpose, the information they need, and the difficulty of the material. You may not have realized it, but you probably use many reading strategies already.

1. **Look at the list of reading materials below. Do you read them all in the same way? Write the methods you use on the lines.**

from start to finish	only in certain parts
slowly and carefully	quickly and selectively

READING MATERIAL	HOW DO YOU READ IT?
1. a telephone book	_____
2. a novel	_____
3. a newspaper or magazine	_____
4. a recipe	_____
5. a personal letter	_____
6. a movie review	_____

When you read in different ways, you are using reading strategies. Three common ways of reading are: *scanning*, *skimming*, and *reading closely*.

Scanning: When we scan, we read quickly looking for specific information.

2. **Look quickly at the movie information below. Circle the movie that is playing at the Palace Theater.**

1. A Slow Boat from Greenland	**4. Parent's Night Out**
(Westminster 2 5:30, 7:40, 9:50)	(Odeon 5, 7, 9)
2. Moon Children	**5. Twice Upon a Time**
(Grand 5:15, 7:15, 9:15)	(Palace 5:20, 7:40, 10)
3. Paper Dolls	**6. Wendy's Wedding**
(Piccadilly 4:50, 6:10, 8:40)	(Westminster 1 5:30, 7:30, 9:30)

What answer did you find? How did you find the answer? If you looked for the word *Palace*, you were probably scanning.

Skimming: When we skim, we read quickly to get a general idea of the reading. One common reason for skimming is to get enough information to decide if we want to continue reading further.

3. **Look quickly at this movie review. What is the reviewer's opinion of the movie? Write it on the line below.**

Paper Dolls
★★

Paper Dolls is one of the most interesting movies to date from director Martin Blackmun; unfortunately, it is not one of his best. *Paper Dolls* is the story of a young woman whose life as a top model is destroyed by a tragic automobile accident. Her face is scarred and disfigured, making it impossible for her to work. As a result, she is rejected by her boyfriend and her former friends. So, she sells all of her possessions and moves to a small town in the Midwest where she knows no one. The movie tells the story of her struggle to learn to live in a world where she must depend on herself. The story moved so slowly in the beginning, that when the car accident occurred, I could only feel relief that something had finally happened. However, the second part of the movie is so good that it makes the first part worth sitting through.

Opinion: _____

Were you able to find the reviewer's opinion? Can you explain it in your own words? Did you find it in less than 15 seconds? If you did, you were probably skimming.

> **Reading closely:** When we read closely, we read more slowly and carefully. We read closely when we want to understand as much as possible. We also read closely to check to be sure that we can find the information we need. Sometimes we even need to read a text several times in order to understand it.

4. **Read the paragraph and find out two things you can do to make your refrigerator work more efficiently. Circle them.**

Refrigerator Efficiency

The refrigerator represents about 30% of most electric bills. To find out how well yours operates, open the door and place a dollar bill against the seal. Then close the door. If you can remove the bill, the seal is not tight enough and should be replaced. Vacuuming the coils behind or below the unit can improve efficiency as well, but be sure to unplug the refrigerator first.

Did you find the information? If you were able to find it, you probably read the paragraph closely.

Handling Unknown Vocabulary Words

One of the most difficult problems when you are reading in a foreign language is knowing what to do about the words that you do not understand.

1. **What do you usually do when you are reading and you find an unknown vocabulary word? Circle your answer.**

   1. I stop and look the word up in a dictionary.

   2. I try to guess the general meaning of the word.

   3. I skip over the word.

   4. I ask someone the meaning of the word.

   Each of the strategies above works sometimes, but not at all times. You will decide the best strategy to use every time you come to an unknown word in a reading. However, the emphasis in this textbook will be on giving you as many strategies as possible for dealing with the meaning of unknown words and for reading successfully.

A note about dictionary use: In the beginning, you may feel that you need to use a dictionary often. However, if you practice strategies for understanding unknown words in other ways, you will find that you will need to use your dictionary much less over time. You will also find that it is only one of several different strategies you can use when you see words that you don't understand.

Developing Your Vocabulary

There are two basic ways of dealing with the problem of unknown vocabulary in reading:

> use strategies for figuring out what vocabulary words mean as you read

> increase your vocabulary as much as possible in this class and others

Good readers use both of these strategies. Remember, the more words you know, the fewer you will have to guess as you read.

2. Now discuss these questions with your class.

1. How do you learn new vocabulary?

2. Where do you find the most useful new words?

An important way to develop a powerful vocabulary is to read, read, and read. We now know that the more you read, the more words you will learn.

The Organization of This Book

It is important to understand the way that this book is organized in order to get the most out of the activities in each unit.

1. **Look at the table of contents at the beginning of this book. The book is divided into four units. Write their titles below:**

   1. _____

   2. _____

   3. _____

   4. _____

2. **The units are divided into four parts. What are they called?**

   Part A: _____

   Part B: _____

   Part C: _____

   Part D: _____

   1. How many readings are in Part A? _____

   2. How many readings are in Part B? _____

   3. What kind of activities are in Part C? _____

   4. What kind of activities are in Part D? _____

   _____

   In Part A, you will be introduced to various reading strategies. In Part B, you will practice them.

3. **Each unit also has one or two Unit Tasks. Look at the table of contents.**

   1. Which units have two Unit Tasks? _____

   2. Which units have only one? _____

   Sometimes you will not do the Unit Task(s) until you have finished all six readings in a unit; sometimes you will do two tasks in each unit. As you are reading, you will be reminded to look for information related to the Unit Task. Some readings will be directly related to the task. They will give you a lot of helpful information. Others will be related only indirectly. They may give you only a little information to help you to do the Unit Task(s). You need to decide which readings are more important, and which are less important, for your purpose. In the end, you will need to put together information from the different readings in order to do the Unit Task(s) well. If you would like to do even more reading on a topic, the appendix at the back of the book contains extra readings for each unit.

$\mathcal{I}$N THIS UNIT

Reading Strategies

- Understanding the use of examples
- Identifying the organization of a reading
- Identifying the author's main idea
- Identifying the author's important points
- Underlining or highlighting the text
- Understanding and using bar graphs
- Finding important ideas

Strategies for Unknown Vocabulary

- Using internal definitions
- Using general meaning
- Identifying punctuation cues
- Finding internal definitions
- Recognizing technical words

The Ad Game

Think About It

*A*dvertising is big business. It is such a profitable business that the cost of advertising a product is often more than the cost of making it. For example, a box of cereal costs three to four dollars. However, the grain only costs about 10 cents, the packaging costs about 90 cents and much of the other two or three dollars pays for advertising. How many cans of soda did the PepsiCo have to sell in order to pay for one Michael Jackson television commercial? About 192,307,692!

From *The History of American Advertising*, James Gilmore

Discuss these questions with your classmates.

1. As a consumer, how do you feel about advertisements? Do you think that they are necessary, helpful, or a waste of money?

2. Do you pay attention to some television commercials or advertisements more than others? Why?

3. Do you often buy things because you have seen them in advertisements or on commercials? Give some examples.

Looking Ahead in Unit One

Look through the unit and answer these questions. Write your answers on the lines.

1. How many readings are there in Part A?

   _____

2. How many readings are there in Part B?

   _____

3. At the end of the unit you will have two Unit Tasks. What page are they on? What are the tasks?

   _____

   _____

4. Is there more information on the unit topic? Where is it?

   _____

5. Which reading sounds the most interesting to you?

   _____

   _____

PART  FOCUS ON SKILLS

Reading in Different Ways for Different Purposes

Scanning

Scanning is reading quickly to find specific information.

Look at the ad on page 5. Scan for this information.

1. How old do you have to be to get a 40% discount on a Eurailpass?

   _____

2. How many countries can you travel to with a Eurailpass?

   _____

3. What's the web address for Eurailpass?

   _____

Skimming

When we skim, we read quickly to understand the author's general idea or ideas. Because we are looking for the main ideas, we don't try to remember all the details.

Look at the ad on page 6. What is the main idea of the ad? Check your answer.

_____ 1. Truck drivers and construction workers love Gardenburgers.

_____ 2. Paul wrote a book and is on TV.

_____ 3. Gardenburgers have no meat.

Reading Closely

When you read closely, you read more slowly and carefully. You also pay more attention to the details. We read closely when we need to understand as much as possible. For example, when we read poetry, we often read closely.

This is the beginning of a very well-known poem by American poet, Joyce Kilmer.

Trees
I think that I shall never see
A poem lovely as a tree...

1. **The two silly poems below were based on Joyce Kilmer's poem. One was written by Jef I. Richards, a professor of advertising. The other was written by Ogden Nash, a famous American poet. Can you guess who wrote each one? Write your answers on the lines.**

Poem A
I think that I shall never see
A billboard lovely as a tree.
Indeed, unless the billboards fall
I'll never see a tree at all.

Poem B
I think that I shall never see
An ad so lovely as a tree.
But if a tree you have to sell,
It takes an ad to do that well.

Author: _____   _____

Cue: _____   _____

2. Compare poems A and B. What is the point of each one? Which one do you agree with?

Comparing Different Ways of Reading

Read the situations below and choose the type of reading that best fits each situation. Check (✓) the correct box or boxes. (Note: Some activities may require a combination of reading strategies.) Be prepared to explain your choices.

	SCANNING	SKIMMING	READING CLOSELY
1. You need to find the meaning of a word in the dictionary.	✓	❑	✓
2. You see a newspaper headline about your favorite singer. You have only one minute before class to find out what happened to him/her.	❑	❑	❑
3. You just bought a new VCR. You need to learn how to use it.	❑	❑	❑
4. You want to find out if your favorite sports team won yesterday.	❑	❑	❑
5. It's fifteen minutes before history class, and you just realized that you forgot to read Chapter 6 last night.	❑	❑	❑

You are now developing the skill of reading flexibly. Changing the way you read according to your purpose and the amount of time you have is an important part of becoming a good reader. Each time you read, think about the different ways of reading and decide which one is best for your purpose.

Finding the Author's Viewpoint

1. **Read the quotations below. Which ones do you agree with?**

I cannot "...think of any circumstances in which advertising would not be an evil." *Arnold Toynbee, historian*

"Advertising is legalized lying." *H. G. Wells, author*

"Next to [religion], advertising is the greatest force in the world. And I say that without...disrespect. Advertising makes people discontented. It makes them want things they don't have. Without discontent, there is no progress, no achievement." *Ray Locke, advertising executive*

2. Look back at the quotations on page 8 and the poems on page 7. Can you figure out the writer's opinion? Is it generally *for* or *against* advertising? Complete the chart below by checking (✓) the correct column.

	generally for advertising	generally against advertising	I don't know
Arnold Toynbee			
H.G. Wells			
Joyce Kilmer			
Ray Locke			
James Gilmore			
Ogden Nash			
Jef I. Richards			

READING 1: "A VERY SHORT HISTORY OF ADVERTISING"

A. Pre-reading the Text

Which reading technique(s) should you use?
❏ skimming
❏ scanning
❏ reading closely

1. Look at the title and the pictures of Reading 1. What do you think this reading will be about? Circle your answer. Why do you think this?

   1. effective advertisements

   2. changes in advertising over time

   3. advertising today

PRE-READING STRATEGY: Using Your General Knowledge

When you read, it is important to connect the ideas in the reading to what you already know about the topic of the reading. This information, what you already know, is called your general knowledge. Even if your knowledge is not very specific, you probably know more than you think.

---

2. Use your general knowledge to make predictions about the reading. When a reading is about history, what do you expect? Circle the statements that you think are correct.

   1. It will include dates.

   2. It will include many statistics.

   3. It will start at the earliest time and move to more recent time.

   4. It will include the author's opinions.

3. **Brainstorm with your class about advertisements in the past. Can you remember any advertisements or television commercials from when you were younger? How were old advertisements different from ones we have now? Circle the statements that you think are correct.**

   1. The people wore old-fashioned clothes.

   2. They sometimes advertised products that we do not use today.

   3. They gave more factual information about the products.

4. **Think about what you did in the pre-reading exercises above and on page 9. Write your answers on the lines below.**

   1. What are some reasons that we pre-read?

   _____

   _____

   _____

   2. Where are some places that you look at when you pre-read?

   _____

   _____

   _____

Which reading technique(s) should you use?
❑ skimming
❑ scanning
❑ reading closely

5. **Now read about the history of advertising. As you read, check to see if any of your ideas appear in the reading.**

6. **Then read the article a second time.**

READING 1

A VERY SHORT HISTORY OF ADVERTISING

From *An Introduction to Advertising*, Richard Taflinger, Ph.D.

INTRODUCTION

1   Advertising is a major tool in the marketing of products, services and ideas. Companies certainly think it's a good way of selling, and they have increased their advertising budgets year after year. In 1985, the March 28 issue of Advertising Age magazine reported the following statistics. In 1983, companies worldwide spent $19,837,800,000 on advertising. In 1984, they spent $23,429,700,000. The March 25, 1991 issue of Advertising Age gave a total of almost $52 billion for 1990. That's a 260% increase in seven years. Clearly, companies believe in advertising.

2 Advertising has been around for thousands of years. Daniel Mannix, in his book on the Roman games, <u>Those About to Die</u>, quotes an ad from the time of the Roman Empire.

WEATHER PERMITTING, 30 PAIRS OF GLADIATORS, FURNISHED BY A. CLODIUS FLACCUS, WILL FIGHT MAY 1ST, 2ND, AND 3RD AT THE CIRCUS MAXIMUS. THE FIGHTS WILL BE FOLLOWED BY A BIG WILD ANIMAL HUNT. THE FAMOUS GLADIATOR PARIS WILL FIGHT.

3 Two thousand years later, these same types of ads were still being used. They were used to promote events such as plays and recruiting for the military. For example, almost two thousand years later, in 1798, the captain of an American ship, the USS Constitution, advertised for a crew:

...ONE HUNDRED and FIFTY

able Seamen, and NINETY-FIVE ordinary[1] Seamen, will have an opportunity of entering into the service of their country for One year, ...To all able-bodied[2] Seamen, ... SEVENTEEN DOLLARS; and to all ORDINARY SEAMEN the sum of TEN DOLLARS ...per month, will be given.

[1] At the time this ad was written, *ordinary* meant "not especially qualified."

[2] *Able-bodied* meant "having special physical strength; especially qualified for this purpose.

4 Advertising remained the same until the early 19th century. Signs hanging outside shops advertised services. For example, shoemakers would hang a shoe-shaped sign outside their shops. These signs told consumers where to buy shoes. However, this was not product advertising. It was service advertising. Yes, the product was shoes, but the shoemaker didn't have a store full of shoes for the consumer to choose from. Instead, he had samples of his work. The customer chose which shoes she or he wanted. Then the shoemaker took the measurements and made the shoes. The customer came back later to pick them up.

5 In these three cases, what was being advertised wasn't products. The purpose of the advertising was to gather people, as audience, as workers, as customers.

PRODUCT ADVERTISING IN THE UNITED STATES

6 It wasn't until after the Industrial Revolution at the beginning of the 19th century that true product advertising began. This was because for the first time products were being mass-produced, that is, made in large quantities.

7 Early consumer advertising was basically "caveat emptor" (Let the buyer beware). Producers said just about anything they wanted in their ads. The following is a typical advertisement for a product of the 1880's, a mechanism called the "Health Chair."

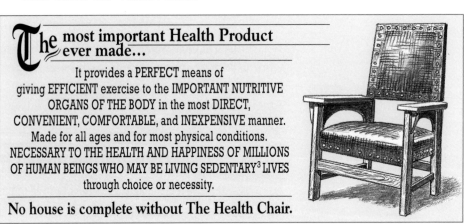

The most important Health Product ever made...

It provides a PERFECT means of giving EFFICIENT exercise to the IMPORTANT NUTRITIVE ORGANS OF THE BODY in the most DIRECT, CONVENIENT, COMFORTABLE, and INEXPENSIVE manner. Made for all ages and for most physical conditions. NECESSARY TO THE HEALTH AND HAPPINESS OF MILLIONS OF HUMAN BEINGS WHO MAY BE LIVING SEDENTARY[3] LIVES through choice or necessity.

No house is complete without The Health Chair.

8 Quite a chair, wasn't it? Actually, it wasn't. It didn't improve anyone's health. This type of advertising made consumers angry and led to laws that required advertisers to substantiate, or prove, their claims. In 1938, the Federal Trade Commission of the United States government was given the power to protect consumers from deceptive, or untrue, and unfair advertising. Since then, advertising has gone through several schools of thought or philosophies.

[3] inactive

HARD-SELL ADVERTISING

9　The 1940's and 50's was the era of the hard-sell approach in the United States. Ads, particularly television commercials, depended on repetition. The basis of this approach was the Unique Selling Proposition–the USP. The USP was one unique feature of the product that was stressed in the ad. Most of these ads did not treat consumers as intelligent people. Many advertisers believed that the consumer couldn't think about more than one point at a time. Therefore, each ad presented one selling feature, repeated over and over.

SOFT-SELL ADVERTISING

10　However, advertisers in the 1960's changed to a new approach, soft-sell advertising. Soft-sell depends less on describing the product and more on how the product will make the consumer feel. In this approach, psychology becomes important, since these ads aim at people's emotions rather than their intellect. It is generally a more interesting and sophisticated approach to advertising.

11　Related to soft-sell is the idea of positioning. Positioning shows how a product compares with other products. In other words, the ad shows where the product fits into the market. For example, everyone uses soap. But different soaps are positioned for different segments, that is, parts of the market. Dove soap is not even called soap. It is called a "beauty bar." It is positioned as a soap for women with dry skin. With a different name and ad campaign it could be positioned as a soap for men with dirty hands.

12　Advertisers have to be very careful about the way that they position their products. In 1997, cigarette makers in the United States were forced to stop advertisements featuring a cartoon camel. The government said that the company had positioned the cigarettes to appeal to children, which was against the law.

13　The French have a marketing strategy that sums up positioning: *Cherchez le creneau* ("Look for the hole"). To find a hole, you have to be able to think in reverse. If everyone is going east, see if you can find a hole by going west. One of the best examples of this kind of thinking was the positioning of the Volkswagen Beetle. For years American car makers made longer, lower cars. Then came the Volkswagen Beetle. It was short, fat and ugly. Normally, advertisers would have tried to minimize its weaknesses and maximize its strengths. But Volkswagen's advertising agency decided that its "hole" was size. It created ads that simply said, "Think small." With two simple words, this headline did two things at once. It stated Volkswagen's position and challenged the idea that bigger was better. There were other small cars on the market before Volkswagen. However, Volkswagen was the first car that said, " I'm better <u>because</u> I'm small."

Think small.

B. Checking Your Comprehension

Which reading technique(s) should you use?
❑ skimming
❑ scanning
❑ reading closely

1. Write the time period when each of these events occurred. An example has been done for you.

1. products made to order <u>early 19th century</u>

2. hard-sell advertising _____

3. mass-production begins _____

4. product advertising begins _____

5. soft-sell advertising (positioning approach) _____

6. laws to control advertising in the United States _____

7. service and location advertising only _____

2. **Label the timeline with the numbers of the events listed above. An example has been done for you.**

◀1800	Industrial Revolution	1900	1938	1940's — 1950's		1960's
1. ___	2. ___	3. _6_	4. ___	5. ___	6. ___	7. ___

3. **Look at the words and phrases below. Each one is closely related to one of the column headings. Write the words in the correct columns. An example has been done for you.**

Industrial Revolution	mass-production	positioning
psychology	repetition ✓	USP

PRODUCT ADVERTISING

_____

_____

HARD-SELL

_repetition_____

_____

SOFT-SELL

_____

_____

C. Topics for Discussion

Discuss the following questions with your classmates.

1. On page 10, you thought about how advertising today is different from earlier advertising. What did you think before you read? What do you think now? Tell your classmates.

2. What is the author's opinion of the topics listed below? Look for clues in the text. Check (✓) the correct column. Discuss your ideas with your classmates. Be prepared to explain your answers

	IN FAVOR	NOT IN FAVOR	I DON'T KNOW
1. hard-sell advertising	____	____	____
2. the Health Chair	____	____	____
3. laws regulating advertising	____	____	____
4. the Industrial Revolution	____	____	____

3. Do you think modern day ads are better or worse for consumers than the ads of long ago? Why?

D. Reading Strategies

1. **Look at the examples taken from Reading 1 below. Why does the author use each example? Write the purpose in the chart below. An example has been done for you.**

EXAMPLE	PURPOSE
Military ad	to show how advertisements were used to gather workers
Roman gladiator ad	_____
Shoemaker's ad	_____
Health Chair ad	_____
Volkswagen ad	_____

2. **How is Reading 1 organized? Check (✓) the answer.**

____ 1. It presents a problem and then a solution.

____ 2. It describes something and then compares something else with it.

____ 3. It presents the information in time order (chronologically).

____ 4. It presents a cause and then its effect.

READING STRATEGY: Identifying the Author's Important Points

When we read, it is important to understand that in almost everything we read, some ideas are more important than others. As readers, we use this knowledge to do different things:

- to find an author's purpose for writing
- to write a summary
- to find specific information we need
- to get a general idea of what we are reading

Which of the following sentences are more important than the others? Which are less important? Discuss your ideas with your classmates. Can you explain your answers?

1. Volkswagen ads used headlines such as "Think Small."
2. There were several distinct time periods in the history of advertising.
3. In 1983, companies spent $19,837,800,000 on advertising.

Sometimes it is not easy to identify an author's important points. However, often information that states a general idea is more important than a specific detail.

3. **Now decide which sentences below are important ideas for this reading, and which ones are details. Check (✓) the correct column.**

IMPORTANT IDEA	DETAIL	
_____	_____	1. a. The Roman games were advertised.
_____	_____	b. People have been advertising for thousands of years.
_____	_____	2. a. The first advertisements were for services and locations.
_____	_____	b. Shoemakers advertised a service, not a product.
_____	_____	3. a. The claims in the Health Chair advertisement were not true.
_____	_____	b. Before regulation, many advertisements were not true.
_____	_____	4. a. Hard-sell advertisements were repetitive.
_____	_____	b. Hard-sell advertisements were often on television.
_____	_____	5. a. Soft-sell advertising is emotional.
_____	_____	b. The Volkswagen was one of the first products advertised by soft-sell.

4. **What do you think was the author's purpose for writing Reading 1? Circle your answer.**

1. to explain about how ads used to be and how they have changed
2. to show that modern day ads are much better than old-fashioned ads
3. to explain the characteristics of good and bad ads

E. Strategies for Unknown Vocabulary

VOCABULARY STRATEGY: Using Internal Definitions

Sometimes the text gives you the meaning of an unfamiliar word if you continue to read further. Specialized words are often explained, even for native speakers of English. These two words and phrases below are often used to signal that an internal definition is coming:

that is (…products were being mass-produced, **that is,** made in large quantities)

or (…advertising has gone through several schools of thought, **or** philosophies.)

Sometimes, an explanation is found between commas or in parentheses.

Sometimes, no signal is given. A definition may simply occur later in the sentence that contains the word.

Which reading technique(s) should you use?
❑ skimming
❑ scanning
❑ reading closely

1. Find these words and their definitions in the text on pages 11–14.

1. substantiate _____

2. deceptive _____

3. schools of thought _____

4. segment _____

2. What do these phrases mean?

1. *caveat emptor* _____

2. *cherchez le creneau* _____

3. What is the definition of USP (unique selling point) in Reading 1?

F. Building Your Vocabulary

Use these steps to build your vocabulary with words from the reading.

1. Look back at Reading 1 and make a list of ten to fifteen new words that you feel are important to learn.

2. Write these words in your vocabulary notebook. Group words that are similar (e.g., *sleepless/restless, anthropology/anthropologist*). Copy a sentence or phrase in which the word appears. Decide on the part of speech of the word and write a definition for it.

3. If you are still unsure of the meaning of this word or the part of speech, look it up in the dictionary and write the definition in your own words. For additional practice, write your own sentence.

G. Writing Your Ideas

Look at the writing topics below. Choose at least one and write about it.

1. In the early days of advertising, the idea of "caveat emptor" allowed advertisers to say almost anything in their ads. What kinds of controls on advertising exist today? Do you think they are adequate? Why or why not? Does your country have these kinds of controls?

2. What kinds of information do you have to have to be a good consumer? Where can you find this information?

READING 2: "BASIC ADVERTISING TECHNIQUES"

A. Pre-reading the Text

PRE-READING STRATEGY: Identifying the Topic

When you pre-read, it is helpful first to identify the topic of what you will read. A topic is usually a word or short phrase describing the general subject of the reading. It answers the question, "What is this reading about?"

---

1. **Where can you look in a reading to find these kinds of information? Circle all the correct answers.**

   title   pictures   graphs   subtitles   words in bold

2. **Now read and find the topic.**

PRE-READING STRATEGY: Using Information about Where a Reading Is from

When we pre-read, we often look to see where the reading came from. Is it from a textbook, a well-known newspaper, or a magazine published by a particular group? If you saw an article on models used in advertisements in *Modern Woman Magazine* and another one on the same topic in a textbook called *Techniques of Advertising*, how would you expect the articles to be different? Why?

We also want to know about the author. Is he or she a journalist, an expert in the field, or someone with a particular point of view? Why might this information be important?

Which reading technique(s) should you use?
❏ skimming
❏ scanning
❏ reading closely

3. **Look at this reading and find the answers to these questions.**

   1. Is this reading from a textbook, a magazine, or a newspaper? How do you know?

   2. Who wrote it?

   3. How will the answers to these questions influence you?

4. **What do you know about this topic? Is this topic the same as the topic of Reading 1? Which of the following do you need to think about before you read?**

   1. why advertisements are good or bad

   2. different ways that advertisements influence us

   3. how much advertisements cost

5. **Now read about advertising techniques. Does the reading mention any of your ideas from question 2 on page 10? You will see that there are questions in the margin on the left side of the reading. Fold a piece of paper and cover these questions when you read the first time. Try to understand as much of the reading as you can.**

6. **Then reread the article. This time use the margin questions to help you.**

READING 2

Basic Advertising Techniques

From *An Introduction to Advertising,* Richard Taflinger, Ph.D.

1 Is the underlined sentence an important idea or a detail? How do you know?

1 One of the first principles that you must understand in advertising is that it is limited in both time and space. Television and radio commercials are usually only 10 to 60 seconds long. Print ads are usually no larger than two pages, and usually much smaller. Therefore, an advertisement must do its job quickly. It must get the consumer's attention, identify the product, and deliver the selling message in a small time or space. In order to do this, advertising often breaks the rules of grammar, image, and even society.

2 Find internal definitions for the two words in bold.

2 The second basic point is that advertisements usually have two parts: copy and illustrations. **Copy** refers to the words in the advertisement. These words give the sales message. **Illustrations** are the pictures or photographs. Most ads are a combination of copy and illustration. Some advertisements have small illustrations and a lot of copy. Some are only an illustration with the name of the product.

3 The decision about how much copy and illustration to use depends on how the advertiser wants to present the **sales message**. Understanding how advertisers make this decision is complex. First you must understand how humans process, or work with, information because we do not process all kinds of information in the same way. We process some kinds of information intellectually. In other words, we think about the information in order to understand it. We process other kinds of information emotionally. This means we use feelings rather than thinking to understand the information.

4 We generally process copy in ads intellectually. That is because both reading and listening are thinking processes. These thinking processes translate symbols (written words) or sounds (spoken words) into meaning. Of course, words, especially if they are spoken, can be very emotional—they can bring memories that make you laugh or cry. However, even though spoken words are often very emotional, we must first translate them. In other words, we do not see words as reality.

5 The mind also interprets drawings and paintings intellectually. Like words, drawings and paintings are not the things themselves, but an artist's idea of them. The viewer must translate the lines, colors and shapes into meaning. Illustrations can have a lot of emotion, but again they are not reality.

3 Why does the author talk about *The 3rd of May 1808?*

6 In order to understand this idea better, think of a well-known painting such as *The 3rd of May 1808 in Madrid: The Executions on Príncipe Pío Hill* by Goya, below. This painting upsets many people. However, think of the same scene in a photograph. Most people would find the photograph even more disturbing. That is because we process photographs emotionally. To us, they are real. Therefore, photographs do not need translation. Research supports this idea. It shows that photographs attract more readers, are more believable and remembered better than illustrations.

7 Just as there are two kinds of mental processes, there are two basic ways of presenting a sales message: intellectually and emotionally. An **intellectual presentation** uses ideas to get a consumer to buy a product or service. For example, computer buyers usually do not think about what the machine looks like or the effect it might have on their social life. They are looking for technical information. How fast does the computer work? How large is its memory?

8 Advertisements that present a message intellectually have a lot of copy. The copy explains the uses and benefits of the product or service. In addition, such ads are not usually seen on television because television ads are very short. It requires time and careful thinking to understand a message which contains a lot of ideas. These kinds of ads usually appear in magazines or newspapers where the consumer has unlimited time to process the information.

9 Ads with an intellectual presentation usually have few illustrations. If they have any illustrations, they will probably be drawings or paintings. In this way, both parts of the ad are processed in the same way. If they have photographs, the photographs will usually be simple, with little emotional content, usually showing only what the product looks like.

10 The second basic way to present a sales message is emotionally. In an **emotional presentation**, the use of the product is often not the most important sales message. Instead, the ad focuses on the buyer's social, psychological or economic needs. For example, an emotional ad may show how the product or service will make the consumers' social life better by increasing their appeal, making them feel more confident, or making them rich. Some of the most effective ads today are ones that use an emotional presentation. These types of ads will be the focus of our next chapter.

B. Checking Your Comprehension

Read each exercise below. Then look back at the reading to find the answers.

1. Complete the following sentences.

   1. Print advertisements have to give their message in a limited

   _____.

   2. Television advertisements have to give their message in a limited

   _____.

2. How are these parts of advertisements processed? Check (✓) the correct column.

	INTELLECTUALLY PROCESSED	EMOTIONALLY PROCESSED
Copy	_____	_____
Drawings	_____	_____
Paintings	_____	_____
Photographs	_____	_____

C. Topics for Discussion

Discuss the following questions with your classmates.

1. Look at the ads in this unit. Which ones do you think are presented intellectually? emotionally? Which ones are a combination of both?

2. Decide which kind of presentation would be better for each product. Check (✓) your answers and discuss your opinions with the class.

	MOSTLY EMOTIONAL	MOSTLY INTELLECTUAL
1. a complicated camera	_____	_____
2. blue jeans	_____	_____
3. a car	_____	_____
4. ice cream	_____	_____
5. an expensive piano	_____	_____

3. The author believes that photographs are processed emotionally and that drawings and paintings are processed intellectually. Compare the painting and the photograph below. Do you agree with him?

D. Reading Strategies

READING STRATEGY: Identifying the Author's Main Idea

Sometimes a reading has one main idea, and all the information in the article is connected to that idea. Often, it is related to the author's purpose for writing or his or her point of view on the topic. Usually, though, a reading contains several important points that support or are directly connected to the main idea. The main idea is also normally stated in a complete sentence.

One way to find the main idea is to begin by identifying the general topic. As you learned in the pre-reading exercise for Reading 2, a topic answers the question, "What is this reading about?"

Then, once you know the topic, identifying what the author says or believes about the topic can help you find the main idea.

Following these two steps can help you find the main idea of a reading:

In order to	Ask this question
Find the topic	"What is this reading about?"
Find the main idea	"What does the author say or believe about the topic?"

1. **Look at the topic you wrote in pre-reading question 2 on page 19 before you read this text. Now that you have finished Reading 2, do you still think this is the topic? If not, why not?**

READING STRATEGY: More Practice in Identifying the Author's Main Idea

When trying to identify the main idea, be careful not to be too general or too specific. A main idea statement needs to include all the information that is given in the text, but not more (too general), and not less (too specific). A statement that is too general will include information that is not found in the text. A statement that is too specific will not include all the information that is in the text.

2. **Which of these sentences gives the main idea of this reading? Circle the number of the correct answer.**

   1. There are many kinds of advertisements.

   2. Ads make use of different techniques to accomplish different purposes.

   3. Ads use both intellectual and emotional presentations.

3. **Can you explain why the other two answers are not correct? (Hint: Are they too general or too specific?)**

4. **Did your answers agree with the following explanations?**

Too general: Answer 1 is not correct because it is too general. The reading does not discuss *all* the different kinds of advertisements.

Too specific: Answer 3 is too specific. This is only one of the ideas that the author discusses.

The correct answer is 2. That is the author's main idea.

READING STRATEGY: Identifying Important Ideas in the Reading

The author's important ideas often support the main idea or offer general statements about one of the aspects of the main idea. They do not usually give information about specific facts or examples, however.

Which of the following sentences is an important point from this reading?

Hint: Does it explain one of the general techniques used in advertising? (Then it is probably an important idea.) Does it give a specific example of one kind of ad? (Then it is probably not an important idea.)

1. Advertisements are limited in space or time.

2. Computer ads usually have a lot of copy.

The answer is 1. Answer 1 explains one of the general principles that can be used in advertising. Answer 2 is a detail. It explains only about one type or example of ads—computer ads—and describes which specific technique it makes use of.

---

5. **Sometimes the author tells you which ideas are important. Look back at the first sentence in Reading 2 (on page 20). Does he think that this statement is important?**

6. **Many times the author does not tell you which ideas are the most important. Then you have to read and decide for yourself. Look at these statements. Based on the reading, decide if each of these points is important or not. Check (✓) the important points.**

1. Advertisements are limited in space and time.   _____

2. *The 3rd of May 1808* is a painting.   _____

3. An intellectual presentation uses ideas.   _____

4. Advertisements contain copy and illustrations.   _____

5. Written words are kinds of symbols.   _____

7. Sometimes the decision between what is an important point and what is a detail is not so clear-cut. What do you think about the statements below? Check (✓) the important points. Compare your answers with your classmates'.

1. The amount of copy versus illustration depends on how the advertiser wants to present the sales message. _____

2. Paintings are processed intellectually. _____

3. Some ads make people feel more confident. _____

4. Photographs are processed emotionally. _____

READING STRATEGY: Underlining or Highlighting the Text

One way of remembering important information is to underline or highlight it. Highlighting can help you to find important information easily or to study for an examination. When you underline or highlight, you must make sure to include enough information so that you will remember the important points. However, if you include too much, the important points might get lost.

This means that as you read, you must constantly decide if something is important or not.

---

8. Look at how three different students underlined the first paragraph of the reading. Which one will be more effective? Why?

____ 1. <u>One of the first principles that you must realize in advertising is that it is limited in both time and space. Television and radio commercials are usually only 10 to 60 seconds long. Print ads are usually no larger than two pages, and usually much smaller</u>. Therefore, an advertisement must do its job quickly. <u>It must get the consumer's attention, identify the product, and deliver the selling message in a small time or space. In order to do this, advertising often breaks the rules of grammar, image, and even society.</u>

____ 2. One of the <u>first principles</u> that you must realize in advertising is that it is <u>limited</u> in both time and space. Television and radio commercials are usually only 10 to 60 seconds long. Print ads are usually no larger than two pages, and usually much smaller. Therefore, an advertisement must do its job <u>quickly</u>. It must get the consumer's attention, identify the product, and deliver the selling message in a small time or space. In order to do this, advertising often breaks the rules of <u>grammar, image</u>, and even <u>society.</u>

____ 3. One of the <u>first principles</u> that you must realize in advertising is that it is <u>limited</u> in both <u>time and space</u>. Television and radio <u>commercials</u> are usually only <u>10 to 60 seconds long</u>. Print <u>ads</u> are usually no larger than <u>two pages</u>, and usually much smaller.

Therefore, an advertisement must do its job quickly. It must <u>get</u> the consumer's <u>attention</u>, <u>identify</u> the <u>product</u>, and <u>deliver</u> the selling <u>message</u> in a <u>small time or space</u>. In order to do this, advertising often <u>breaks the rules of grammar, image</u>, and even <u>society</u>.

9. **What kinds of words and phrases did Student 3 underline? Which were left out?**

10. **Underline or highlight the important information in Reading 2 (pages 20–22). Compare your work with your classmates'.**

E. Strategies for Unknown Vocabulary

VOCABULARY STRATEGY: More on Internal Definitions and Explanations

The phrase **in other words** can also be used to introduce a definition or an explanation:

in other words (…spoken words are often very emotional, we must first translate them. **In other words,** we do not see words as reality.)

---

1. **Scan Reading 2 on pages 20–22 to find the words below. What definitions or explanations are given within the reading?**

   symbols _____

   process _____

   sounds _____

   emotionally _____

   intellectually _____

2. **Scan to find the words *copy* and *illustration* in the text. Then use the words to describe the parts of the ad on page 5.**

VOCABULARY STRATEGY: Using General Meaning

Even when the text does not give you an exact definition of a word, you can often guess the general meaning of the word. A general idea is often good enough to let you continue reading without stopping to look at a dictionary. If you stop to look at a dictionary, it is easy to forget what you were reading about.

---

3. **Look for the word *disturbing* in paragraph 6 of Reading (page 21). Which of these is a good general meaning?**

   1. difficult   2. interesting   3. upsetting

4. **Look for the word *appeal* in the last paragraph (page 22). Circle the best ending for this definition.**

Appeal describes something that people...

    1. don't want to have.

    2. want to have more of.

    3. have too much of.

F. Building Your Vocabulary

Use these steps to build your vocabulary with words from the reading.

1. Look at your reading list from Reading 1. Put a checkmark (✓) next to any words that also appeared in Reading 2. Then look back at Reading 2 and make a list of five to ten new words that you feel are important to learn.

2. Write these words in your vocabulary notebook. Group words that are similar (e.g., *advertising/advertisement, emotional/intellectual*). Copy a sentence or phrase in which the word appears. Decide on the part of speech of the word and write a definition for it.

3. If you are still unsure of the meaning of this word or the part of speech, look it up in the dictionary and write the definition in your own words. For additional practice, write your own sentence.

G. Writing Your Ideas

Look at the writing topics below. Choose at least one and write about it.

1. Look in a magazine for an advertisement with a mostly emotional presentation and one with a mostly intellectual presentation. Are they effective? Explain why you think so.

2. Have you ever bought something that you didn't really need because of an advertisement? What did you buy? How did the ad convince you to buy it?

READING 3: "CHARACTERISTICS OF GOOD ADS"

A. Pre-reading the Text

1. **What is the topic of this reading? Use your general knowledge. The title says "Characteristics of Good Ads." Think of some good advertisements that you have seen. What do you think makes them effective?**

2. **Below are the subtitles of three of the sections of the following article. Try to match them with the purpose of each section. Then look quickly at these three sections of the reading.**

SUBTITLE	PURPOSE OF SECTION
Introduction	to give the results of the research
Methodology	to describe how the research was done
Findings	to give background information about why the research was done

Which reading technique(s) should you use?
❏ skimming
❏ scanning
❏ reading closely

3. **Now think about your purpose for reading. If your purpose is <u>to find the characteristics of effective advertisements</u>, which section will probably be the most useful?**

Introduction   Methodology   Findings

4. **Now read the entire article. Does it mention any of your ideas? Pay careful attention to the characteristics of effective ads. Remember to cover the margin questions the first time that you read.**

5. **Read the article again. Use the questions in the margin to help you.**

READING 3

CHARACTERISTICS OF GOOD ADS

Dennis Kropmeyer
Consumer Research Department
Morgan Advertising Research Company

INTRODUCTION

1 Notice the internal definition.

1   The advertising industry has done a lot of research on "stopping power"—the combination of characteristics that makes readers stop, notice, and read an advertisement. Advertisers want to know what makes one advertisement have more stopping power than another. There are, obviously, many elements which combine to make an effective advertisement—for example, it must be imaginative. The goal of this report is to discover the common characteristics of the ads that our readers have found to be the most effective. Some of the questions answered in the following analysis are:

   • How are photographs and illustrations used in effective ads?

2 What do these questions tell you?

   • What characteristics and techniques are the most common?

METHODOLOGY

2 To produce this report, Morgan Research Company analyzed 996 effective advertisements from 1989 and 1990. These advertisements were taken from 45 different magazines.

3 Morgan Advertising Performance Studies are conducted in this way:

3 Why is this information marked with a bullet (•)?

- Readers are asked to look at a magazine when they first receive it.

- Two weeks later, they are asked to look at it again.

- Researchers then ask them which advertisements they remember from their first reading.

- Researchers may also ask several other questions about the advertisements, articles or editorials in the magazine.

- The first 100 answers received are used in the study.

4 The ten advertisements with the highest "remember seeing" scores in each of 393 Morgan Advertising Performance Studies were included in this analysis. In some cases, more than 10 advertisements were included because of tie scores.

FINDINGS
Photographs and Illustrations

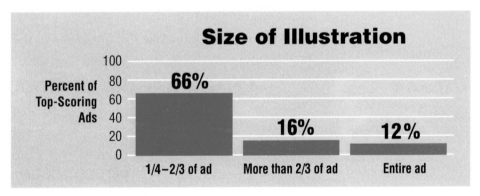

5 The photograph or illustration in an advertisement is very important to its stopping power. Ninety-eight percent of top-scoring ads contain a photograph or illustration. In most of these ads, the photograph or illustration is quite large. In two-thirds of top-scoring ads, the photo or illustration covers 1/4–2/3 of the ad, in another 16% of the ads, the photo covers more than 2/3 of the ad, and in 12% of these ads, the photo covers the entire ad.

4 This paragraph contains an internal definition. What is it for?

6 The results of the research about the most common messages for top-scoring ads is extremely interesting. More than a third of top scoring ads (36%) show "borrowed interest" photos. A "borrowed interest" photo is one that seems to connect the product with the photo but is actually unrelated to it.

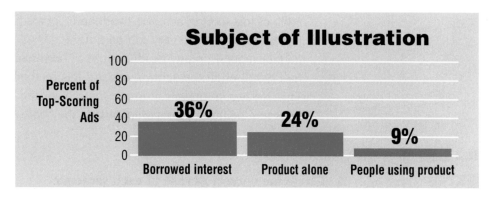

Subject of Illustration

Percent of Top-Scoring Ads

- Borrowed interest: 36%
- Product alone: 24%
- People using product: 9%

For example, a picture of a lovely mountain scene may be used in a cigarette advertisement. (Cigarettes have no connection to mountains but the advertiser hopes that readers will make an emotional connection between the two.) In addition to photographs, there are also "borrowed interest" messages. These show up in almost every part of our analysis (photos, headlines, and copy). But "borrowed interest" is not the only message that creates stopping power. Nearly one quarter (24%) of top scoring ads show the product alone, and another 9% show people using the product.

Descriptive Copy

7 The study does not show that copy has a lot of "stopping power." However, after readers stop to look at the advertisement, the copy becomes very important. Advertising copy, in fact, seems to be an essential part of advertising. Ninety-five percent of top scoring ads have more than 25 words of copy. Nearly seven of ten top ads had copy of average length (26–200 words). However, 65% had more than 100 words, and 27% had more than 200 words.

8 The most common messages contained in ad copy are the product's characteristics (33% of top ads) and the usefulness of the product (27% of top ads). In other words, copy is used to show the consumer the benefits of the product.

Headlines

9 In addition to the photograph or illustration, the headline is also a key element for getting the reader's attention. On average, five times as many people read a headline as read the body copy. In this case, ninety-eight percent of top-scoring ads contain a headline, but in most cases, the headline is not very large. In 59% of the ads in this study, for example, the headline is small (1/2 inch high or less). In only 10% of the ads were the headlines large (1 inch high or more).

10 Similarly, the length of the headline in 75% of top ads is short, but powerful—between 1–12 words. In 36% of top ads, the headline was limited to 1–6 words. The placement of the headline does not seem very important. In

17% of top scoring ads, the headline is located in the top 1/3 of the page and in 16%, it is the very top part of the ad. As in the case of photographs and illustrations, many headlines use a "borrowed interest" message. Nearly half (48%) of all top-scoring ads use this method—usually in a funny way. This creates a powerful image or makes the reader see a connection between the product or company and the "borrowed interest" idea.

B. Checking Your Comprehension

1. Circle the correct phrase in each sentence.

1. Advertisers try to write ads with <u>a lot of/very little</u> "stopping power."

2. If an ad has "stopping power," many people will <u>read it/not buy the product</u>.

3. Copy has <u>a lot of/very little</u> "stopping power."

2. Answer these questions.

1. According to the study, what makes an effective headline?

2. Look at the advertisements in this unit. Which ones do you think have effective headlines?

3. Find an advertisement in this unit that has a "borrowed interest" photograph and another with a "borrowed interest" message. What is the "borrowed interest" in each case?

4. Find an advertisement with no headline. Is it effective?

C. Topics for Discussion

Discuss the following questions with your classmates.

1. If you were an executive in an advertising company, how would you use the information in this report? For example, would you decide to copy all the techniques of the top-scoring ads? Why or why not?

2. The research in this report was based on how many people remembered seeing each advertisement. Would you buy a product because you remembered seeing the advertisement? Can you think of any better ways of finding out which ads are the most effective?

3. Advertisers often use statistics (e.g., "97% of people prefer our brand to Brand X"). Why do advertisers use statistics? Should you always believe statistics? Do they always tell the whole story? (In the example above, it might be that 97% of our *employees* prefer our brand!)

D. Reading Strategies

READING STRATEGY: Understanding and Using Bar Graphs

Charts and graphs present information in easy-to-read, visual form. They help us find information quickly.

We usually look at charts and graphs to find specific pieces of information. For that reason, we usually scan them. When we scan, we use our knowledge about how the information is organized in order to find what we are looking for. For example, a bus schedule can be organized according to where the bus is going, according to the day, or according to the time.

Dover—Guilford—Putney—Keene Airport			
DAILY	**LEAVE DOVER**	**LEAVE GUILFORD**	**LEAVE PUTNEY**	**ARRIVE KEENE AIRPORT**
Daily	6:00 A.M.	6:30 A.M.	7:10 A.M.	7:35 A.M.
Daily	6:30	7:00	7:40	8:05
M-F	7:30	8:00	8:40	9:05
Daily	10:30	11:00	11:40	12:05 P.M.
Daily	12:30 P.M.	1:00 P.M.	1:40 P.M.	2:05
Daily	2:00	2:30	3:10	3:35
Daily	3:30	4:00	4:40	5:05
Daily	5:30	6:00	6:40	7:05
M-F	7:00	7:30	8:10	9:35

---

1. **How is the information organized in the graph on page 30?**

   1. What does the vertical line show?

   2. What does the horizontal line show?

2. **Now scan both graphs to answer these questions. Use your knowledge about how the information is presented in order to find your answers.**

   1. What percentage of ads have illustrations that cover the entire ad?

   2. What percentage of ads have a "borrowed interest" photograph?

3. **How did you use the organization of the graphs to decide where to look for the answers?**

READING STRATEGY: Finding Important Ideas

All the information in a reading is not of equal importance. Some ideas will be more important than others. The first question to answer when you are deciding which information is the most important for you, is what is your purpose in reading. The next step is to think about general information versus details. Although the details are sometimes important for a particular purpose, many times the details simply support or explain the author's main idea.

---

4. **Which section of this article contains the most useful information for an advertising executive? Why?**

   Introduction   Methodology   Findings

5. Are all the statistics in this article of equal importance? Why or why not?

6. Look at the statements below. Then look back at the section of the article about headlines. Which three of the following statements give important information about headlines?

    1. Most ads contain a headline.

    2. Headlines can be larger than one inch.

    3. Most headlines have 1–12 words.

    4. Some headlines are at the top of the page.

    5. Headlines can have a "borrowed interest" message.

7. How did you decide which ones were important? Now go back and underline or highlight this information in the article.

8. Look back at the sections called *Photographs and Illustrations* and *Descriptive Copy*. Underline or highlight the important information. Compare your work with your classmates'.

9. Use the sections that you underlined or highlighted to complete the following about the most successful ads in each category. An example has been done for you.

    The most successful ads have these characteristics:

    1. <u>They contain a headline.</u>
       (headline)

    2. _____
       (length of headline)

    3. _____
       (size of illustration)

    4. _____
       (subject of illustration)

E. Strategies for Unknown Vocabulary

VOCABULARY STRATEGY: Recognizing Technical Words

Sometimes specialized vocabulary or technical words and phrases are used in quotation marks. These marks show that the author is using these words in a special way.

1. Which of these phrases are given in quotation marks in Reading 3? Check (✓) your answers.

    ____ 1. remember seeing (scores)   ____ 3. stopping power

    ____ 2. performance studies   ____ 4. borrowed interest

2. **Look back at the reading. Find definitions for** *borrowed interest* **and** *stopping power* **and write them here:**

borrowed interest _____

stopping power _____

3. **Which sentence below uses the phrase** *remember seeing* **in the same way that the author uses it in the article?**

1. I remember seeing that advertisement in a magazine.

2. This ad received the highest remember seeing score.

F. Building Your Vocabulary

Use these steps to build your vocabulary with words from the reading.

1. Look at your reading list from Readings 1–2. Put a checkmark (✓) next to any words that also appeared in Reading 3. Then look back at Reading 3 and make a list of five to ten new words that you feel are important to learn.

2. Write these words in your vocabulary notebook. Group words that are similar (e.g., *effective/imaginative, combine/combination*). Copy a sentence or phrase in which the word appears. Decide on the part of speech of the word and write a definition for it.

3. If you are still unsure of the meaning of this word or the part of speech, look it up in the dictionary and write the definition in your own words. For additional practice, write your own sentence.

G. Writing Your Ideas

Look at the writing topics below. Choose at least one and write about it.

1. Try the "remember seeing" test on yourself. Look at a magazine. The next day try to see how many advertisements you can remember. Did you remember advertisements with the same characteristics as the study showed? Write about your results.

2. Advertisers generally do a lot of research. They often conduct telephone surveys. Have you ever been asked to answer an advertising survey? Would you answer one if you were asked? Why or why not?

H. Making Connections

When you are reading, it is important to make connections between different articles. Look back at Readings 2 and 3. Which of the concepts described in these readings relate to "soft-sell advertising" as described in Reading 1?

intellectual presentation

sales message

illustration

borrowed interest

emotional presentation

copy

stopping power

PART  FOCUS ON READING FOR A PURPOSE

When you read, you always read for a purpose. In Part A of this unit, your purpose was to find and understand the author's important points. You often read for this purpose. For example, a teacher may assign you to read a chapter from a textbook and expect you to understand its content.

However, you also read for other purposes. For example, you may need to find out about a specific topic and put together information from different books or articles. You might need the information in order to write a research paper, prepare for an essay exam, or make an oral presentation. The information you need may be part of the author's important ideas or it may not be. In these situations, you need to approach the reading in a new way. In Part B, you will learn how to do this. However, you will still use the skills and strategies that you learned in Part A.

Steps in Reading for a Purpose

Before You Read

Pre-Step: Identify the Information You Need—Decide what kind of information you need to find and predict where you might find it.

One of your purposes in this unit is to evaluate some advertisements to see if they are effective or not. What kind of information do you think you will need for this? Write your answer in your notebook. You probably wrote that you will need some kind of information on what qualities make an effective ad.

Step 1: Preview—Look quickly at a reading to see if you can find the kind of information you indentified in the Pre-Step.

Two ways to preview are:

Skimming: Reading quickly to get a general idea of what the article says, so you know if the article is useful for your purpose or if you should look in a different place.

Scanning: Reading quickly to find some key words or specific clues that will give you a hint about the usefulness of the article.

If you think the article has useful information or if you're not sure if it does, you can move on to Step 2. If the article does not have useful information, you can stop reading it and go on to a different one.

While You Read

Step 2: Read Closely—Carefully check out the parts of the article that you think will contain useful information for your purpose.

When you think you have found some information that may be useful, you change the way you read. Reading carefully allows you to find the details in a text.

After You Read

Step 3: Note Useful Information—Highlight, underline, make notes, or summarize the important information.

If you have found some information that is useful for your purpose, you need to note it or mark it in some way so that you can remember it. You can do this by underlining, highlighting, or taking notes on another piece of paper. You can also do this by paraphrasing the information—writing the important ideas in your own words.

If you have not found any useful information, you may need to look in a different place, or you may need to think again about the kind of information you need.

STEPS IN READING FOR A PURPOSE
Think About the Task: What is your purpose for reading this time?

BEFORE YOU READ
Pre-Step: Identify the information you need
Predict: What kind of information do you think you will need?
Where do you think you will find it?

Step 1: Preview
Look quickly at a reading to find the information you need.

Reading 1: Characteristics of Good Ads

WHILE YOU READ
Step 2: Read Closely
Read carefully those parts of the reading you think will be useful.

Characteristics of Good Ads

important characteristics of ads are

AFTER YOU READ
Step 3: Note Useful Information
Identify and note the important information

Characteristics of Good Ads

important characteristics of ads are
catch customers' attention

Qualities of Good Ads
1.
2.
3.

Finally, put together all the useful information that you have found in the different readings.

Reading 1 + Reading 2 + Reading 3 + Reading 4

Qualities of Good Ads
1.
2.
3.

Unit Tasks: Evaluating Ads, Writing an Effective Ad

When you have finished Readings 1–6, you will complete two Unit Tasks:

Unit Task 1: Analyze the advertisements in Unit 1. Use the information in the readings to decide which ads are the most and least effective. Be prepared to defend your opinions.

Unit Task 2: Use the information from the readings to design and write your own ad.

Try Reading for a Purpose

You have learned how reading for a purpose is different from reading to find an author's main ideas. Now you will try reading for a purpose, thinking about the Unit Tasks. You have already determined that in order to do them, you need information on the qualities of good ads. In Unit Task 1, you will need to evaluate the effectiveness of some ads—that is, you will decide whether or not the ads work. You have read some information about the advertising industry. Some of it will help you do Unit Task 1 and some of it will not.

1. **Now look back at Readings 1–3. Scan the titles and skim the articles to help yourself remember what is in them and decide how useful each article will be for the Unit Tasks. Then check (✓) your answers below.**

VERY USEFUL	A LITTLE USEFUL	NOT USEFUL	
_____	_____	_____	Reading 1 ("A Very Short History of Advertising")
_____	_____	_____	Reading 2 ("Basic Advertising Techniques")
_____	_____	_____	Reading 3 ("Characteristics of Good Ads")

2. **Look ahead to Readings 4–6. Scan the titles and skim the articles to decide how useful each article will be in helping you evaluate ads. Check (✓) your decisions.**

VERY USEFUL	A LITTLE USEFUL	NOT USEFUL	
_____	_____	_____	Reading 4 ("Twelve Steps to Creating Successful Ads")
_____	_____	_____	Reading 5 ("What's in a Name?")
_____	_____	_____	Reading 6 ("Improve Your Creativity in Five Minutes a Day")

3. **Now look at the titles of Readings 1–6. Which one looks like it will not be very helpful for Unit Task 1, evaluating ads, but could be very useful for Unit Task 2, writing an advertisement?**

READING 4: "TWELVE STEPS TO CREATING SUCCESSFUL ADVERTISEMENTS"

Step 1: Preview

Which reading technique(s) should you use?
❏ skimming
❏ scanning
❏ reading closely

1. **Preview Readings 4A and 4B. Do you think Readings 4A and 4B will be useful for the Unit Tasks? Where can you look to find out?**

PREVIEWING STRATEGY: Looking at the Format of a Reading

When a written text is printed in a book, magazine, or newspaper, it is made to look a certain way. What a reading looks like can give you important information about it. For example, could you recognize a newspaper article written in Russian? a business letter written in Greek? How? What are the formal characteristics of these two different types of written material?

What other types of written material can you recognize?

> Madrid, 22 de enero de 1999
>
> Curtidos Hermanos González
> C/Mayor, 11
> Salamanca
>
> Estimados señores:
> Les hago saber que este lunes pasado nuestros almacenes se han trasladado a nuestra fábrica de Alcalá de Henares. Para pedidos y para confirmar el envío de pedidos, pónganse en contacto con

---

2. **Take one minute to skim Readings 4A and 4B. Then answer these questions.**

   1. Where is Reading 4A probably from?

   2. Does Reading 4A seem useful for the Unit Tasks? Why or why not?

   3. Who wrote Reading 4B?

   4. Who was Reading 4B probably written for?

   5. Does Reading 4B seem useful for the Unit Tasks? Why or why not?

Step 2: Read Closely

1. **Read these two texts closely and check the predictions that you made in questions 2 and 3 on page 39. Remember not to look at the margin questions the first time that you read.**

2. **Reread the texts using the margin questions to help you.**

MAR 303

WRITING ADVERTISING COPY (3 credits) fall/winter
Prereq.: MAR 115 Introduction to Advertising or permission of the professor

An introduction to writing advertising copy for print ads and radio/television commercials. Students will learn to write copy for large corporations as well as small businesses. Basic elements of design for print ads will also be covered.

MAR 315

MARKETING IN THE GLOBAL ECONOMY (3 credits) fall/winter/summer
Prereq.: MAR 105 Introduction to Marketing

The challenges as well as the opportunities offered by the global marketplace.

Professor Allan Burstein
Marketing 303

January 15, 1998

Twelve Steps to Creating
Successful Advertisements

1. Have a Clear "Call to Action"

Selling more is not the immediate purpose of most advertisements. Advertisements need a more specific "call to action." The call to action is what you want the consumer to do after they read the ad.

Examples:
- Call the phone number listed by 5:00 PM on Friday to buy tickets for the concert.
- Walk into the store to see the new stereo equipment.
- Mail in the coupon for their free sample.

You should have just one, simple call to action. All ads help consumers to learn about a product or a service, so that is usually a secondary objective and is not part of the call to action.

1 Do you see any technical vocabulary?

2 What does it mean?

3 How do you know?

4 Can you get a general idea of the word *objective*?

5 What do you think it means?

Complete this sentence:

As a result of reading this advertisement, I expect
_____ to _____.
(types of individuals)   (take this specific action)

As you write the ad, you should look back at this
call to action and ask yourself if your ad copy will
achieve it.

2. Write the Headline

An ad's headline is very closely related to the
objective. They work together to make the same point
in two different ways.

Suppose your client sells a great kitchen cleaner and
your objective is:
To have housewives call to get a free sample.

The headline might be:
Norm is so sure you'll love Hyperclean kitchen
cleaner, he wants to give you a free sample!

If you are writing for a small business, the headline
must immediately tell people what they are selling.

3. Add Action to the Headline

An "action" verb makes a stronger headline.

6 What is an *action* verb in
this context?

"Make Your Windows the Focus of Your Room" is more
powerful than "Beautiful Windows for Every Room in
Your Home."

"Beat Rising Energy Costs Six Ways" is more powerful
than "New Energy-Saving Thermostat."

4. Create the Body

Think of your ad as a sandwich.

headline → makes the reader stop
body → gives more information
call to action → gives them an action to take

7 What does *that is* signal?

When you write the body, you should try to imagine
your client's prospects, that is, his or her possible
customers. What would he or she say to them as one
person to another? That's the way you want to write
your ads—like one person talking to another.

8 What does *in other words* signal?

5. Tell the Truth

It's very important to tell the truth. Lies and exaggerations are not helpful. In other words, do not overstate the good points of the product or service. Consumers do not trust advertisements that make unbelievable promises. Lies and exaggerations do not get new customers, at least not for very long.

6. Shorter Is Better

Short sentences
Short paragraphs
Short words

Fast cure is better than *timely resolution*.

7. Talk Like a Real Person

The best ads use the same language as normal people when they are speaking.

Homework. Try this exercise: using a tape recorder, describe what your client has to offer in fifty words or less. Then transcribe the tape and change it as little as possible.

8. Use a Great Illustration

Every business is selling quality. Great illustrations and copy show that quality is important to your client. Consumers will know they can expect good products or service.

9. Offer Choices

Most people think that ads which offer a choice seem more honest. When you give a consumer a choice, the copy becomes more like friendly advice than advertising.

"Ask your doctors, or go to your local drug store and buy... "

10. Make One Clear Point

The readers get confused when an ad has too much information. Give the most important benefit of your client's product or service in the ad. When customers contact your client, they can learn about any other benefits.

9 Notice that *or* is not always used for definitions!

11. Offer Something for Nothing

One good reason to respond to or answer an ad is to get something for free. However, the free gift has to be valuable to customers. Many ads offer a free brochure or booklet but this doesn't have a lot of value. A free offer will be more effective if it is important <u>or</u> useful to customers. For example, an educational guide, a government publication or a small tool are all valuable free gifts.

Let people see a photo or illustration of the free gift. They will want it more if they can see what they are going to get.

12. Let the Customers Give the Message

Customers can say good things about your client's product or service that would seem untrue if your client said them.

"Morris windows gave my house a whole new look."

10 Can you get a general meaning for *consultation?*

This quotation along with a photo of the customer is very believable and leads to this call to action: "To see what Morris windows can do for your house, simply call for a free consultation…"

A. Checking Your Comprehension

Read each question below. Then look back at the reading to find the answers.

1. What is the purpose of Reading 4A? What is the purpose of Reading 4B?

2. In groups, discuss the advertisement below using the 12 ideas given in Reading 4B. How could you change the ad to make it more effective? Compare your ideas with the ideas of other groups.

DO YOU LIKE EARLY AMERICAN FURNITURE?

The Williamsburg Furniture Company has been making really good Early American furniture since 1903. It has been owned and operated by the same family since that time. Williamsburg employs only master carpenters. And each piece of Williamsburg furniture is built to last. We use only the best hardwood, such as maple, oak, and cherry. In addition, our furniture is built by hand. Williamsburg specializes in Early American furniture, and each piece is an exact copy of real Early American furniture. It is also made in the same way that our ancestors in Williamsburg made their furniture. Our furniture has no glue and no nails.

For a catalogue of our fine furniture write:
Williamsburg Furniture Company, Williamsburg, Virginia

B. Topics for Discussion

Discuss the following questions with your classmates.

1. As a consumer, which of the 12 points in Reading 4B are most important to you? Why?

2. Do you think that most advertisers follow the 12 points? Why or why not?

Step 3: Note Useful Information

1. Find Useful Information

1. **Is there a single main idea in this reading? Why or why not?**

2. **Is it easy to find the important points in this reading? Why?**

3. **How many of the author's important ideas in Reading 4B have valuable information for Unit Tasks 1 and 2? (a lot, some, not very much)**

   a lot   some   not very much

2. Highlight or Underline the Important Information

When an article contains a lot of useful information, you must be especially careful not to highlight or underline too much.

This article is basically a list of useful information. The author divided the list into 12 parts. Each part has a subtitle. Sometimes, the subtitle alone gives you all the important information in that part. For example, look at number 5 below.

> **5. Tell the Truth**
>
> It's very important to tell the truth. Lies and exaggerations are not helpful. In other words, do not overstate the good points of the product or service. Consumers do not trust advertisements that make unbelievable promises. Lies and exaggerations do not get new customers, at least not for very long.

The information in the paragraph explains why you should tell the truth. However, after you read this once, you do not need to remember the explanation. The information that you need to remember is in the subtitle. Now look at point number 1 below.

> **1. Have a Clear "Call to Action"**
>
> Selling more is not the immediate purpose of most advertisements. Advertisements need a more specific "call to action." The call to action is what you want the consumer to do after they read the ad.
>
> Examples:
> • Call the phone number listed by 5:00 PM on Friday to buy tickets for the concert.
> • Walk into the store to see the new stereo equipment.
> • Mail in the coupon for their free sample.
>
> You should have just one, simple call to action. All ads help consumers to learn about a product or a service, so that is usually a secondary objective and is not part of the call to action.

This point introduces the term "call to action" and gives useful information about it. Here, it is helpful to highlight or underline more than just the subtitle. What other information in point number 1 is important for you to remember in order to do the Unit Tasks?

1. **Look back at Reading 4B. Which of these subtitles contains the most useful information from that section? Check (✓) your answers and discuss with your classmates.**

	USEFUL	NOT USEFUL
2. Write the Headline	____	____
4. Create the Body	____	____
7. Talk Like a Real Person	____	____
12. Let the Customers Give the Message	____	____

2. **Look at all the other sections. For each point, decide what information will be the most important to remember when you are evaluating or writing an advertisement, and highlight or underline those ideas.**

3. **Compare your work with your classmates'. Explain your choices.**

C. Building Your Vocabulary

Use these steps to build your vocabulary with words from the reading.

1. Look at your reading list from Readings 1–3. Put a checkmark (✓) next to any words that also appeared in Reading 4. Then, look back at Reading 4 and make a list of five to ten new words that you feel are important to learn.

2. Write these words in your vocabulary notebook. Group words that are similar (e.g., *consumers/customers, true/untrue*). Copy a sentence or phrase in which the word appears. Decide on the part of speech of the word and write a definition for it.

3. If you are still unsure of the meaning of this word or the part of speech, look it up in the dictionary and write the definition in your own words. For additional practice, write your own sentence.

D. Writing Your Ideas

Look at the writing topics below. Choose at least one and write about it.

1. Do you think that most of the ads that you see are effective or ineffective? Why? Explain and give examples whenever possible.

2 Which are more effective, ads in newspapers or ads in magazines? Why? Explain your point of view.

E. Making Connections

1. **Compare Reading 4B with Readings 1–3 and 4A. Is the information in Reading 4B most similar to the information in Reading 1, 2, 3 or 4A?**

2. **How are the two articles similar? Check (✓) your answer. Give examples to support your answer.**

   _____ 1. They are both based on research.

   _____ 2. They are both written by an advertising research company.

   _____ 3. They both talk about creating effective advertisements.

3. **How are they different? Check (✓) your answer. Give examples to support your answer.**

   _____ 1. One is written by an advertising professional and the other is written by an advertising student.

   _____ 2. One is written for advertisers and the other is written for consumers.

   _____ 3. One presents the results of research; the other presents the results of experience in advertising.

READING 5: "WHAT'S IN A NAME?"

Step 1: Preview

1. **Look at the format of this reading. Where is it probably from? How do you know?**

2. **Where should you look to find the general topic of the reading? Do this now. What do you think the general topic is?**

3. **Is this reading likely to be helpful in the Unit Tasks? Why or why not?**

Step 2: Read Closely

1. **Read the text closely. Remember not to pay attention to the margin questions the first time that you read.**

2. **Reread the text, using the margin questions to help you.**

READING 5

1 What examples are given in this paragraph? How can they help you to understand *brand names*?

WHAT'S IN A NAME?

1 Creap coffee creamer is a big seller in Japan, and Bimbo bread is extremely popular in Mexico, but people in English-speaking countries would be unlikely to buy these products. Why? Because their names have unfortunate meanings in English. As companies go global, it is becoming increasingly important to find brand names that can travel from country to country.

2 In a recent article from Reuters News Service, Bridget Ruffell, a director of The Brand Naming Co., which specializes in creating brand names for clients, said, "Finding the right name for an international brand is expensive, time-consuming and fraught with difficulty."

3 "In addition to the problems of meaning and pronunciation, all names have to be legally registered, which involves long and expensive searches to make sure that they have not already been taken by another company," she said.

4 Finding the right product name–and avoiding the wrong ones–is so important that The Brand Naming Co. has created a "black museum" of products with names that make them virtually unsellable in English-speaking countries.

2 Do you need to understand the exact meaning of *skum* and *bum*?

5 There's "Skum," a brand of candy in Sweden, for instance, and "Nuclear," a clothes whitener in Spain.

6 The Brand Naming Co. also cautioned about a Turkish cookie called "Bum" and a Mexican beer called "Nude," although consumers in Ankara and Mexico City told Reuters they had never heard of those products.

3 What or who is Reuters?

7 Companies from English-speaking countries that want to sell their products in non-English-speaking countries also have a lot of problems finding good product names. The sounds R and L, for instance, are often confused among some speakers of Asian languages.

8 Jonathan Mercer, managing director of Brand Guardians, a firm that specializes in creating brand names, said companies have to be careful to avoid names with unfortunate meanings.

9 One of the most famous stories about a brand-naming problem involves an American car. The marketing department at Chevrolet decided to name their new car "Nova." They thought that they'd found a good name. *Nova* means "star" in Latin. However, in Spanish, the two words *no va* mean "doesn't go"–not a very suitable name for a car.

10 There is more than one way to find a name for a new product. Sometimes, to avoid the problems that choosing a real word might cause, companies actually make up a word that (they hope) does not exist in any language. One very successful made-up name is Kodak. It was chosen because it is pronounceable by people who speak many different languages.

4 What is *Kodak* an example of?

11 However, even when a company invents a name, it can still have name problems. For example, a number of years ago, Esso Oil Company wanted a new name for their gasoline that would be acceptable all over the world. After spending a lot of time and even more money, they came up with "Exxon." Unfortunately, it didn't work well in Japan. The Japanese pronounce it "Eki-son," which sounds like the Japanese phrase meaning "loss of profit."

12 Because English is now a global language, companies sometimes choose to use simple English words that describe their new product. A well-known example of this kind of naming technique is the "Walkman." The Sony company chose this name for its personal stereo because it describes the product–you can use it to walk and listen to music at the same time.

13 It can take a long time to find the right name for a new product. First, a company hires a group of creative people to brainstorm a list of possible names. This list may have as many as 100 names on it. Then they often ask consumers to choose the names that they like the best. This technique can have surprising results. A few years ago a French publishing company was going to publish a new series of English-language textbooks. Until they could think of a name for the series, they called it "Method Orange" (like calling a product "Brand X"). When the publishers sent their list of possible names to consumers, someone added this name to the list. To everyone's surprise, it was the most popular name on the list, and the series "Method Orange" was born.

5 Can you guess what *Brand X* means?

14 When a company has found a name that consumers seem to like, the naming process is still not over. They must then research the name to make sure that it is not the name of another product. They usually research the best three or four names so that they can be certain of finding one that works. This research takes a long time because each name must be searched in every country. For example, if you wanted to name a laundry detergent "Fresh," in addition to searching the names of laundry soap in each country, you would also have to look at the names of other types of products that you think might have that name. A search can cost $500 per name per country.

A. Checking Your Comprehension

1. The following are some important points of the article. Write the names of the products that are given as examples of these points:

1. Some product names have unacceptable meanings in English.

   _____

2. Some English product names have unacceptable meanings in other languages. _____

3. One of the best ways to name a product is to make up a new name.

   _____

4. A simple English phrase can make an effective product name.

   _____

2. What three steps do companies go through to name a new product?

1. First they _____

   _____

2. Then they _____

   _____

3. Finally they _____

   _____

B. Topics for Discussion

Discuss the following questions with your classmates.

1. Are there any products whose names you feel are very effective? ineffective?

2. Have you ever not bought a product because you didn't like the name?

Step 3: Note Useful Information

1. Does this reading contain any information that is directly useful to Unit Task 1? If so, what? If not, why not?

2. How might the information in this task help you to do Unit Task 2?

C. Building Your Vocabulary

Use these steps to build your vocabulary with words from the reading.

1. Look at your reading list from Readings 1–4. Put a checkmark (✓) next to any words that also appeared in Reading 5. Then look back at Reading 5 and make a list of five to ten new words that you feel are important to learn.

2. Write these words in your vocabulary notebook. Group words that are similar (e.g., *seller/unsellable, pronounceable/acceptable/suitable*). Copy a sentence or phrase in which the word appears. Decide on the part of speech of the word and write a definition for it.

3. If you are still unsure of the meaning of this word or the part of speech, look it up in the dictionary and write the definition in your own words. For additional practice, write your own sentence.

D. Writing Your Ideas

Look at the writing topics below. Choose at least one and write about it.

1. Shakespeare said, "...a rose by any other name would smell as sweet." Explain why you agree or disagree. Give examples when possible.

2. Think about advertisements for imported products in your country. Are the companies sensitive to the culture of your country? Explain and give examples.

READING 6: "IMPROVE YOUR CREATIVITY IN FIVE MINUTES A DAY"

Step 1: Preview

1. **Reading 6 is an article from an Internet Web site. Imagine for a moment that you were looking through a Web site and you noticed this article. Imagine, too, that it didn't seem to be exactly what you were looking for, in searching for information to help you with your task, but it looked interesting. Answer these questions.**

   1. How can you decide whether or not you should read it?

   2. What parts of it can you look at?

   3. What reading strategies and technique(s) would you use?

2. **How might this article help you with the Unit Tasks?**

Step 2: Read Closely

1. **This reading begins with a quiz to find out how creative you are. Read the first section and take the quiz. Then decide if you need to read the rest of the article closely. If you decide to read the rest of the text, do steps 2 and 3, below.**

2. **Read this text closely and check the predictions that you made in questions 1 and 2 above. Remember not to look at the margin questions the first time that you read.**

3. **Reread the text using the margin questions to help you.**

IMPROVE YOUR CREATIVITY IN FIVE MINUTES A DAY

1 Most of us would like to become more creative. Try this quiz and find out about yourself.

2 You work for a large ad agency. One of your clients, a clothing store, is thinking about using another agency. Your boss has given you until tomorrow to think of a new headline for the announcement of their summer clothing sale.

3 Give yourself ten minutes to write down or draw as many ideas as you have. When you are finished, score your results.

1 What is your score?

4 Scoring: Give yourself 1 point for each idea.

7–10 points	You're a creative genius.
4–6 points	Think about going into advertising.
2–3 points	You have some creativity.
0–1 point	You need some work.

LEARNING CREATIVITY

5 When you took the quiz, was anything stopping you from having ideas? Were you telling yourself "that isn't practical" or "you can't do that in an ad"? It is this "self-talk" that keeps us from having ideas.

QUANTITY EQUALS QUALITY

2 Do you believe this statistic?

3 Does it matter if it's true or not?

6 The average adult thinks of three to six possible answers for any problem. The average five-year-old thinks of sixty. Research has shown that, in creativity, quantity equals quality. The more ideas you have, the better your final solution will be. That is because the best ideas usually appear at the end of the list.

7 So, to improve your creativity you need to learn to make longer lists. To do this you should focus on four areas:

1. Understanding how creative thinking works

4 What is the internal definition for *suspend judgment?*

2. Suspending judgment—and turning off our internal critic

3. Finding sources of ideas all around us

4. Applying the key success factors of creative thinking

TWO TYPES OF THINKING STRATEGIES

5 Is there a definition of *convergent* and *divergent?*

6 Do you need one?

8 There are two types of thinking strategies. They are called divergent and convergent thinking. Divergent thinking creates possibility. Convergent thinking creates practicality. However, most adults try to do both kinds of

thinking at the same time. That creates problems. For example, if you think of an idea for improving your job and at the same time decide that your boss won't like it, you will never use that idea.

7 How does the author help you understand these words?

9   In divergent thinking, judgment is turned off. No negative self-talk is allowed. No criticism. No evaluation. Do not think about practicality, profit, approval, or advantage. Divergent thinking is about the creation of ideas without thinking about their usefulness. Let yourself think about both the obvious and the imaginative.

10 In convergent thinking, judgment is turned back on. It is often helpful to first decide how you will measure the value of an idea. How will you decide how good it is? Then use convergent thinking—which of your ideas has the most value to you? How can you combine your best ideas to make a great solution?

8 Why does the author talk about cars and brakes here?

11 The secret to creativity is this: separate idea creation from idea evaluation. In other words, don't drive the car of your mind with one foot on the gas and the other on the brake. Get into the habit of thinking up lots of ideas, then selecting from that list. Create possibility, then practicality. You'll be surprised at the results.

SUSPENDING JUDGMENT

12 First, become aware of your internal critic, that inner voice that tells you to "quit wasting time," or "think of something useful." It is sometimes helpful to make a list of these phrases. You don't have to forget them completely—we all need to be able to judge. You only have to hold these phrases back for five minutes or so. It's difficult at first, but practice makes perfect.

13 In nature, about 95% of new species die out quickly. You could say that nature has only about five good ideas in every hundred. Fortunately, nature does not concentrate on the bad ideas; it just keeps creating new ideas. Suspending judgment, that is, not judging immediately, allows you to create huge lists of ideas. This increases the probability that you will think of a really good idea.

14 Second, be aware of how you judge others. Notice your language when you evaluate someone's ideas. Have a conversation with someone and try not to judge their ideas; simply state your own opinion. You will see that it is extremely difficult to stop judging people. The next time you are in a store, choose a person and notice your impressions of him or her. What is his or her situation in life? How educated is he/she? How much money does he/she make? Notice that you make up stories and you don't know whether they are true. Yet we often consider these stories "facts" when we make decisions about people. We allow our judgment to limit our relationships with others. Remember, the more aware we become of judgment, the easier it is to turn it off.

9 Do this activity.

15 Make a list of new toy ideas for kids ages six to eight. Each time you're stopped, write down your thoughts on a separate list. Continue until you have at least six "idea stoppers." Now go back and write down ideas that deliberately violate, or disobey, every one. Perhaps you wrote "kids won't like it." Write down some unlikeable toy ideas. On a recent comedy television show they showed a toy called Sad Sara, a doll who does nothing but cry.

16 Even your internal critic can be a source of ideas! We have found that there are several factors that help to increase creativity in individuals and groups. When these factors are present, people are the most creative.

Remember these four success factors:

- Safety

- No Judgment

- Have Fun

- Practice

Safety

17 It is often our fear of criticism that keeps us quiet. This is why traditional brainstorming sessions are difficult for most people. This problem is easy to correct. You simply need to create a "safe space" for yourself. In your safe space, you can create ideas without fear of judgment.

18 To create a safe space, allow yourself to think divergently. Record every idea you have. Then decide what ideas you want to share with others. In meetings, you can write your ideas down first, and then choose some to present to the group.

19 Listen to what you tell yourself about your ideas. Notice how you think about others' ideas. Try not to judge immediately—you will get a chance later. However, you must be careful. Don't get judgmental about your judgment. Don't start criticizing yourself because you're having a problem not judging. Remember, waiting to judge is like exercising a muscle. The more you do it, the easier it will get.

Fun

20 You've never seen a serious five-year-old when she's being creative. Have fun! If it isn't fun, change how you're doing it. Play with your problem—change your point of view. How would a doctor, a lawyer, a beauty queen, or a banker handle your problem? Get down on the floor and be a child again—now what ideas do you have?

10 Is this statistic realistic? Does it matter if it's true?

21 We have found that it is possible to increase creativity by 400% in less than an hour. But it only persists in those that practice holding off judgment regularly. We recommend five minutes a day for thirty days—and you'll be thinking up six impossible things before breakfast!

22 Also, notice the creative efforts of others. Watch kids. Even commercials on TV can have a high degree of creativity. What makes a clever idea, or a creative product?

23 Imagine that you have inherited your rich uncle's business. You are so excited that you immediately go out and spend a lot of money. Then you find out the unhappy truth. Your uncle got rich making glass milk bottles! You have inherited thousands of them but hardly anyone wants to buy them because most people prefer plastic bottles. What can you do with them? Remember, suspend judgment, have fun, and go for quantity first.

A. Checking Your Comprehension

1. Check (✓) the correct column for each statement.

	CONVERGENT THINKING	DIVERGENT THINKING
1. You criticize your ideas.	_____	_____
2. You make long lists of ideas.	_____	_____
3. You think about practicality.	_____	_____
4. You are judgmental.	_____	_____

2. Circle all the ideas that are true according to Reading 6.

1. Divergent thinking comes before convergent thinking.

2. Convergent thinking is never necessary.

3. Divergent thinking should be fun.

3. How can this reading help ad writers?

4. Did the reading help you do the practice activity in paragraphs 21–23? Why or why not?

B. Reading Strategies

> ### READING STRATEGY: More Practice in Finding Important Ideas
>
> As you learned in Reading 3, sometimes the author states his or her main idea. In Reading 6, the author tells us what his main idea is. Can you find it?
>
> Part of being a good reader is being able to figure out what the author's other important points are, even if the author doesn't tell you. For example, look at these three statements. Which one states an important point from Reading 6?
>
> 1. The average adult thinks of three to six possible answers for any problem.
> 2. Research has shown that, in creativity, quantity equals quality.
> 3. Some children and some adults are creative.
>
> The correct answer is 2. (Answer 1 is an interesting detail that the author gave us to support answer 2. Answer 3 is too general.)

Put a checkmark (✓) next to the statements that you think are the author's important points. (For some statements, you and your classmates may not agree.)

_____ 1. There are two types of thinking strategies: convergent and divergent thinking.

_____ 2. In divergent thinking, no evaluation is allowed.

_____ 3. In convergent thinking, judgment is allowed.

_____ 4. Suspending judgment increases the probability that we will be able to think of a really good idea.

_____ 5. It is difficult to stop judging people.

_____ 6. Having fun is an important part of being creative.

_____ 7. Try getting down on the floor and acting like a child again as a way to get new ideas.

_____ 8. Everyone can learn to be more creative.

_____ 9. In order to be creative, it is important to feel safe with our ideas.

_____ 10. There are many ways to be creative.

C. Topics for Discussion

Discuss the following questions with your classmates.

1. Read the following two quotes. How do they relate to the ideas in the reading? Do Linus Pauling, Leo Burnett, and Vincent Parillo agree on the topic of creativity? Give a reason for your answer.

   "If you want to have a great idea, have lots of ideas." _Linus Pauling, Nobel Prize winner for chemistry_

"To [stop] making mistakes is very easy. All you have to do is [stop] having ideas." *Leo Burnett, advertising executive*

2. Do you think most people are creative? Why or why not? What is an example of a time when you were especially creative?

Step 3: Note Useful Information

1. **How is the information in Reading 6 different from the information in Readings 1–5?**

2. **How will the information in Reading 6 help you to do the Unit Tasks?**

3. **Go back to Reading 6 and highlight the information that will help you to do the Unit Tasks.**

D. Building Your Vocabulary

Use these steps to build your vocabulary with words from the reading.

1. Look at your reading list from Readings 1–5. Put a checkmark (✓) next to any words that also appeared in Reading 6. Then look back at Reading 6 and make a list of five to ten new words that you feel are important to learn.

2. Write these words in your vocabulary notebook. Group words that are similar (e.g., *create/creation/creative, practicality/probability*). Copy a sentence or phrase in which the word appears. Decide on the part of speech of the word and write a definition for it.

3. If you are still unsure of the meaning of this word or the part of speech, look it up in the dictionary and write the definition in your own words. For additional practice, write your own sentence.

E. Writing Your Ideas

Look at the writing topics below. Choose at least one and write about it.

1. Do you know any very creative people? Write about someone whom you think is creative. Why do you think that they are creative? How do they get their ideas? (Don't be afraid to write about yourself!)

2. Do you think that children are more creative than adults? Why or why not?

Building Your Vocabulary: Summary

Look back at the vocabulary lists that you have made for this unit. On another piece of paper copy down any words from the list that have two or more checkmarks (✓). These are important because they occur more than once. Look at the first list and find words that you think you may need to use for the Unit Tasks. Add these words to the second list. Group any similar words together.

The second list will be your active vocabulary. These are words that you will want to learn to use in speech and in writing. The other, longer, list is your passive vocabulary. These are words that you want to learn to recognize but not necessarily use. In your vocabulary notebook make two sections, one for active vocabulary and another for passive vocabulary. Copy the words into the correct section. Remember to include an example sentence or phrase and the part of speech. For active vocabulary, you should also add your own sentence or phrase. Ask another student or your teacher to check to see if you have used the word correctly.

There are many strategies for learning new vocabulary. Some people draw pictures to help them. For example, if you wanted to remember the meanings of *headline, copy, illustration* and *imagination*, you could make a drawing such as this:

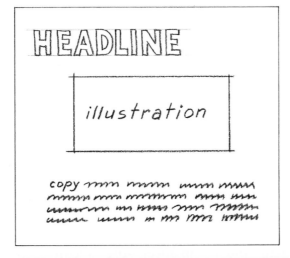

UNIT TASK 1:
Evaluating Advertisements

In Unit Task 1, you will analyze the advertisements in Unit 1. Use the information in the readings to decide which ads are the most and least effective. Be prepared to defend your opinions.

1. Look back at the sections that you underlined or highlighted in Readings 1–6. Prepare for a group discussion by making a list of the information that you think is the most important.

2. With a small group of your classmates, use the information in Readings 1–6 to list five of the most important characteristics of effective advertisements. Rewrite the information in your own words. Do not write complete sentences. Explain to the class why you chose these items.

3. Look at the advertisements in this unit or bring in other ads and discuss them in groups. Imagine you are an advertising professional. Decide which ad is the most effective and which is the least effective. Use the information in the readings to defend your opinions. Discuss your choices with your group.

UNIT TASK 2:
Writing an Effective Advertisement

In Unit Task 2, you will use the information from the readings to design and write your own ad.

---

1. Look back at the sections that you underlined or highlighted in Readings 1–6. Think about the information that will help you write a good ad.

2. In groups, choose a product or a service and design an advertisement for it. Think about *positioning, illustration, headlines,* and *copy.* Use the information you have learned from the readings about characteristics of good ads.

3. Present your group's advertisement to the rest of the class. Explain why you designed your ad the way that you did.

4. Look at the ads designed by the other groups and listen to their explanations. Think about and discuss how they applied the ideas from this unit.

PART EXPANSION ACTIVITIES

Applying Your Knowledge

1. Imagine you are an advertising executive. Your job is to evaluate the ads your classmates designed in Unit Task 2. First, read the critique below. Underline the compliments and circle the criticisms. Then choose one of your classmates' ads and write an evaluation of it, using the information you have learned from your reading. Find some good qualities in the ad. Also make some suggestions about how your classmates could make the ad more effective.

I think that Group 1's advertisement for tennis shoes is very effective. The picture was very amusing. I think that it would have good stopping power. But since teenagers are the biggest market for tennis shoes, it would be better to have a younger person in the picture. The woman in the picture is about thirty. Teenagers might think that these shoes are meant for older people. The headline was also good but it seemed a little small. It might be better to make the headline larger and move it to the top of the page.

2. Imagine that you are a member of a consumer watchdog organization. Your job is to evaluate ads for their truthfulness and helpfulness to consumers. Choose one of your classmates' ads and write an evaluation of it, using the information you have learned in your reading. Make suggestions about how the ad could be improved from the consumer's standpoint. For more information, look at Additional Reading 1 on page 220.

The Electronic Link

1. Look on the Internet to find more information about advertising. Some possible Internet sites for information on advertising are:

   The advertising graveyard   http://www.zeldman.com/ad.html

   Advertising Age magazine   http://www.adage.com/

   Chiat Day Advertising Agency   http://www.chiatday.com/web/

   You can find many more Internet sites devoted to advertising by using these key words to search:

   advertisements

   "advertising agency"

   "advertising department"

   "advertising links"

   "advertising resources"

   marketing

2. Present your findings to the class.

3. Choose one Web site.

   Name of site _____

   URL (Web address) _____

   Who created this Web site? _____

   Is it reasonable to think that the information in this site is correct? _____

4. List up to four new facts you learned from the Web site that were not included in the readings in this unit.

1. _____

2. _____

3. _____

4. _____

For More Information

The Federal Trade Commission Act requires all advertising to be truthful and nondeceptive or misleading. If you have questions or concerns about advertisements, or for a free copy of Best Sellers, a list of all the FTC's consumer and business publications, write:

Consumer Response Center

Federal Trade Commission

Washington, D.C. 20580

Your comments help the FTC in its law enforcement efforts.

For additional information about advertising, write to:

Council of Better Business Bureaus, Inc.

845 Third Avenue

New York, N.Y. 10022

 See Additional Readings for this unit on pages 220–224.

Essay Questions

Choose one of the topics below and write an essay about it.

1. Now that you have learned a great deal about the advertising industry, how do you feel about it? Do you think that advertisements are helpful or a waste of money?

2. Some people feel that advertisements always lie because they minimize a product's bad points and maximize its good points. Do you agree or not? Why?

3. Do consumers need more laws to protect them from false advertising? Why or why not?

4 In this unit, you have read primarily about print advertising. In what ways is television advertising the same? In what ways is it different? What advantages does each one have over the other?

1997 AUTOMOBILE OF THE YEAR.
IT'S MORE THAN JUST A DREAM.

Automobile | AUTOMOBILE OF THE YEAR *Automobile Magazine* assembled some of the world's finest vehicles for a head-to-head competition, all vying for the coveted 1997 Automobile of the Year award. And the winner was Toyota's RAV4. 2 door or 4 door. Front-wheel or full-time 4-wheel drive. 4-wheel independent suspension. Fully caffeinated engine. Tons of people and cargo space. Plus see-above-traffic visibility. Of course, winning this prestigious award validates what we've known all along. That the RAV4 is more than just a dream, it's a fantasy vehicle for the real world.

Call 1-800-GO-TOYOTA or visit our website at: http://www.toyota.com for a brochure or full-line CD-ROM plus the location of your nearest dealer. ©1997 Toyota Motor Sales, U.S.A., Inc. Buckle up! Do it for those who love you. Toyota reminds you to Tread Lightly!® on public and private land. Vehicle shown with optional equipment.

TOYOTA RAV4
I love what you do for me

3:13 p.m.
San Francisco
Concierge
Addis Rezene

Conversant in Japanese and French. Fluent in English and 2-year-old.

Radisson
HOTELS WORLDWIDE
The difference is genuine.

The difference. You notice it the minute you arrive. In people like Addis Rezene. And the rest of our staff. People who are helpful and courteous not because it's their job. But because it's their nature. We invite you to experience the difference at any Radisson.

For reservations call 1-800-333-3333, visit us at www.radisson.com or contact your travel professional.

Evaluating Your Progress

**Think about the skills and strategies that you used in this unit.
Check (✓) the correct boxes that apply to you.**

	NEVER	SOMETIMES	OFTEN	ALWAYS
1. My classmates and I agreed with one another on the author's important points.	☐	☐	☐	☐
2. When I scanned, I was able to find specific information easily.	☐	☐	☐	☐
3. When I skimmed, I was able to get a general idea of the reading.	☐	☐	☐	☐
4. I was able to find internal definitions.	☐	☐	☐	☐
5. I was able to get a general meaning of a word defined in the text.	☐	☐	☐	☐
6. I thought about the author's point of view as I read.	☐	☐	☐	☐
7. My underlining/highlighting helped me to find useful information quickly.	☐	☐	☐	☐
8. I understood and could use the three steps in reading for a purpose.	☐	☐	☐	☐
9. The best ways for me to preview were to:				
skim all or part of the reading	☐	☐	☐	☐
scan key words	☐	☐	☐	☐
scan subtitles	☐	☐	☐	☐
look at pictures, charts, and graphs	☐	☐	☐	☐

Setting Your Reading Goals

Choose three items from the list above that you would like to improve. Write them below.

Goal #1: _____

Goal #2: _____

Goal #3: _____

$\mathcal{I}$N THIS UNIT

Reading Strategies

- Recognizing how information is organized
- Evaluating support for ideas and opinions
- Using examples to find an author's important ideas
- Understanding where a reading comes from
- Making local inferences
- Recognizing referents
- Understanding the organization of a comparative reading

Strategies for Unknown Vocabulary

- Using synonyms
- Using parallellism to find synonyms
- Using repetition and parallelism
- Using lists to get a general meaning of a word
- Using examples to guess meaning
- Recognizing parts of speech

This Thing Called Love

Think About It

A man and a woman are at a party. They are strangers. Suddenly, the woman sees the man across the room. He is talking to a couple of friends. She notices that he has a nice smile. She moves to be in his line of vision and glances at him to see if he has noticed her. He has. Their eyes meet for a second. She begins talking to the people near her, waiting to see if he will approach. He does. He walks over to look at a picture on the wall near where she is standing. Their eyes meet again, this time for a little longer, and they smile in recognition. She moves over to where he is standing and comments on the painting. He agrees with her comment, and they smile with greater warmth. They look at each other a little longer than normal. She smiles brightly, turns her head, and tosses her hair. They find a place to sit away from the crowd. As they talk, he edges closer to her. He is excited and a little nervous. The pupils of his eyes widen. They talk as if no one else is in the room. Each tries to present his or her best self. However, they reveal more about themselves than they normally do on first meeting someone. Gradually, they begin to mirror each other's gestures. When she turns her head, he turns his head. When he takes a drink, she takes a drink. At home after the party, each feels hopeful yet uncertain. They know that although they feel excited and full of hope, love fails many more times than it succeeds. It is the same all over the world. Other couples are falling in love in Finland and Patagonia. They are courting in Madagascar and the Philippines. Despite their different cultures, all these courting couples would understand the hope and excitement that this couple feels.

Discuss these questions with your classmates.

1. Compare the description of the party on page 67 to a meeting between a man and a woman in your culture. What would be the same? What would be different?

2. The writer says that this couple feels hopeful and uncertain. Why do they feel that way?

3. The writer believes that romantic love can be found in all cultures. Do you agree? Why or why not?

4. What is *courting*? Where and how does courtship occur in your culture?

Looking Ahead in Unit Two

Look through the unit and answer these questions.

1. Find the titles of the readings and write them on the lines.

Reading 1: _____

Reading 2: _____

Reading 3: _____

Reading 4: _____

Reading 5: _____

Reading 6: _____

2. Which reading looks the most interesting? Why?

3. What is the Unit Task that you will complete at the end (page 114) of this unit?

 PART A   FOCUS ON SKILLS

READING 1: "WHY HIM? WHY HER?"

A. Pre-reading the Text

1. **Which parts of the reading should you look at in order to quickly predict the topic? Circle your answers.**

   1. title   2. subtitle   3. author's name   4. illustrations

2. **Now look at those places in Reading 1. What do you think the topic is?**

   _____

3. **Use your general knowledge. Write three reasons that people fall in love.**

_____

_____

_____

PRE-READING STRATEGY: Reading the First and Last Paragraphs

A good way to get a more detailed idea of a reading is to read one or two paragraphs at the beginning or end. In many types of readings, the first paragraph serves as an introduction that explains what the reading is about. The last paragraph is often a conclusion that restates the most important points of the reading.

One major exception to this type of organization is the news story. In a news story, the latest or newest information usually comes in the first paragraph. The paragraphs that follow contain background information on the story. The last paragraph is usually not a summary.

---

4. **Read the first and last paragraphs of Reading 1. Which one was the most informative? Do you think that the reading will include any of your ideas about why people fall in love?**

5. **Read the text closely. Remember to cover the margin questions when you read the first time.**

6. **Read the text again and use the margin questions to help you.**

READING 1

Why Him? Why Her?

From
The Anatomy of Love,
Helen Fisher, Ph.D.

1 What definition of _infatuation_ does the writer give?

1   Almost everybody knows what infatuation, or falling in love, feels like. Those sleepless nights and restless days. You daydream during class or business meetings, forget your coat, drive past your house, sit by the phone, or plan what you will say—obsessed, waiting for the next meeting with "him" or "her." You take foolish risks, say stupid things, laugh too hard, tell all of your secrets, talk all night, walk at dawn, and are generally oblivious to the rest of the world.

2   Why do we fall in love with Ray as opposed to Bill, Sue instead of Cecilia? Why him? Why her?

"The heart has its reasons which reason knows nothing of," wrote philosopher Blaise Pascal. Scientists can, however, provide some "reasonable" explanations for this hurricane of emotion.

Love Maps

2 Is *love map* a generally recognized term?

3   Researcher John Money believes that all human beings have something he calls a "love map." Long before you fall in love with a particular person, you have developed a mental map which determines with whom you will fall in love.

4   Children develop these love maps, Money thinks, between ages five and eight (or even earlier) in response to family, friends, and other people they meet, as well as their experiences. For example, as a child you get used to the way your mother listens, scolds, and pats you and how your father jokes or walks or smells. You like certain things about your friends and relatives; you don't like others or you connect them with unpleasant occurrences. Gradually, these memories begin to form a pattern in your mind.

3 What does this example illustrate?

4 What information do paragraphs 4–6 provide?

5   As you grow up, this unconscious map takes shape and an image of the ideal sweetheart gradually becomes clearer. Then, in teenage years, when sexual feelings flood the brain, your love map becomes quite specific. You imagine exactly how your true love will look—his or her hair and eye color, and height and weight—as well as personality, manners, and other features. You soon not only have a mental picture of your perfect partner but you also have dreams about the places you will go together and the kinds of conversations the two of you will have.

5 Look at the use of *vary* in paragraphs 7 and 8. Can you guess what it means?

6 In paragraph 7, what is the purpose of these lists?

6   So, long before your true love walks into your life, you have already constructed some basic elements of your ideal sweetheart. Then, when you actually see someone who seems to fit the image, you fall in love with him or her and project your unique love map onto this person. The recipient is generally quite different from your ideal. However, you pay little attention to the differences. Hence, Chaucer's famous words, "Love is blind."

7   These love maps vary from one individual to the next. Some people are attracted to a business suit or a doctor's uniform, others by small feet, or a certain kind of laugh. Her voice, the way he smiles, her spontaneity, his patience, her energy, his sense of humor, her interests, his dreams, her athletic ability—an endless number of obvious as well as subtle elements work together to make one person more attractive than another. We can all list a few specific things we find attractive, but in our unconscious minds there are many more.

Beauty

8   Although some people would try to deny it, research has shown that at least part of attraction is a

Standards of beauty vary the world over.

7 What do these examples show?

8 Is the point of this paragraph to show how people are the same or different?

9 In paragraph 10, what groups are the same? What two groups are different?

10 What is the definition of *innate* in paragraph 11?

11 In paragraph 11, what is the purpose of this list?

person's looks. However, as you might guess, standards of beauty vary the world over. When Europeans first went to Africa, Africans thought that their blonde hair and white skin was hideously ugly. Women in Tonga traditionally diet to stay slim, while Siriono women of Bolivia eat continually to stay fat. In fact, there is seemingly no end to the variety of features that different cultures consider attractive: stretched necks, molded heads, filed teeth, pierced noses, and scorched or "tanned" skin. Beauty truly is in the eyes of the beholder.

9 Despite dissimilar standards of beauty and sex appeal, there are a few widely shared opinions about what incites romantic passion. Men and women around the world are attracted to those with good complexions. In addition to clear skin, people everywhere are drawn to partners whom they regard as clean. Likewise, in most places, men generally prefer plump, wide-hipped women to slim ones.

Position and Power

10 Money is just as important as appearance. From a study of thirty-seven cultures in thirty-three countries, psychologist David Buss uncovered a distinct male/female difference in sexual preferences that illustrates this point. From rural Zulus to urban Brazilians, men are attracted to young, good-looking, energetic women, while women are drawn to men with goods, property, or money. Americans are no exception. Teenage girls are excited by boys with expensive cars, and older women are impressed by men with houses, land, boats, or other expensive accoutrements. Therefore, a gentle, poetic carpenter will probably not attract as many women as an insensitive rich banker.

11 These male/female preferences are probably innate; that is, we are born with them. It is to a male's genetic advantage to fall in love with a woman who will produce healthy offspring. Youth, clear skin, bright eyes, vibrant hair, white teeth, a supple body, and a lively personality indicate the good health and energy important to his genetic future. To women, money indicates power, prestige, success, and the ability to provide. It is to a woman's biological

advantage to fall in love with a man who can help support her young. As Montaigne, the sixteenth-century French essayist, summed it up, "We do not marry for ourselves, whatever we say; we marry just as much or more for our posterity."

Mystery

12 A degree of unfamiliarity is essential to infatuation. People almost never become captivated by someone they know well, as a classic Israeli study by Shepher clearly illustrates. In this study, very young children were placed in groups during the day while their parents worked. Before the age of ten these children often played together, yet as they moved into adolescence, boys and girls became inhibited and tense with one another. Then, when they were teenagers, they developed strong brother-sister bonds. Almost none married within their peer group, however. A study of 2,769 marriages found that only 13 occurred between people who had been in the same groups, and that in each of these marriages, one partner had left the original group before the age of six. Apparently during some time in childhood, most people lose the ability to develop sexual desire for those people whom they see regularly. Mystery, then, is critical to romantic love.

Difficulties

13 Barriers also seem to provoke infatuation. If a person is difficult "to get," they seem more interesting. In fact, this element of conquest is often central to infatuation. This has become known as the Romeo and Juliet effect. If real impediments exist, such as the family feud in Shakespeare's play, these obstructions are likely to intensify one's passion. It is not surprising that people fall for a person who is married, a foreigner, or someone separated from them by an obstacle that appears almost insurmountable. Yet, generally,

12 In paragraph 13, what do you know about Romeo and Juliet that may help you to understand this concept?

Some octogenarians fall crazily in love.

13 Can you guess the meaning of the phrase *head over heels?*

there must also be at least a small possibility of fulfillment in order for people to fall "head over heels" in love.

receptive, though, he or she is in danger of falling in love with the next acceptable person who comes along.

Timing

14 What is the purpose of this list?

14 In addition to beauty, mystery, and difficulties, timing plays an important role in infatuation. When individuals are looking for adventure, craving to leave home, lonely, displaced in a foreign country, passing into a new stage in life, or financially and psychologically ready to share themselves or start a family, they easily fall in love. From her questionnaires and interviews with over eight hundred Americans, psychologist Dorothy Tennov reported that infatuation occurred only after one had become ready.

15 Can you guess the meaning of the idiom *puppy love?*

16 Can you find a definition for *positive assortive mating* in paragraph 16?

15 Infatuation generally first takes place shortly after puberty. But it can happen at any stage in life. Children experience puppy love; some octogenarians fall crazily in love. Once an individual becomes

Similarity

16 Last, as a rule we are drawn to people like ourselves. Individuals of the same ethnic group, with similar physical traits and levels of education generally marry each other. Anthropologists call this positive assortive mating.

Putting it All Together

17 It is these factors appearing *all at once*—including timing, barriers, mystery, similarities, a matched love map—that make you fall in love. Then, when that potential love object turns his or her head, smiles, or looks at you, you get that feeling of excitement. It can happen gradually or in a second. When it happens very quickly, it is often called "love at first sight."

What Features Do Americans Consider Attractive?

American tastes in romantic partners show some definite patterns. In a test done in the 1970s, 1,031 Caucasian college students at the University of Wyoming rated what they found sexually appealing. Their answers confirmed what you might expect. Men tended to prefer blondes, blue eyes, and lighter skin color, while women liked darker men. But there were some surprises. Few men liked very large breasts or a slender, boyish female figure, and almost none of the women were attracted to extremely muscular men. In fact, both sexes preferred the average. Too short, too tall, too slight, too pale or dark—the extremes were not chosen. Averageness still wins. In a more recent study, psychologists selected thirty-two faces of American Caucasian women and made a computer picture of "average" faces. Then they showed these computer pictures to college students. Of ninety-four photographs of real female faces, only four were rated more attractive than the computer images.

B. Checking Your Comprehension

Complete the following list. Restate the ideas from the reading in your own words.

FACTORS THAT MAKE ROMANTIC LOVE MORE LIKELY TO OCCUR

1. _____

2. _____

3. _____

4. _____

5. _____

C. Topics for Discussion

Discuss the following questions with your classmates.

1. Are there any ideas in Reading 1 that you do not agree with? Why?

2. Which of the ideas in Reading 1 can you find in this song?

STRANGERS IN THE NIGHT

Kaempfert/Singleton/Snyder

Strangers in the night exchanging glances
Wond'ring in the night
What were the chances we'd be sharing love
Before the night was through.
Something in your eyes was so inviting,
Something in you smile was so exciting,
Something in my heart,
Told me I must have you.
Strangers in the night, two lonely people
We were strangers in the night
Up to the moment
When we said our first hello.
Little did we know
Love was just a glance away,
A warm embracing dance away and
Ever since that night, we've been together.
Lovers at first sight, in love forever.
It turned out so right,
For strangers in the night.

3. Do you know any songs (in English or in your own language) about the feeling of being in love? Bring them to class.

4. Which ideas from Reading 1 can you find in your culture?

D. Reading Strategies

READING STRATEGY: Recognizing How Information Is Organized

In Unit 1, you learned about chronological order, or sequence, as one method of organizing a reading. There are several other kinds of organization, such as:

Problem-solution   States or describes a problem and gives one or more possible solutions

Listing   Describes or explains something by listing items or examples

Comparison and contrast   Describes similarities and differences of two or more things

Each type of organization orders information in a specific way.

---

1. **Look at this chart of the organization of Reading 1. Write the main idea of each section. An example has been done for you.**

   INTRODUCTION

   States that the article will explain why people fall in love. _____

   Love Maps _____

   _____

   Beauty _____

   _____

   Position and Power _____

   _____

   Mystery _____

   _____

   Difficulties _____

   _____

   Timing _____

   _____

   Similarity _____

   _____

   CONCLUSION

   Restates main ideas and adds a final thought. _____

2. What kind of organization is used in the reading?

3. Is it useful to know the organization of a text before you read? Why?

READING STRATEGY: Evaluating Support for Ideas and Opinions

When authors present a new idea or a controversial opinion, they usually defend it by providing support. There are several different kinds of support. Some of these are:

- giving examples
- giving evidence from research
- quoting (using the words of) an authority or famous person

As you read, look carefully at the support the authors give. What kind of support is it? How well does it support their idea or opinion? Does it convince you that the author is correct?

---

4. Find the examples below in the reading. What idea is supported by each example?

   1. Romeo and Juliet

      <u>People are more likely to fall in love when barriers exist.</u>

   2. Siriono women in Bolivia

      _____

   3. houses, land, boats, and other expensive accoutrements

      _____

   4. Shepher's research in Israel

      _____

5. In this reading, the author mentions the four names shown in the chart below. Find these names in Reading 1. What idea does each person's work support? What kind of support is used?

RESEARCHER	IDEA SUPPORTED	KIND OF SUPPORT
Money		
Buss		
Shepher		
Tennov		

6. The author also quotes several well-known writers. Look for the names on page 77 and complete the chart. Write a question mark if the answer is not in the text.

WRITER	WHO HE WAS	QUOTATION
Pascal	_____	_____
Montaigne	_____	_____
Chaucer	_____	_____

What kind of support is this? Do these quotations support the writer's argument? Why or why not?

7. **Do you think the author's arguments are convincing? Why or why not? Which points do you agree with? Are there any that you doubt?**

READING STRATEGY:
Using Examples to Find an Author's Important Ideas

An author often gives examples to explain or support an idea. They are usually too specific to be considered one of the important ideas of an article. However, looking for examples can help you discover the important ideas because a writer will often include examples of things that he or she thinks are important. Most examples occur after an important idea.

Look at the paragraph below. The important idea is circled. The examples are underlined.

However, as you might guess, standards of beauty vary the world over. When Europeans first went to Africa, Africans thought that their blonde hair and white skin was hideously ugly. Women in Tonga traditionally diet to stay slim, while Siriono women of Bolivia eat continually to stay fat.

---

8. **Now reread paragraph 14 from Reading 1, shown below. Circle the most important idea. Underline the examples.**

In addition to beauty, mystery, and difficulties, timing plays an important role in infatuation. When individuals are looking for adventure, craving to leave home, lonely, displaced in a foreign country, passing into a new stage in life, or financially and psychologically ready to share themselves or start a family, they easily fall in love. From her questionnaires and interviews with over eight hundred Americans, psychologist Dorothy Tennov reported that infatuation occurred only after one had become ready.

9. **Look for more examples in Reading 1. Reread paragraphs 1–10. Put a vertical line (|) in the margin next to the examples. Look at the sentence or sentences before the examples. Circle the important idea that the examples support.**

10. **Read these statements from paragraphs 1–10. Put a checkmark (✓) next to the ones that you think are main ideas.**

_____ 1. Love maps develop during childhood.

_____ 2. Most people imagine their ideal mate's hair and eye color.

_____ 3. Some people are attracted by uniforms.

_____ 4. Everyone's love map is different.

_____ 5. Africans thought that blonde hair and blue eyes were ugly.

_____ 6. People in most cultures find clear skin attractive.

_____ 7. Carpenters are not as attractive to women as bankers.

_____ 8. Women choose men who can support them well.

11. **Now reread paragraphs 11–17. Find the examples. Then find the important ideas and write them below.**

_____

_____

_____

_____

E. Strategies for Unknown Vocabulary

VOCABULARY STRATEGY: Using Synonyms

Generally, when we are talking about a topic, we need to refer to the same ideas or concept again and again. Good writers often use synonyms or synonymous phrases to avoid repeating the same words. Often it is possible to use these synonyms to understand the meanings of other words nearby.

1. **Find synonyms for these words in the paragraphs listed.**

	PARAGRAPH NUMBER	SYNONYMS		
1. lover	5	_____	_____	_____
2. barrier	13	_____	_____	_____
3. love	1, 2, 15	_____	_____	_____

Writers sometimes repeat an idea using the same grammatical structure but different words. In this way the structures are made parallel. Parallel structures also often use synonyms. If you understand the words in one phrase, you can often guess the meaning of the other.

Look at this example:

Long before you fall in love with Ray **as opposed to** Bill, Sue **instead of** Cecilia...

If you know the meaning of **instead of**, you can probably guess the meaning of **as opposed to**.

2. **Look for these phrases in the reading and find synonyms in the reading for the words in bold type.**

	PARAGRAPH NUMBER	SYNONYM
1. "...women are **drawn to** men with goods..."	10	_____
2. "...women are **impressed by** men with houses..."	10	_____
3. "It is to a woman's **biological advantage...**"	11	_____

VOCABULARY STRATEGY:
Using Lists to Get a General Meaning of a Word

The author of this reading has included many lists of examples. The items in each list have at least one thing in common. They are all examples of the same general point or category. Look at this sentence from paragraph 1:

You take foolish risks, say stupid things, laugh too hard, tell all of your secrets, talk all night, walk at dawn, and are generally oblivious to the rest of the world.

How many examples are in this list? What general category do these examples belong to?

Do you completely understand the phrases **oblivious to the rest of the world** or **take foolish risks**? Do you need to? What do you know about them even if you do not understand them completely?

3. **Underline the lists of examples in the sentences below. Then circle the words that you do not understand. What general category does each group belong to? An example has been done for you.**

1. When individuals are <u>looking for adventure, craving to leave home, lonely, displaced in a foreign country, passing into a new stage in life, or financially and psychologically ready to share themselves or start a family</u>, they easily fall in love.

Category: _Different life situations_

2. In fact, there is seemingly no end to the variety of features that different cultures consider attractive: stretched necks, molded heads, filed teeth, pierced noses, and scorched or "tanned" skin.

Category: _____

3. Youth, clear skin, bright eyes, vibrant hair, white teeth, a supple body, and a lively personality indicate the good health and energy important to his genetic future.

    Category: _____

4. Her voice, the way he smiles, her spontaneity, his patience, her energy, his sense of humor, her interests, his dreams, her athletic ability—an endless number of obvious as well as subtle elements work together to make one person more attractive than another.

    Category: _____

E. Building Your Vocabulary

Use these steps to build your vocabulary with words from the reading.

1. Look back at Reading 1 and make a list of ten to fifteen new words that you feel are important to learn.

2. Write these words in your vocabulary notebook. Group words that are similar (e.g., *courting/courtship, oblivious/unconscious/obvious*). Copy a sentence or phrase in which the word appears. Decide on the part of speech of the word and write a definition for it.

3. If you are still unsure of the meaning of this word or the part of speech, look it up in the dictionary and write the definition in your own words. For additional practice, write your own sentence.

F. Writing Your Ideas

Look at the writing topics below. Choose at least one and write about it.

1. Think of a romantic story you have read or heard about, or a romantic movie you have seen. Then think about the ideas proposed in Reading 1 about the effect of mystery, timing, and barriers on infatuation. Explain how these ideas support or contradict the events in the story or movie.

2. Do you have an ideal mate? What is he or she like? If you are already in a relationship, how is your mate similar to your ideal? How is he or she different?

3. Chaucer said, "Love is blind." Do you agree or not? Support your argument with evidence from the reading and/or your own opinion and experience.

READING 2: "ROMANCE IS UNIVERSAL"

A. Pre-reading the Text

1. Look at Reading 2. Think about these questions.

1. What is the topic of this reading?

2. Where is this reading from?

3. Do you think the writer is an expert in the field?

4. How will the answers to questions 2 and 3 affect your interpretation of the reading?

2. Use your general knowledge. Do you think animals "fall in love"? Why or why not?

3. Read the text closely. Remember to cover the margin questions the first time that you read the article.

4. Read the text a second time and use the margin questions to help you.

READING 2

Romance Is Universal

Scientists find evidence of romance in most cultures and in many species.

1 In paragraph 1, what is this a list of?

1   Is romance permitted in your culture? Is it a part of everyday life, or is it forbidden in public places? Recent research now shows that there is a good chance that romance can be found almost everywhere. Dr. Helen Fisher, the author of a book called *The Anatomy of Love*, writes about romance, saying, "…studies have shown that romantic love exists in virtually every culture." In fact, from their survey of 168 cultures, anthropologists William Jankoviak and Edward Fischer were able to find direct evidence that romantic love exists in 87 percent of them. No matter what most human cultures say about romance, love stories, myths, legends, poems, songs, love potions, love charms, lovers' quarrels, and other romantic rituals have been and still are an important part of life around the world.

2   Almost all cultures have courtship customs that would-be lovers are expected to follow. For example, in some Latin American countries young men and women come together in the public square on certain days. The women walk in a circle one way, while the unmarried men make a larger circle and

2 What clues may help you to understand the words *go-betweens* and *matchmakers?*

3 The author changes the focus with the phrase *But animals?* What do you predict they are going to talk about now?

4 Can you find an internal definition for *courtship feeding?*

5 Can you guess the meaning of the idiom *bring home the bacon?*

6 In paragraph 4, why does the author use such different animals in her list of examples?

7 Can you find the internal definition of *tamarin* in paragraph 4?

walk in the opposite direction. In some other countries, even where go-betweens and matchmakers make most of the contact between families with unmarried men and women, romance still finds ways to fit into the age-old traditions. Whatever the ritual, it can be seen that romantic love is part of the human experience.

3 But animals? They don't have romantic feelings—or do they? Amazingly, many biologists now believe that human beings are not the only creatures who experience romantic love. Many animals not only touch each other but actually look at one another affectionately while they are courting. According to anthropologist Diane Smuts, watching baboons court is like watching a young man and woman meet for the first time in a singles bar. Another researcher, Diane Ackerman, claims that animals even have their own version of a dinner date. Anthropologists call it a "courtship feeding," a kind of animal behavior in which the male animal feeds food that he has gathered to the female he is courting. The purpose of the "courtship feeding" is to prove that the male will be a good provider to future children that they may have. In human terms, this would mean that he will literally be able to "bring home the bacon."

4 In the human world, we usually think that men begin most relationships, but studies are showing that women are often the first to show interest. It is often the females who give small signs that tell the male that she is interested

in him. Again there are parallels in the animal world. Among nonhumans, males put on "courtship rituals," which are usually elaborate shows for the females. These courtship displays can take many different forms. They include the courtship dances of spiders, the vocal courtship of bullfrogs, and the fighting courtship among male deer. In most cases, the females then decide which males they want. Diane Ackerman describes the surprising behavior of the cottontop tamarins, small forest-dwelling monkeys of South America. In this species, according to Ackerman, males do much of the child care. Therefore, a male tries to get a female's attention by visiting her while he is carrying a baby cottontop on his back. What the male is actually saying is, "See what a caring father I would be? I would be great with your kids."

5 There are many things a female looks for in a mate. One of the most important of these is health. It is easy to understand why females are not attracted to males who seem weak or sick. The female wants the healthiest male that she can get in order to produce offspring with the best chance for survival. In some species, she also needs a strong male to help her build a nest, find food, and protect their offspring from predators. That is why the courtship ritual is so important. It has two purposes. It shows the female that the male is serious and also proves that he is healthy and strong. She may learn this in several different ways. Many times adult males actually have to

fight to win the right to mate with a particular female. Although the fighting may end in death, more often it is just a show of strength. For example, male deer are famous for fighting each other with their large antlers. However, according to biologist George Goodwin, deer antlers are branched so that they will not normally cause a serious wound during mating battles. The branches only allow the antlers to go a certain distance before they get caught on each other and stop the deer.

8 Why does the scientist use the phrase *a fat wallet* in paragraph 6?

6 Females looking for mates are also looking for wealth. Of course, many women would like to marry rich men too, but in the animal world, wealth has a different meaning and form than it does in the human world. A female animal wants a generous male who will protect and support her offspring. For example, when a male Pyrochroidae beetle is trying to impress a female, he shows her a well in his forehead. If it is very deep, in beetle terms he is a strong, handsome beetle. This well is important because that is where the male beetle carries a poison that will protect the female's future eggs from ants and other predators. "It's as though he's showing her a fat wallet," entomologist Tom Eisner explains, "and saying, 'There's more in the bank where that came from.'"

Male cottontop tamarins do much of the childcare.

9 What may help you to understand *dexterity* and *endurance* in paragraph 7?

7   One of the most complex courtship rituals in the animal world is that of the bowerbird in New Guinea. Male bowerbirds compete for females by building bowers that can be as much as nine feet tall. Female bowerbirds choose males who collect the most decorations, design the most beautiful nests, and put on the best dance. So, males build beautiful constructions and then they decorate them with flowers, shells, butterfly wings, small bits of feathers, seeds, ballpoint pen tops, toothbrushes, or other ornaments. Researchers have counted as many as 500 decorations on a single bower. Some nests are even painted with a mixture of saliva and dried grass, charcoal, or fruit. And this is not the end of his work. He must then defend it from other males who will try to steal his best decorations. Therefore, a nest with many ornaments will advertise a male's power. Females are attracted to males with large, beautifully decorated nests. Jared Diamond, a researcher who has studied these unusual birds, explains that a male must have many skills: physical strength, dexterity, and endurance, in addition to searching skills and memory, in order to build a good nest. In human terms, female bowerbirds choose husbands according to who is most successful in a very difficult athletic contest, combined with a chess game and a sewing exercise.

8   One group of male spiders goes through one of the unhappiest courtship rituals. They have complex courtship rituals in which the male may wrap the female in some silk, or "dance" in a series of complex steps. Males in this group who are lucky in love can also be unlucky at the same time. In some of the species, the females, which are larger than the males, may eat the males during or after mating.

9   Whatever the courtship ritual, the purpose here is the same: the male is demonstrating to the hopeful female that he will be the best mate for her in the contest to ensure the survival of their species.

B. Checking Your Comprehension

Read each question below. Then look back at the reading to find the answers.

1. What percentage of cultures that the two anthropologists have studied *do not* have a tradition of romantic love?

   _____

2. What is a *courtship feeding*?

   _____

   _____

3. Who do researchers say really has the power of beginning relationships?

   _____

4. What two things do females look for in males?

   _____

5. What is the purpose of a *courtship display*?

   _____

   _____

6. Which of the following kinds of information could logically be added to this reading? Explain.
   a. information about the relationship of humans and their pets
   b. information about female animals who have raised young animals from another species
   c. information about animals who "marry" for life

C. Topics for Discussion

Discuss the following questions with your classmates.

1. The author states that a dinner date is the same as a courtship feeding. Do you agree? How similar are they? How different? What functions does a dinner date serve?

2. In many cultures, people believe that men decide when a relationship begins. However, this article claims that females actually control the beginning of courtship. Which is true in your culture?

D. Reading Strategies

READING STRATEGY: Understanding Where a Reading Comes from

In Unit 1, you learned that the format of a reading can give you information about its source, and that you can use this information to interpret what it says.

---

1. Complete the chart below with a classmate. Then discuss your answers.

GENRES	small print	large print	one column	many columns	many pictures	chapter headings	key words in bold	graphs/charts
A tabloid newspaper		✓		✓	✓			
A serious newspaper								
A textbook								
A newsmagazine								
A novel								
A research report								

2. Use the features in the chart above to answer these questions.

1. Where do you think Reading 2 might be from?

2. What are some other clues to the genre or type of reading?

3. Would you expect to find all the genres in this textbook? Explain.

4. How many of the genres above can you find in this textbook?

5. Would you treat the information in all these genres the same? Give an example to explain your answer.

READING STRATEGY: Making Local Inferences

As you saw in Unit 1, some of the information in a reading may not be stated directly. You can use logic and your general knowledge to infer or guess things that the author doesn't say. In English, we call this "reading between the lines." Making inferences is an important part of reading well.

Some inferences can be made using the information stated in just one or two sentences. They are called local inferences. Read the sentences below.

Jim heard a loud bang and looked up quickly, just in time to see a large group of birds rise from among the leaves. As the birds took off in a V-shape, heading south, he shivered and pulled his coat tighter around him. He took a deep breath, feeling the peaceful silence of the greenness around him. He wiped away a tear.

What can you infer, or guess, from this paragraph? Circle all possible answers. Explain your reasons for each answer.

1. It is almost summer.
2. It is almost winter.
3. Jim is feeling sad.
4. Jim is at home in the city.
5. Jim is sitting near some trees.

3. **Look at these sentences from Reading 2 and circle the reasonable local inferences. Remember to base your inferences only on the sentences given here. Explain your answers. For each sentence, more than one inference may be possible.**

1. Jared Diamond, a researcher who has studied these birds, explains that a male must have physical strength, dexterity, and endurance, plus searching skills and memory, in order to build a good nest. (paragraph 7)

   a. Physical strength is the most important of these characteristics.

   b. All of these characteristics are necessary for survival.

   c. Jared Diamond likes animals.

   d. Scientists understand bowerbirds completely.

2. Amazingly, many biologists now believe that human beings are not the only creatures who experience romantic love. (paragraph 3)

   a. In the past, many biologists did not accept this idea.

   b. This idea has not been accepted by all biologists.

   c. Many biologists are doing research on this concept.

   d. Infatuation can be found in all parts of the animal world.

READING STRATEGY: Recognizing Referents

Some words in a reading refer back to ideas that were stated earlier. When you read, you must be able to figure out which words or concepts are being referred to. These are called referents.

This and **that** are two important referring words. For example:

In some countries, people elect representatives. **This** is called indirect democracy.

What does the word **this** refer to?

---

4. **Look for these sentences in Reading 2 and find the referents for the words in bold type.**

1. **That** is why the courtship ritual is so important. (paragraph 5)

2. And **this** is not the end of his work. (paragraph 7)

3. She may learn **this** in several different ways. (paragraph 5)

VOCABULARY STRATEGY: Using Examples to Guess Meaning

In the exercise on page 79, you learned that knowing the category that a word belongs to can help you to guess its meaning. Sometimes, however, it may be the category word that you do not understand. In that case, you can often use the examples to help you guess its meaning. Look at this sentence:

Unpleasant **sensations** such as pain, hunger, and thirst are warning signs.

What can help you to understand the word **sensation**?

---

1. **Read each sentence below and use the items in the list to guess the meaning of the word in bold type.**

   1. ...[Male bowerbirds decorate their nests with]...flowers, shells, butterfly wings, small bits of feathers, seeds, ballpoint pen tops, toothbrushes, or other **ornaments**.

   2. No matter what most human cultures say about romance, love stories, myths, legends, poems, songs, love potions, love charms, lovers' quarrels, and other romantic **rituals** have been and are still an important part of life around the world.

   3. ...the male beetle carries a poison that will protect the female's future eggs from ants and other **predators.**

VOCABULARY STRATEGY: Recognizing Parts of Speech

Some words can be used in more than one part of speech, even if no suffix is added. In this case, you must use other grammatical clues to figure out the part of speech. Be careful—the same word can have very different meanings! Look at this example:

...he shows her a **well** in his forehead...

You may recognize the word **well** because it looks like the adverb form of **good** as in the sentence **She sings well**. However, in this example, the word **a** comes before **well**. Since you know that **a** is always linked to a noun, in this case, the word **well** must be a noun. Once you know that it is a noun, you can begin to figure out what it means.

---

2. **Below are words that can be more than one part of speech. Look for them in Reading 2 and decide which part of speech they are.**

WORD	PARAGRAPH NUMBER	LINE	PART OF SPEECH
1. shows	4	12	_____
2. displays	4	13	_____
3. caring	4	31	_____
4. end	5	23	_____
5. searching	7	33	_____

F. Building Your Vocabulary

Use these steps to build your vocabulary with words from the reading.

1. Look at your reading list from Reading 1. Put a checkmark (✓) next to any words that also appeared in Reading 2. Then look back at Reading 2 and make a list of five to ten new words that you feel are important to learn.

2. Write these words in your vocabulary notebook. Group words that are similar (e.g., *health/healthy, serious/generous*). Copy a sentence or phrase in which the word appears. Decide on the part of speech of the word and write a definition for it.

3. If you are still unsure of the meaning of this word or the part of speech, look it up in the dictionary and write the definition in your own words. For additional practice, write your own sentence.

G. Writing Your Ideas

Look at the writing topics below. Choose at least one and write about it.

1. According to Reading 2, romance also exists in animal life. Do you think humans and animals are similar in this way? If so, how are they similar? If not, what are the differences? Give examples to support your ideas.

2. The author says that most female animals look for mates that will give them healthy offspring in order for their species to survive. Is this true for humans? Can you think of any ways that animals and humans are alike in this respect?

H. Making Connections

Reading 2 is mainly about animals, while Reading 1 discusses humans. However, there still may be some common ideas. Which of these ideas are contained in both readings? Circle all possible answers.

1. the concept of love maps

2. an explanation of how a mate is chosen

3. the concept of inborn preferences

4. the importance of mystery in choosing a mate

After you finish Readings 1–6, you will complete the Unit Task, investigating the concept of romance in your culture. You will be asked to prepare a report on this topic. A more complete description of the Unit Task can be found on page 114. Your purpose in reading the rest of Unit 2 is to gather information and ideas for the Unit Task.

As you learned in Unit 1, these are the steps in reading for a purpose.

Pre-Step: Identify the Information You Need is a preparatory step that you complete before you look at any of the readings closely. In this step, you think about what information you will need in order to complete the task and which readings are likely to give you that information. Then, when you read each selection, you go through the following process:

Step 1: Preview (look briefly at the reading, predict what will be in it, and think about whether the reading will contain useful information for your task)

Step 2: Read Closely (take a more careful look at the reading)

Step 3: Note Useful Information (look again at the reading to underline, highlight, or take notes on information that will help you do the task)

This section will take you through the preparatory step of deciding which information will be useful for the task.

Pre-Step: Identify the Information You Need

1. **Start to think about the information that you will need for the Unit Task. Even though the readings in this unit are not specifically about your culture, they may raise questions which will help you think about your culture. The questions below may be helpful for your task. Write your own questions in your notebook.**

   1. Who begins a romantic relationship?

   2. What is the role of money in courtship?

   3. What makes people fall in love?

   4. Is courtship public or private?

   5. What is the relationship between marriage and romance?

2. **Can you think of any other questions that will help you do the Unit Task? Brainstorm with your class, and add new questions to your notebook.**

3. **Think about Readings 1 and 2. Did they discuss any of the questions in Exercise 1? If so, write the question numbers in the chart below.**

READING NUMBER	TITLE	QUESTIONS DISCUSSED IN THE READING
1	Why Him? Why Her?	_____
2	Romance Is Universal	_____

4. **Now look ahead to Readings 3–6. Which of the readings do you think will address the questions above? Write the question numbers in the chart.**

READING NUMBER	TITLE	QUESTIONS THAT THE READING MIGHT DISCUSS
3	Body Talk	_____
4	Dating: A Twentieth Century Invention	_____
5	Playing Hard to Get	_____
6	The Place of Romance in Love	_____

You will not find all of the information that you need for the Unit Task in the readings. Some of it will come from your culture. What sources in your culture might give you useful information?

5. **Now continue on to Readings 3–6, keeping the Unit Task in mind. Remember, you will not have to perform the Unit Task until the end of the unit.**

READING 3: "BODY TALK"

Step 1: Preview

1. **Look at the title. What do you predict the reading will be about? Skim parts of the text. Were your predictions correct?**

2. **The reading is a description. From the subtitles, what will it probably describe?**

   1. a group of people   2. a process   3. a period in history

3. **How is the information probably organized in the reading?**

   1. listing   2. problem/solution   3. time order

4. **Where is this reading probably from? Who probably wrote it? Who was it probably written for?**

5. Do you know what "body talk" is? Do you think this is related to romance? How? Can you think of any examples of it? Share these ideas with your classmates.

Step 2: Read Closely

1. Look back at the questions on page 90. Which ones might be discussed in this reading? Read the text closely to check your predictions. Do not look at the margin questions the first time that you read.

2. Read the text a second time and use the margin questions to help you.

READING 3

BODY TALK

From *The Anatomy of Love*, Helen Fisher, Ph.D

1 What is this a list of?

2 Guess what kind of behavior *flirting* is.

3 Here is more information on flirting. Did you guess correctly?

4 Notice the words *first* and *then*. What do these words signal?

1 In the 1960s Irenaus Eibl-Eibesfeldt, a German ethnologist, noticed a pattern to women's courting behavior. Eibl-Eibesfeldt used a camera with a secret lens so that when he pointed the camera straight ahead, he was actually taking pictures to the side. In this way he was able to take pictures of couples secretly. In his travels to Samoa, Papua New Guinea, France, Japan, Africa, and the Amazon, he recorded numerous examples of flirting behavior. Then, back in his laboratory at the Max Planck Institute for Behavioral Physiology, near Munich, Germany, he carefully examined each courting episode, picture by picture.

2 A universal pattern of female flirting emerged. Women from places as different as the jungles of Amazonia, the salons of Paris and the highlands of New Guinea apparently flirt with the same sequence of expressions. First, the woman smiles at her admirer and quickly lifts her eyebrows as she opens her eyes wide to look at him. Then she drops her eyes, tilts her head down and to the side, and looks away. Frequently she also covers her face with her hands, giggling. This sequential flirting gesture is so distinctive that Eibl-Eibesfeldt is convinced it is innate, or inborn, a human female courtship strategy that evolved thousands of years ago.

3 Could these courting cues be part of a larger human mating dance? David Givens, an anthropologist, and Timothy Perper, a biologist, think so. Both scientists have spent several hundred hours watching college men and women in bars in the United States and Canada. They watched as young men and women tried to pick each other up and found the same general pattern to the courting process. According to these investigators, American singles-bar courtship has several stages. I shall divide them into five.

THE FIVE-STAGE PICKUP

Stage 1: Attention-getting

5 What helps you to understand *establish a territory*?

6 If you do not understand *exaggerate*, what might help you?

4 The first is the "attention-getting" phase. Young men and women do this somewhat differently. As soon as they enter the bar, both males and females typically establish a territory—a seat, a place to lean, a position near the jukebox or dance floor. Then they begin to attract attention to themselves. Tactics vary. Men tend to roll their shoulders, stretch, stand tall, and move from foot to foot. They also exaggerate their body movements. For example, instead of using the wrist to stir a drink, men often use the entire arm. They light a cigarette with a whole-body gesture, ending by shaking their arms from the elbow to blow out the match. In addition, they may often laugh more loudly than normal.

Singles bars were the scene of Givens and Perper's research on body talk.

7 Which words help you understand the phrase *advertise their availability*?

5 Older men advertise their availability in other ways. They wear expensive jewelry and clothing which show their success. But all of these signals can be reduced to one basic, three-part message: "I am here; I am important; I am harmless."

8 What point do these lists illustrate?

6 Young women begin the attention-getting phase with many of the same maneuvers that men use—smiling, gazing, shifting, swaying, stretching, and moving in their territory to draw attention to themselves. Often they use a number of feminine moves as well. They twist their curls, tilt their heads, look up coyly, giggle, raise their brows, blush, and hide their faces in order to signal, "I am here."

Stage 2: Recognition

9 Does the reading provide enough information to understand the word *risky*? If not, is it important enough to look further for the meaning?

7 Stage two, the "recognition" stage, starts when eyes meet eyes; then one or the other of the potential lovers acknowledges the recognition with a smile or slight body shift, and the couple moves closer to be able to talk. This can be the beginning of the romance. But it is nowhere near as risky as the next major escalation point: stage three—talk.

Stage 3: Grooming Talk

10 Read the first two sentences. Can you guess what *risky* means now?

11 Does *or* signal a definition or a choice here?

8 Talking is dangerous for an important reason. The human voice is like a second signature that also reveals your background, education, and other things about your character that can make a potential mate accept or reject you in moments. Actors, public speakers, diplomats, and talented liars regularly adjust their voices. Movie actors often raise their voices to adopt sweet, flowing tones when "flirting." And smart liars avoid lying on the telephone for good reason. It is a purely auditory medium where small changes in emphasis and intonation are easily noticed. We are taught from childhood to control our facial expressions, as when our parents tell us to "smile for Grandma," but most of us are unconscious of the power of our voices.

12 What two words describe *conversation*? Do you understand both of them?

13 What does *singsong* describe? Can you guess its meaning?

9 This idle, often meaningless conversation, which Desmond Morris calls grooming talk, is distinctive because voices often become higher, softer, and more singsong-tones one also uses to express affection to children and concern for those in need of care.

14 What three words describe *hello*? Do you understand them all?

15 How can *but* help you to understand the meaning of *go astray*?

10 Grooming talk starts with such simple statements as "I like your watch" or "How's the food?" The best leads are either compliments or questions, since both require a response. Moreover, what you say often matters less than how you say it. This is critical. The moment you open your mouth and speak, you state your intentions with your inflection and intonation. A high-pitched, gentle, mellifluous "hello" is often a sign of sexual interest, whereas a short, low, matter-of-fact, or indifferent "hi" rarely leads to love. If a prospective mate laughs more than necessary, she or he is probably flirting too. Both Givens and Perper saw many potential love affairs go astray soon after conversation started. But if a couple get through this step successfully and each begins to listen actively to the other, they often move to stage four: touch.

Stage 4: Touch

16 What might help you understand *intention cues*?

11 Touching begins with "intention cues"—leaning forward, resting one's arm toward the other's on the table, or moving one's foot closer if both persons are standing. Then the turning point—one person touches the other on the shoulder, the forearm, the wrist, or some other acceptable body part. Normally the woman touches first, in a way that seems casual but has actually been carefully planned.

17 How can *but* help you to understand the word *casual*?

18 How can *yet* help you to understand *insignificant*?

12 How insignificant this touching looks, yet how important it is. The receiver notices this message instantly. If he shrinks back, the pickup is over. If he moves away, even a little, she may never try to touch again. If he ignores the advance, she may touch once more. But if he leans toward her, smiles, or returns the gesture with his own deliberate touch, they have overcome a major barrier well known in the animal community.

13 Touch has been called the mother of the senses. No doubt this is true, because every human culture has codes that indicate who may touch whom and when, where, and how. Imaginative and resourceful in their variety,

19 What point does this list illustrate?

these touching games are basic to human courting too. So if our pair continue to talk and touch—bobbing, tilting, gazing, smiling, swaying, flirting—they usually achieve the last stage of the courtship ritual: total body synchrony.

Stage 5: Keeping Time

20 Are there any clues to help you to guess the meaning of *body synchrony?*

14 Body synchrony is the final and most interesting component of the pickup. As potential lovers become comfortable, they pivot or turn until their shoulders become aligned, their bodies face-to-face. This turning toward each other may start before they begin to talk or hours into conversation, but after a while the man and woman begin to move together. At first this movement is brief. When he lifts his drink, she lifts hers. Then they desynchronize. In time, however, they mirror each other more and more. When he crosses his legs, she crosses hers; as he leans left, she leans left; when he smoothes his hair, she smoothes hers. They move in perfect rhythm as they look into each other's eyes.

15 Is the five-stage pickup universal to men and women? We do not know. Certainly not everybody in the world displays all of the behavior patterns that Givens and Perper found in American bars. People in most societies do not meet in bars. Many do not even court one another openly; instead, their marriages are arranged. And few anthropologists have studied the postures, gestures, and expressions that men and women in other cultures use when they interact. But there is a great deal of secondary evidence to suggest that at least some of these patterns are universal to humankind.

A. Checking your Comprehension

1. Look at these pictures and put them in order (1–5) according to the information in Reading 3. An example has been done for you.

2. Use the pictures to write a short description of each stage of the "pick-up." Then go back to the reading to check your answers.

B. Making Inferences

1. Why did Eibl-Eibesfeldt take people's pictures secretly?

2. Do you think that Givens and Perper divided the pick-up process into five stages themselves? Why or why not?

3. What is one of the main reasons that young adults in the United States go to bars?

C. Topics for Discussion

Discuss the following questions with your classmates.

1. How do men and women in your culture meet? Where? Have you ever observed all or part of this process? Have you observed any other steps or processes?

2. How do men and women in your culture signal interest in each other?

Step 3: Note Useful Information

Sometimes the author's purpose for writing is different from your purpose for reading. In this case, the author's important ideas may not be the ones that are most useful for you. Answer the questions below.

1. What are the author's important ideas in this reading?

2. Is knowing this information essential for your purpose? Why or why not?

3. If you answered *no* to question 2, is there any general information in the reading that may be helpful to you in doing the Unit Task?

D. Building Your Vocabulary

Use these steps to build your vocabulary with words from the reading.

1. Look at your vocabulary list from Readings 1 and 2. Put a checkmark (✓) next to any words that also appeared in Reading 3. Then look back at Reading 3 and make a list of five to ten new words that you feel are important to learn.

2. Write these words in your vocabulary notebook. Group words that are similar (e.g., *face/facial, posture/gesture*). Copy a sentence or phrase in which the word appears. Decide on the part of speech of the word and write a definition for it.

3. If you are still unsure of the meaning of this word or the part of speech, look it up in the dictionary and write the definition in your own words. For additional practice, write your own sentence.

E. Writing Your Ideas

Look at the writing topics below. Choose at least one and write about it.

1. With a friend, go to a place where young men and women meet, such as a restaurant or a dance. Think about the process described in the reading. Observe the behavior in this place. Then write about your observations.

2. In groups, write short skits based on the five-stage pickup. Act them out for your class.

3. Compare popular pictures from your culture that show romance with pictures or photos of romance in the United States (e.g., magazine ads, movie posters). How is the "body language" the same or different? What else is different?

F. Making Connections

1. **What research methodology was used to study men and women in bars? How is it similar to the research methodology used to study the effectiveness of ads that you read about in Unit 1, Reading 3? How is it different?**

2. **What are the similiarities and differences between the types of findings that each study produced?**

READING 4: "DATING: A TWENTIETH CENTURY INVENTION"

Step 1: Preview

1. **Look at the title of this reading. Is there anything surprising about it?**

2. **What country or countries do you think the reading is going to refer to? Write your predictions below.**

_____

3. **If dating is a twentieth-century invention, what do you think people did before that? Do you think that this reading will tell you?**

Step 2: Read Closely

1. **Look back at the questions on pages 90-91. Which ones might be discussed in this reading? Read the text closely to check your predictions. Do not look at the margin questions the first time that you read.**

2. **Read the text again and use the margin questions to help you.**

READING 4

DATING: A TWENTIETH CENTURY INVENTION

From *From Front Porch to Back Seat*, Beth Bailey

1 What was a *"call"*?

1 One day in the 1920's, a young man asked a city girl if he might call on her. When he arrived at her home, she had her hat on. It may not seem like a very meaningful story to us today, but any American born before 1910 would have understood. The hat signaled that she expected to leave the house. He came on a "call." He expected to sit in her family's living room, to talk, to meet her mother, perhaps to have something to eat or to listen to her play the piano. She expected a "date," to be taken "out" somewhere and entertained. In the end, he spent four weeks' savings fulfilling her expectations.

2 Look back at this paragraph. What is the most important idea?

2 In the early Twentieth Century, this new style of courtship, dating, had begun to take the place of the old system of calling. The change was swift. By the mid-1920's calling was gone and dating had transformed American courtship. Dating moved courtship into the public world. Courtship was relocated from living rooms and community events to restaurants, theaters, and dance halls. At the same time, couples were transferred from the watchful eyes of family and local community to the anonymity of public places. Courtship among strangers offered couples new freedom.

3 Dating not only transformed the outward modes and traditions of American courtship, it also changed the distribution of control and power in courtship.

3 When you see *one change*, what do you expect to see next?

4 Does *while* connect two opposing ideas here?

5 Do the words *restrictive* and *repressive* probably have positive or negative meanings?

6 Read the first three sentences. Can you guess the meaning of *took the initiative*? What information helped you?

7 *Conventions* occurred in paragraph 3. Does it help you to understand *conventionally*?

8 What is this paragraph about?

One change was generational: the dating system decreased parental control and gave young men and women more freedom. The other change was sexual. It took the power from women and gave it to men. Calling gave women a large portion of control. First of all, courtship took place within the girl's home—in women's "sphere," as it was called in the nineteenth century—or at entertainments largely devised and directed by women. Dating moved courtship out of the home and into man's sphere—the world outside the home. Female controls and traditions lost much of their power outside women's sphere. And while many of the conventions or rules of female behavior were restrictive and repressive, they had allowed women (young women and their mothers) a great deal of immediate control over courtship. The transfer of spheres brought about a transfer of control as well.

4 Second, in the calling system, the woman took the initiative. Etiquette books and magazine advice columns were clear on that point: it was the "girl's privilege" to ask a young man to call. Furthermore, the man was not allowed to take the first step. In 1909, a young man wrote to the *Ladies' Home Journal* adviser asking, "May I call upon a young woman whom I greatly admire, although she had not given me permission?" The adviser replied that a man must never call without an invitation.

5 There was some confusion caused by this reversal of initiative, especially during the twenty years or so when going out and calling coexisted as systems. (The unfortunate young man in the story above, for example, had asked the city girl if he might call on her, so perhaps she was conventionally correct to think that he meant to take her out.) The issue of money also raised many questions. One young woman, "Henrietta L." wrote to the magazine the *Ladies' Home Journal*, to ask whether a girl might "suggest to a friend going to any entertainment or place of amusement where there will be any expense to the young man." The reply: "Never, under any circumstances." The adviser explained that the invitation to go out must "always" come from the man, for he was the one who had to pay. This same adviser insisted that the woman must "always" invite the man to call; clearly she realized that money was central.

6 Courtship in America had always been somewhat dependent on money (or family background). A poor clerk or factory worker would not have called upon the daughter of a rich family, and men were expected to be economically secure before they married. But in the dating system, money entered directly into the relationship between a man and a woman as the symbolic currency of exchange in even casual relationships. Access to the public world of the city required money. Money—men's money—became the basis of the dating system and, thus, of courtship. And this change fundamentally altered the balance of power between men and women in courtship until very recently.

A. Checking Your Comprehension

Decide if each statement is true or false according to the reading. Write _T_ or _F_ on the line. An example has been done for you.

___T___ 1. The system of "calling" no longer exists in the United States.

_____ 2. The change from calling to dating took place about 50 years ago.

_____ 3. Women usually take the initiative in dating.

_____ 4. In the calling system, money was not important at all.

_____ 5. Dating is a public form of courtship.

_____ 6. Women had more control in calling than they do in dating.

B. Making Inferences

1. **What is the significance of the hat in paragraph 1? What does this tell you about the way women probably dressed at that time?**

2. **Was this article probably written by a man or a woman? Why do you think this?**

3. **Where did young men and women get information about conventions and traditions in the early twentieth century?**

C. Topics for Discussion

Discuss the following questions with your classmates.

1. What are advantages and disadvantages of the calling and dating systems of courtship?

2. How have women's roles in American society or in your society changed in the past 100 years?

3. How have the changes in women's roles changed the conventions of dating?

4. How is dating today similar to the author's description here? How is it different?

D. Additional Strategy Practice

READING STRATEGY:
Understanding the Organization of a Comparative Reading

In Unit 1, you learned that a reading may be organized by the order in which events happened in time. This is called chronological order. In this unit, Reading 1 was organized as items in a list. Reading 3 was an example of a reading organized to show the steps of a process. Readings may also be organized in other ways. In Reading 4, above, the information compares two different systems for men and women to get to meet and know each other: calling and dating.

Two of the common ways that a reading can compare two things are presented below. One way is to present all the information about the first subject, then all the information about the second subject. Another way is to present the ideas one by one, giving information about each idea first from Subject A and then from Subject B.

Comparison Method 1	Comparison Method 2
Introduction	Introduction
Subject A	Point #1
Point #1	Subject A
Point #2	Subject B
Subject B	Point #2
Point #1	Subject A
Point #2	Subject B
Conclusion	Conclusion

In which way was the information in Reading 4 organized? Make an outline like the one in the box above.

Step 3: Note Useful Information

1. **In a reading that compares two things, the most useful ideas are the points of comparison. Look at the concepts below. Check (✓) the points on which the calling and dating systems are different. Compare your ideas with your classmates'.**

   _____ what time of day men and women met

   _____ where they met

   _____ what the role of money was

   _____ what types of activities they took part in

   _____ who the people involved were

   _____ who had the power to take the initiative

   _____ what the purpose of the activity was

2. Sometimes it is more efficient to make notes of the important points than to highlight or underline them. When you are making notes of a comparison, a good way to do it is with a chart like the one below. Make a chart and put in all the points that you checked (✓) in question 1. Compare it with a classmate's. Which of these points is important for the Unit Task, investigating the concept of romance in your culture?

POINT	CALLING	DATING
Place	woman's home	in public

E. Building Your Vocabulary

Use these steps to build your vocabulary with words from the reading.

1. Look at your vocabulary list from Readings 1–3. Put a checkmark (✓) next to any words that also appeared in Reading 4. Then look back at Reading 4 and make a list of five to ten new words that you feel are important to learn.

2. Write these words in your vocabulary notebook. Group words that are similar (e.g., *conventions/conventionally, transformed/transferred*). Copy a sentence or phrase in which the word appears. Decide on the part of speech of the word and write a definition for it.

3. If you are still unsure of the meaning of this word or the part of speech, look it up in the dictionary and write the definition in your own words. For additional practice, write your own sentence.

F. Writing Your Ideas

Look at the writing topics below. Choose at least one and write about it.

1. If you could choose, would you choose the calling or dating system? Why? Take a position and support it with reasons and explanations.

2. Have you ever dated? What did you do? Where did you go? Describe your dating experience using some of the points of comparison in the chart above.

3. Do young people meet in your society? If so, how? Is the system similar to calling, dating, or is it another system altogether? Describe it using the same categories given in Step 3.

READING 5: "PLAYING HARD TO GET"

Step 1: Preview

1. **Preview this reading. Where do you think it is from? Why?**

2. **Look at the title and predict the topic.**

    1. Did the title give you enough information to make a prediction? If not, look at the subtitle and try again.

    2. Did you find the topic? If not, read the first paragraph carefully and predict the topic.

3. **Why do you think it says *Rule #5, Rule #17* and *Rule #20*? How are rules related to romance? Discuss your ideas with your classmates.**

Step 2: Read Closely

1. **Look back at the questions on page 90. Which ones might be discussed in this reading? Read the text closely to check your predictions. Do not look at the margin questions the first time that you read.**

2. **Read the text again and use the margin questions to help you.**

READING 5

1 How can *but* help you to understand the verb *sets back*? Is it positive or negative?

2 Can you guess what *word-of-mouth* success means?

Playing Hard to Get
A fast-selling book called *The Rules* sets the dating game back 30 years—but fans promise that it works.

Rule #5: Don't Call Him and Rarely Return His Calls

1 Men have not figured it out yet but a communication revolution is sweeping America. They can leave a woman a message; she does not call back. They send her roses; there is no thank-you call. They flirtatiously hand a woman a business card and say "Give me a ring—we'll have lunch." The tactic used to work, but now the phone sits silent.

2 The era that has resurrected Jane Austen and girdles seems to have produced a new sort of woman—someone who doesn't call herself a woman at all but a Rules Girl. A Rules Girl is "a creature unlike any other." A Rules Girl would never ask a man out—or even talk to a man first; she is "easy to be with" but hard to get because she is very, very busy. All this is the result of a new self-help book on dating, *The Rules: Time-Tested Secrets for Capturing the Heart of Mr. Right* (Warner Books, $5.99).

3 This little paperback has become a word-of-mouth success, selling 50,000 copies in the past month alone; 235,000 copies have been shipped to stores

since its publication in early 1995. *The Rules* is not just a book; it's a movement. Around the country Rules Girls are forming Rules support groups. They are paying $45 to attend Rules seminars and $250 an hour for phone advice from authors, Ellen Fein and Sherrie Schneider. Hollywood producer Wendy Finerman has bought the movie rights for $250,000.

3 Who is Kirshbaum? Has his company made a lot of money from this book? What idiom describes this situation?

4   Laurence Kirshbaum, CEO of Warner Books, admits that at first he could not believe women in the '90's would want this book: "My reaction to it is one of great sadness," he says, "in that if this is what relations between the sexes have come down to, I think we're in trouble." Kirshbaum is weeping all the way to the bank: *Rules II* is already being written.

Rule #17: Let Him Take the Lead

4 What is a synonym for *thesis?*

5   Fein and Schneider preached the rules to friends for years before deciding to write them down. Their thesis, or belief, is a simple one, familiar to evolutionary scientists (and most older women): men are hunters who are thrilled by the chase. In recent years, the authors claim, women have made the game too easy. "Feminism," explains Schneider, "has not changed men."

6   Fein and Schneider have clearly hit a nerve among women like Kathy, a thirtyish Hollywood movie producer, who says, "The results of the Rules are wonderful. You need a series of behaviors that are kind of consistent." That need explains why women at a recent Rules seminar in New York City asked the authors questions such as, "If I'm in a long-distance relationship, how long am I allowed to stay on the phone with the man?" The Rules answer: 10 minutes.

Rule #20: Be Honest but Mysterious

7   Fein and Schneider promise results that are nothing short of revolutionary. "When you do the Rules, you cut down on domestic violence," says Schneider, with amazing confidence. "[Men] are so crazy about you, they never ignore or abuse you." She goes on to claim they don't cheat on you either.

8   If nothing else, Rules Girls have a spirit of adventure. "Sherrie and Ellen assure me that it works, " says Randi, a California Rules Girl. "I'll try something else if it doesn't."

Story: Elizabeth Gleick

A. Checking Your Comprehension

Read each exercise below. Then look back at the reading and find the answers.

1. What is the purpose of the Rules?

2. According to the Rules, who should take the initiative in a relationship?

3. What is the point that *The Rules* authors are trying to make?

4. What are some benefits of the Rules, according to the authors?

5. Which of these statements correctly summarizes the ideas of *The Rules* authors? Circle your answer.

   a. Women and men should be completely open and honest with each other.

   b. A woman should let a man run after her until she catches him.

   c. Modern courtship is very different from courtship 50 years ago.

   d. Marriage is bad for both men and women.

B. Making Inferences

1. **After reading the article, can you guess the meaning of the idiom "playing hard to get"?**

2. **Which of these statements would the authors of *The Rules* probably agree with? Check (✓) all possible answers.**

   ____ 1. A woman should not ask a man out on a date.

   ____ 2. A man should not ask a woman out on a date.

   ____ 3. A woman should not accept an invitation made on the same day.

   ____ 4. A woman should not buy a man an expensive present.

   ____ 5. A woman should compliment a man on his clothing.

3. ***The Rules* has been very, very successful. What can you infer about American society from this?**

4. **This book is very controversial (people have strong feelings about whether it is good or bad). Why do you think this is so?**

C. Topics for Discussion

Discuss the following questions with your classmates.

1. Do you agree with the Rules described in this article? Why or why not?

2. Would the Rules be accepted or rejected by most members of your society?

Step 3: Note Useful Information

Reading 5 discusses courtship only in the United States. However, it may still be useful for the Unit Task. Thinking about the concept of romance in one culture will help you to examine it in your own.

1. **Is the Rules philosophy similar to your society's beliefs about how to find a partner? Reread the article and highlight any similarities you find. Then go back and underline any differences you find.**

2. **Did this article suggest any new questions that will help you with the Unit Task? If so, add them to the list on page 90.**

D. Building Your Vocabulary

Use these steps to build your vocabulary with words from the reading.

1. Look at your vocabulary list from Readings 1–4. Put a checkmark (✓) next to any words that also appeared in Reading 5. Then look back at Reading 5 and make a list of five to ten new words that you feel are important to learn.

2. Write these words in your vocabulary notebook. Group words that are similar (e.g., *revolution/revolutionary, communication/publication*). Copy a sentence or phrase in which the word appears. Decide on the part of speech of the word and write a definition for it.

3. If you are still unsure of the meaning of this word or the part of speech, look it up in the dictionary and write the definition in your own words. For additional practice, write your own sentence.

E. Writing Your Ideas

Look at the writing topics below. Choose at least one and write about it.

1. Write some suggestions of your own for someone who wants to find a partner.

2. What are the rules for finding a wife? Are they any different from the rules for finding a husband? How? Why?

3. Many cultures view marriage positively and remaining single negatively. Why do you think this happens? How do you feel about this? Does your culture place a strong emphasis on getting married? How does this affect the society as a whole? How does it affect individuals in the society?

F. Making Connections

1. Is the main point of *The Rules* authors supported by the information in Reading 1? Why or why not?

2. How does this reading relate to Reading 4? According to *The Rules* authors, how has dating changed? How do they think dating should be?

READING 6: "THE PLACE OF ROMANCE IN LOVE"

Step 1: Preview

1. Look for the items in column 1 in the chart below and complete columns 2 and 3.

FEATURE	Is it in this reading?	Information given	Prediction about the reading
Title of the reading	yes	the place of romance in love	It will explain the difference between love and romance
Subtitle(s)	no		
Author's name/title			
Name of book/magazine/ newspaper			
Audience it was written for			
Format of the reading			
Pictures/graphs			
First/last paragraph			

2. Make predictions based on the information you found and fill in column 4.

Step 2: Read Closely

1. Look back at the questions on page 90. Which ones might be discussed in this reading? Read the text closely to check your predictions. Remember not to look at the margin questions the first time that you read.

2. Read the text again, using the margin questions to help you.

THE PLACE OF ROMANCE IN LOVE

From *The Psychologist's Book of Self-Tests*, Louis Janda

1 Who is the audience? How do you know?

2 What can help you guess what the idiom *of two minds* means?

3 What is the point Hunt is trying to make here?

4 Does *while* connect two opposing ideas here? What are they?

5 Can you guess the meanings of *lifelong* and *clear-headed* by looking at the parts of the words?

6 Can you guess the meaning of *regardless?*

1 As a marriage counselor, I have been invited here to speak to you today about love and marriage. I am happy to do this because I feel that American society today has completely confused romance with love. Furthermore, I believe that it is this confusion which has caused the divorce rates to increase so dramatically and you, as young adults, will become the next victims unless you learn to put romance in its place.

2 Morton Hunt, the prolific social science writer, has observed that we Americans are of two minds when it comes to love; we believe in every principle of romantic love, but we know perfectly well things don't really work that way. I agree with Hunt, but I would expand his thesis to suggest that your belief about romantic love depends on the state of your own love life. When we are in love, we tend to believe romantic ideas such as "Love conquers all." But after we have been in a love relationship for a few years, we strongly believe that "Love is not enough." As in so many areas of life, experience makes it difficult to remain idealistic about romantic love.

3 Studies have shown that college students tend to be more romantic than older, more experienced adults. That is why your parents may seem hopelessly conservative and cautious about love. They probably weren't always that way. They simply have the wisdom that sometimes comes with age.

4 I realize I myself may sound cynical about romantic love, and perhaps I am. While I do believe there isn't a feeling that even comes close to being as exciting as being in love, I also have seen too many couples who based their decision to marry on their intense emotional attachment for each other, only to learn later that they were completely incompatible in every other way. Being in love is a wonderful experience, but it is not sufficient justification for making a decision that will affect the rest of your life. When choosing a lifelong partner, we need to be as objective, rational, and clearheaded as possible. Unfortunately, being in love often makes it difficult to summon these qualities. Several researchers have documented the common observation that we overlook the defects or imperfections in our lovers. It is only after love has worn off that we can see their deficiencies.

5 As you may suspect, there are differences between men and women when it comes to romantic love, although the nature of the differences may surprise you. Until recently, men have typically been shown to be more romantic than women on psychological tests. They were more likely to believe that people should marry for love regardless of differences in background, attitudes, or personality. Women have tended to be more practical, perhaps even calculating—reluctant to marry a man they were in love with if he did not possess other qualities they were looking for.

7 What difference is being referred to here?

6   The explanation for this difference was that, traditionally, a woman's standard of living was largely determined by the man she chose to marry. Men could afford to be romantic. Their choice of a wife was not going to decide the neighborhood they could live in, the quality of the clothes they could wear, or whether they could afford to send their children to college. Women had good reason to ignore their hearts.

7   However, a generation ago, increasing numbers of women began to pursue their own careers. Several social scientists thought that as women started to achieve more financial independence, they might also become more romantic; and this does seem to have happened. Surveys conducted during the past few years have found few, if any, differences between college men and women in how they respond on psychological tests of romanticism.

8   Nevertheless, some differences between the sexes seem to remain. Dr. Zick Rubin, one of the foremost "love researchers," has found that men are more likely than women to want to fall in love, they are less likely to end a relationship, and they suffer more when a relationship ends. Interestingly, even when a relationship is more important to the woman than it is to the man, the woman is more likely to end it if she feels it will not be best for her in the long run. Women still seem to be capable of more objectivity when it comes to love than men.

9   Let us return, for a moment, to Hunt's remark that we are firmly of two minds when it comes to romantic love. What he meant was that most of us are smart enough and rational enough not to let our hearts control our lives. We all want to fall in love, but we have the wisdom to fall in love with people who are similar to ourselves in terms of background, temperament, and values—factors that are important to a stable relationship. Even if we seem romantic, part of us remains objective enough to make relatively good choices when it comes to selecting a partner.

10   People who are very romantic allow their emotions to overcome their reason. For instance, young women who have an unwanted pregnancy have higher romanticism scores than those who do not. A more common problem among the extremely romantic is the tendency to make commitments too quickly, and then to become disappointed once the feelings of romantic love inevitably begin to fade.

8 What point does this example illustrate?

11   I know one woman in her 40's, Janet, an otherwise bright and successful individual, who is planning her third divorce after being married this time for less than two years. She fell hard for Allen, and she really wanted to have a child with him before she was too old. But after the baby was born, she decided that Allen was dull and uninteresting. Now she is planning to leave him. Sadly for Janet, she does not have enough insight into her pattern to realize how her romanticism is hurting her life.

9 What point does this
example illustrate?

12 Barbara, on the other hand, has Janet's romantic ideals, but she has learned to keep them in their place. Consider her story: She married Tim when she was 19 because she was, in her words, hopelessly in love with him. It didn't take her long to realize that they were totally incompatible. She was lucky enough to get out of the marriage before they had children. She swore she'd never make the same mistake again. When she met Ray, she was deeply in love before a month passed, but she told him that she wouldn't marry him until they had lived together for a while. After two years, when her heart no longer pounded when she expected to see him, she knew that she could be objective enough to make the right decision. They got married, and they're still happy five years later.

10 What does *the icing on the cake* mean here? Can you guess?

13 Barbara's story may not be the most romantic, but her life is much better than Janet's. Being romantic is nice, I suppose, and being in love is truly wonderful, but most people would be much better off if they could view it as the icing on the cake rather than as the basis for making a commitment to a relationship.

A. Checking Your Comprehension

Which statements would the speaker agree with? Check (✓) your answers.

_____ 1. Romance and love are the same.

_____ 2. Many people decide to get married too quickly.

_____ 3. Love conquers all.

_____ 4. Love is not enough.

_____ 5. Compatibility is more important than love.

B. Making Inferences

1. Is the speaker sympathetic to young people?

2. Does the speaker probably think that it is good or bad that women have become more romantic?

3. Does the speaker probably believe that divorce is bad?

C. Topics for Discussion

Discuss the following questions with your classmates.

1. Imagine that you have a son or daughter who is thinking about getting married. What advice would you give to him or her?

2. Would older adults in your culture generally agree with the opinions in this lecture? Why or why not?

D. Additional Strategy Practice

> ### READING STRATEGY:
> ### More on Evaluating Support for Ideas and Opinions
>
> In the Reading Strategy section on page 76, you learned how to evaluate support for an opinion. Three kinds of support were used in Reading 1:
>
>   a. giving examples
>
>   b. giving evidence from research
>
>   c. quoting an authority
>
> There are also other kinds of support:
>
>   d. giving logical explanations
>
>   e. giving reasons
>
>   f. criticizing reasons that support the opposing point of view

1. **Look at Reading 6. What is the author's opinion or main point? State it below in your own words.**

   _____

   _____

2. **What kind of support does the author give for this opinion? Look at the different examples of support below. Find the word or phrase from the list in the box that best describes it. Write the letter on the line.**

   _____ 1. For instance, young women who have an unwanted pregnancy have higher romanticism scores than those who do not.

   _____ 2. I know one woman in her 40's, Janet, an otherwise bright and successful individual, who is planning her third divorce after being married this time for less than two years.

   _____ 3. Morton Hunt, the prolific social science writer, has observed that we Americans are of two minds when it comes to love; we believe in every principle of romantic love, but we know perfectly well things don't really work that way.

   _____ 4. I realize I myself may sound cynical about romantic love, and perhaps I am. While I do believe there isn't a feeling that even comes close to being as exciting as being in love, I also have seen too many couples who based their decision to marry on their intense emotional attachment for each other, only to learn later that they were completely incompatible in every other way.

   _____ 5. Until recently, men have typically been shown to be more romantic than women on psychological tests. They were more likely to believe that people should marry for love regardless of differences in background, attitudes, or personality. Women have tended to be more practical, perhaps even calculating—reluctant to marry a man they were in love with if he did not possess other qualities they were looking for.

_____ 6. The explanation for this difference was that, traditionally, a woman's standard of living was largely determined by the man she chose to spend her life with. Men could afford to be romantic. Their choice of a wife was not likely to determine the neighborhood they could live in, the quality of the clothes they could wear, or whether they could afford to send their children to college. Women had good reason to ignore their hearts.

3. How well has the author above made his case? Are there any opinions that you disagree with?

Step 3: Note Useful Information

1. What ideas in this reading may tell you where to look when you are thinking about the concept of romance in your own culture?

2. What are the similarities or differences between your culture and the situations presented in this reading?

E. Building Your Vocabulary

Use these steps to build your vocabulary with words from the reading.

1. Look at your vocabulary list from Readings 1–5. Put a checkmark (✓) next to any words that also appeared in Reading 6. Then look back at Reading 6 and make a list of new words that you feel are important to learn.

2. Write these words in your vocabulary notebook. Group words that are similar (e.g., *romance/romantic/romanticism, cynical/rational*). Copy a sentence or phrase in which the word appears. Decide on the part of speech of the word and write a definition for it.

3. If you are still unsure of the meaning of this word or the part of speech, look it up in the dictionary and write the definition in your own words. For additional practice, write your own sentence.

F. Writing Your Ideas

Look at the writing topics below. Choose at least one and write about it.

1. Relate the story of Romeo and Juliet (or a similar romantic story) to the views about love and marriage in this reading. How would the author have counseled the lovers?

2. Do you think that there is room for romance in an arranged marriage? Explain your viewpoint.

G. Making Connections

1. **Do you think that the authors of *The Rules* would agree with the opinions in this lecture? Why or why not?**

2. **How is the style of this reading different from the previous readings?**

 PART **C** DOING THE UNIT TASK

Building Your Vocabulary: Summary

Look at your vocabulary lists for this unit. Make a list of all the words that appeared more than once. Group any similar words together. Add any other words that you feel will be important for doing the Unit Task. These are probably the most important words for your active vocabulary.

There are many different ways to learn vocabulary but one of the best is to make connections among the words that you are trying to learn. One way to do this is to create a word web. A word web is a visual representation of how words are related to a central idea.

Look at this word web for the word *love*.

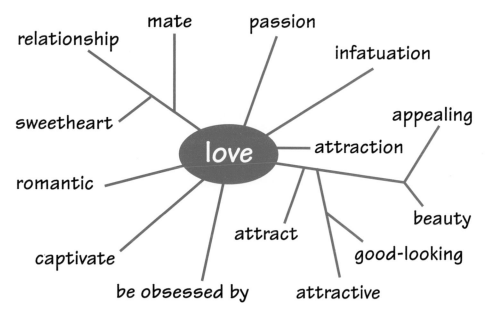

Now make a word web for the word *date*. Compare your word web with a classmate's. How are they the same? How are they different?

UNIT TASK:
Investigating the Concept of Romance in Your Culture

Prepare an oral or written report describing different aspects of romance in your culture. You may choose to look at how romance is depicted in books, movies, and songs in your culture. Also, consider common attitudes about romance, courtship behavior, and traditions.

Work in groups or pairs to develop your ideas for the Unit Task. If there are other students from your country or a country with similar traditions, form a group with them. However, even if your group is made up of students from countries with very different customs, it will still be helpful to you to discuss your ideas and listen to theirs.

1. Look back at the questions for the task on page 90. Choose three questions that interest you and write them here:

   _____

   _____

   _____

   Do you have any other points that you would like to discuss?

2. Look back at the readings and your notes. Which ones contain useful information on the points you want to discuss? Make a list of them with the key points you want to use.

3. What books, music, movies, television shows, advertisements or observations do you plan to use as sources for your report?

4. Look back at the questions you wrote above. Can you make connections between them? Are they all really separate questions, or do their answers overlap? In what order would you like to present the information?

5. Now prepare your report alone or in a group. Use the information and ideas from your discussion.

PART EXPANSION ACTIVITIES

Applying Your Knowledge

1. Talk to a senior citizen in your community. Find out how courtship rituals have changed since he or she was young. Make a report to the class comparing the two.

2. Watch a movie such as *Emma, Sense and Sensibility,* or *Persuasion* (all based on novels by 19th-century British author, Jane Austen). Compare the courting behavior of the characters with the courtship rituals described in this unit. How are they the same? How are they different?

3. In groups, write a letter about a romance problem you are having. Give your letter to another group. They will write an answer to your letter with a suggestion to solve your problem.

4. Bring in a person from your culture who can discuss courtship patterns of a non-American culture. Ask questions such as, "How do people meet?" and "Who must agree to the relationship?"

5. Find the book *The Rules*. Read it and write a critique of it.

The Electronic Link

1. Do an Internet search. Use the search words *marriage customs* in quotes. What sites did you find? Compare your answers with your classmates'.

2. Now choose one Web site and fill in the information requested below. Try to find a site that gives information about a culture other than your own.

   Name of site _____

   URL (Web address) _____

   What country is this site from? _____

3. What did you learn about their marriage customs by looking at this site?

   _____

   _____

   _____

   _____

   _____

4. How are their customs different from or similar to marriage customs in your own country?

   _____

   _____

   _____

   _____

   _____

For More Information

The Anatomy of Love: The Natural History of Monogamy, Adultery, and Divorce. Helen Fisher, Ph.D., New York: Norton, 1992.

The Psychology of Romantic Love: What Love Is, Why Love Is Born, Why It Sometimes Grows, Why It Sometimes Dies. Nathaniel Branden, Ph.D., Los Angeles: J. P. Tarcher, 1980.

The Rules: Time-tested Secrets for Capturing The Heart of Mr. Right. Ellen Fein and Sherrie Schneider, New York: Warner Books, 1995.

From Front Porch to Back Seat: Courtship in Twentieth Century America. Beth Bailey, Baltimore: Johns Hopkins, 1988.

 See Additional Readings for this unit on page 224.

Essay Questions

Choose one of the topics below and write an essay about it.

1. Contrast the view of romance in your culture with what you have learned about romance in the United States from books, movies, television programs, and the readings in this textbook. If you live in the United States, you may also use evidence from your life experience.

2. Compare the concept of romance in your culture today with the concept of romance 50 years ago. How has it changed? How has it remained the same? What are some likely causes of any changes that have occurred?

3. Do you disagree with any of the theories that have been discussed in these readings? Which one or ones? Explain the basis of your disagreement.

Evaluating Your Progress

**Think about the skills and strategies that you used in this unit.
Check (✔) the boxes that apply to you.**

	NEVER	SOMETIMES	OFTEN	ALWAYS
1. I was able to find the author's important points.	☐	☐	☐	☐
2. When I previewed, I thought about where a reading came from.	☐	☐	☐	☐
3. When I previewed, I thought about the audience.	☐	☐	☐	☐
4. I was able to guess meanings by using lists.	☐	☐	☐	☐
5. I was able to get a general meaning of new vocabulary.	☐	☐	☐	☐
6. I judged the author's support for his/her ideas as I read.	☐	☐	☐	☐
7. My underlining/highlighting helped me to find useful information quickly.	☐	☐	☐	☐
8. I looked for synonyms when I read.	☐	☐	☐	☐
9. I could recognize organization by comparison and contrast.	☐	☐	☐	☐
10. I thought about parts of speech when I was trying to figure out the meaning of unknown words.	☐	☐	☐	☐

Setting Your Reading Goals

Choose three items from the list above that you would like to improve. Write them below.

Goal #1: _____

Goal #2: _____

Goal #3: _____

$\mathcal{I}$N THIS UNIT

Reading Strategies

- Recognizing parallel organization
- Using transition words to predict
- Writing margin notes
- Summarizing a reading
- Using margin notes to highlight information

Strategies for Unknown Vocabulary

- Recognizing collocations
- Choosing the right definition
- Using larger contexts to guess meaning
- Deciding when to look for further information

Mind Over Matter

Think About It

*A*fter learning that he might lose his job, a salesman who has never missed a day of work because of illness in years of work repeatedly comes down with the "flu."

A man given a diagnosis of an "incurable" disease and told he would never walk again cures himself with positive thinking and laughter.

Professional athletes practice psychological techniques such as meditation as a regular part of their training in order to improve their performance.

An amazing scientific discovery links emotions with physical changes, not just in the brain but in every cell in your body.

Discuss these questions with your classmates.

1. Which of the items above do you think is the most surprising? the least surprising?

2. Can you think of a time when your mind affected your physical health or your abilities? What happened?

3. The relationship between the mind and the body is sometimes called "the mind-body connection." What is your culture's attitude toward it? For example, do doctors take their patients' mental condition into account when treating them?

Looking Ahead in Unit Three

Look through the unit and answer these questions.

1. With your class, find the titles of the readings in this unit. Write them on the lines.

Reading 1: _____

Reading 2: _____

Reading 3: _____

Reading 4: _____

Reading 5: _____

Reading 6: _____

2. Which reading looks the most interesting?

3. What different genres, or types of sources, can you find?

4. What is the Unit Task?

PART  FOCUS ON SKILLS

READING 1: "THINKING YOURSELF HEALTHY"

A. Pre-reading the Text

1. **Put checkmarks (✓) in the columns to show what kind of information each item usually gives you. An example has been done for you.**

	General topic	Intended audience	Reliability of information	More detailed information about the topic
Titles	✓	✓		
Authors				
Subtitles				
Source				
Introduction				
Conclusion				

2. **Complete the predictions below. Fill in the blank or circle the correct word.**

From the title I can predict that the reading is about _____.

The author <u>uses/does not use</u> a title such as "Doctor" or "Professor" before her name, so she probably <u>is/is not</u> a doctor or a health professional. Therefore, this article was probably written for <u>the general public/health professionals</u> and probably <u>will/will not</u> contain a lot of technical vocabulary.

3. **Look at the reading and find the rest of the items listed in the chart in question 1. Then discuss them with a classmate and write a prediction about the article for each one. Compare your predictions with your classmates'.**

4. **With your class, brainstorm your general knowledge on this topic. Make a list of the ideas that might be in this reading.**

5. **Read the text closely. Remember to cover the margin questions when you read the first time.**

6. **Reread the text, using the margin questions to help you.**

READING 1

Thinking Yourself | **Healthy**
by Cathy Perlmutter
From *Prevention Magazine*

1 What might help you to guess the main idea of the article?

1   In the area of mind/body research, having the right attitude or "spark" can do great things for us. Those of us who can control this positive energy seem to enjoy better health, happiness and even longevity. But what exactly is "The Spark"? And, more important, if we don't have it, how can we get it?

2   There are many theories about this. But we wanted to weigh all the possibilities to determine which count most. That's why we turned to you, our readers. In *Prevention's* "Spark of Life" survey, we asked a wide variety of questions regarding your attitudes—as well as questions about your friendships, relationships, interests, goals and anything else that might contribute to a positive mental attitude. We also asked about your physical health and sense of well-being. We then compared these answers with the others. More than 12,000 people responded. In the final analysis, what emerged was that people who really had "The Spark" had at least six of seven positive attitudes. Fully 30% of the respondents fell into this category.

ATTITUDES THAT MATTER MOST _____

2 Look ahead to the rest of the reading. What purpose does this list serve?

3   So, what are the seven positive attitudes that, according to our survey, define "The Spark of Life"? Here's what we found:

   1. Being very optimistic
   2. Having a strong belief in a higher power
   3. Thinking of the future, not the past
   4. Thinking people are good
   5. Being very trusting
   6. Thinking you control your life
   7. Thinking you control your health

3 Read paragraphs 4–6. What is the author's purpose?

4   We cannot ignore the growing body of medical evidence linking optimism with healthier, longer lives. And, at the very least, positive people are happier and have a greater sense of well-being than their negative neighbors. So thinking positive is a goal worth striving for. The question is: Can we learn optimism?

5   We asked the experts, prominent psychologists and physicians who study the mind/body connection. The first step, they agreed, is having a desire to change, and that means understanding that our negative attitudes are harmful—and that the positive ones can be beneficial.

6   So here's the information on each of the positive attitudes that our survey asked about, what they meant to people who answered, some of the research that shows they're important, and how to cultivate them.

LIGHTING THE SPARK

Being very optimistic

7   Most of the survey respondents look on the bright side. Fifty-four percent are very optimistic and an additional 37% said they're somewhat optimistic. Good for them, because there are many direct ways that negative thoughts can harm us. That's what researchers at Brown University concluded when they analyzed reports from 1,391 people over age 70 on their daily activities and health. After four years, the seniors who had listed old age as the main cause of their health problems had a 78% greater risk of death compared with seniors who did not blame their problems on old age. They concluded that people who blame old age tend to take worse care of themselves. They expect bad health and as a result, they get it.

4 Is this a reasonable conclusion?

8   Turning a pessimist into an optimist is not easy, says Harvard psychologist Ellen Langer, Ph.D., author of *Mindfulness* (Addison-Wesley, 1990). That's because pessimists think they're realists. Both the optimists and pessimists think they're right.

5 What point does this example illustrate?

9   "Take the example of someone who's just lost her job," says Dr. Langer. "A pessimist will surely see that as negative. But the optimist may see that situation as an opportunity to begin life anew. She can arrange her life based on who she is now, not who she was 20 years ago, when she made her first career decision. In contrast with the pessimist who sees only chaos and negative consequences, the optimist sees lots of opportunities."

10   Pessimists can unlearn negative thinking. You can begin the process yourself, says Dr. Langer, by beginning to notice your negative thoughts. "When that happens, just ask yourself, `How else can I see this?' By noticing things rather than just accepting ideas that were given to us in the past, anything that's negative can be reframed," says Dr. Langer.

Having a strong belief in a higher power

11   Readers who responded are a faithful group: 74% say they have a very strong belief in a higher power, and an additional 17% say their belief is moderately strong. Just 4% are nonbelievers.

12   Clergy have always said that faith heals, but nowadays an increasing number of physicians agree with them. "Religious belief is consistently associated with better health," notes Harvard cardiologist Herbert Benson. He has reviewed dozens of studies comparing believers with nonbelievers and finds a consistent trend: "The greater a person's religious commitment, the fewer psychological symptoms, the better the general health, the lower the blood pressure and the longer the survival."

13   Why is religion so helpful? "Faith in an eternal or life-transcending force is a supremely comforting belief," Dr. Benson speculates. "It disconnects unhealthy logic and worries." He adds that it's not just people who regularly attend religious services who will benefit. Research points to health benefits for other people who have a strong sense of spirituality. That means that just about everyone might be able to improve their health by cultivating their spiritual side. Dr. Benson teaches a simple but powerful way to do this, eliciting his well-known "Relaxation Response."

6 The words *Relaxation Response* are capitalized. What does that tell you about this concept?

14   The Relaxation Response is evoked by a simple set of instructions. It involves sitting quietly and focusing silently on a word or phrase for a period of 10 to 20 minutes twice a day, gently brushing aside any everyday thoughts that distract. (If you're interested in learning this simple technique, see Dr. Benson's book *Timeless Healing: The Power and Biology of Belief* [Scribner, 1996]).

Think of the future, not the past

15   Overall, some 78% of readers who answered our survey say they think more about the future than the past. In contrast, only one in five (19%) thinks more about the past.

16   How can you get your thoughts out of the past? University of Kansas psychology professor C. R. Snyder, Ph.D., author of *The Psychology of Hope: You Can Get There from Here* (Simon and Schuster, 1994), suggests setting goals. "Goal-setting is a way to cultivate hope," says Dr. Snyder. And he offers this advice on goal-setting.
- Set goals in many different areas of your life, such as family, work, and hobbies.
- Break the long-range goals into smaller sub-goals.
- Don't set very easy or exceedingly difficult goals.

Thinking people are good, and being trusting

17   Our survey asked readers whether they think that people are generally "good," "more good than bad," "more bad than good," or "bad." Results: Thirty-eight percent think people are "good" and another 57% think people are "more good than bad." Similarly, 39% describe themselves as "very" trusting, and an additional 52% are "somewhat trusting." All in all, those in our survey who

liked and trusted people enjoyed better health and energy than those who didn't.

18   Our findings made perfect sense to psychologist James Billings, director of the psychology program for the Preventive Medicine Research Institute. "If you constantly think you're about to be cheated by every person you look at, you're in a state of negative arousal, which is harmful to your body. Alternatively," says Dr. Billings, "if you expect safety, trust, accommodation and understanding, your body's in a much more relaxed state. When we look at all the medical research, it's clear that social isolation is strongly related to heart disease, and probably other illnesses as well." In other words, people who don't have strong ties to others are more likely to have health problems.

19   There are several ways to reach out to other people. A warm, accepting group situation can be very helpful. Dr. Dean Ornish, who runs a very successful program for heart attack survivors, says that many participants credit their recovery from heart disease to the group support sessions which are an important part of the program.

Thinking you control your health and your life

20   Most of our respondents (60%) feel they control their lives more than their lives control them. Similarly, 74% of them think they have a great deal of control over their own health. In our survey, both of these attitudes were strongly linked to health. People who feel in control of their lives (37%) are more likely to say they're in excellent health compared to those who don't feel in control of their lives (19%). Likewise, people are much more likely to report excellent health who feel in control of their health (42%) compared with those who don't feel in control of their health (8%).

21   Dr. Langer's work reached similar conclusions. Her research found that giving elderly people more mindful control over their lives may help them live longer. In one of her most famous studies, Dr. Langer "empowered" one group of senior citizens in nursing homes. That group was encouraged to make more decisions, such as where to receive visitors and when to see movies. They were also given plants to tend. Another group of seniors was not given the same choices. And although they were given plants, they were told that the staff would water them. Results: The health and emotions of the group with more control improved dramatically. Most striking of all, those seniors lived longer.

22   Dr. Langer's solution for feeling out of control? "Become more conscious that you do have choices. Challenge yourself to learn and do more." Says Dr. Snyder, "Our research shows that positive people have an on-going dialogue with themselves that goes something like this: `I can do this, I can do this.' Sheer repetition makes those kinds of thoughts fill your head, and eventually you'll start to feel in control."

23   Consider cultivating all of these positive attitudes. Our results didn't point to any one of the seven attitudes as greatly more important than the others. "It's having a whole lot of them that seems to make the difference," says our market research director, Ed Slaughter, who analyzed the survey results. So start thinking positive—very, very positive!

7 Can you guess if *accommodation* is good or bad?

8 According to the writer, what idea do these statistics support?

B. Checking Your Comprehension

Look back at Reading 1 and complete the chart.

ATTITUDE	HOW TO GET IT
1. _____	_____
	_____
2. _____	_____
	_____
3. _____	_____
	_____
4. & 5. _____	_____
	_____
	_____
6. & 7. _____	_____
	_____
	_____

C. Making Inferences

1. **What do you think is the main focus of *Prevention Magazine?***

2. **Why do you think this magazine published an article about the way readers responded to a survey? Why did they do the survey with readers and not the general public?**

D. Topics for Discussion

Discuss the following questions with your classmates.

1. How many of the seven key attitudes do you have? Which ones?

   Besides these seven attitudes, are there any others that you think are important?

2. Do you know anyone whose health has been affected by his or her attitude toward life? How did it affect the person?

3. Do you think that it is possible to learn optimism? What do you think it requires?

4. Do you think the results of this survey are true for society as a whole? Why or why not?

E. Reading Strategies

READING STRATEGY: Recognizing Parallel Organization

When authors want to give the same type of information several times, they often use parallel organization. That means that different information is given in the same order each time.

A television guide uses a simple kind of parallel organization. It gives the time, the name of the program, and a brief description. This type of organization helps the reader to find information more easily.

TIME	CHANNEL	PROGRAM
9 pm	3	**The Boy Next Door**/comedy/ Ben and Bridget recall the first time that they met but their recollections are very different. Peter Martech, Rachel Suskind
	4	**The Crusades**/drama/Part 2 of 5-part series. Tonight Richard the Lion-Hearted sets out for the Holy Land. Anthony Mason, Terence Campbell, Margaret Butterworth
	5	**All About Science**/educational/Different kinds of animal languages are explored in tonight's program. Host: Caroline Carter
	6	**Doctors and Nurses**/drama/Dr. Vazquez has to decide whether to perform a dangerous operation on his own daughter. Victor Ventura, Kate Winsby, Erika Chambers
	8	**Tuesday Night Football**/sports/The Missouri Bucaneers meet the California Bobcats in Sacramento, California.
	3	**The Ruskins**/comedy/Perry and Marilyn decide to start a restaurant; however neither of them can cook. Martha Dudley, Philip Penfield
9:30	3	**Anthea Cooper Attorney at Law**/drama/Anthea defends a man accused of stealing money from his children. Patricia Leone, Fred Stimzek
10:00	5	**Live from the Met!**/music/Highlights of the Metropolitan Opera Company's latest production of Verdi's *La Traviata*. Host: Richard Beeston
	6	**G-Men**/drama/The FBI has 24 hours to find a mad bomber before he strikes again. Timothy McDuff, Brian Palmer, Cynthia Sheldon

Parallel organization works in the same way in a longer article.

---

1. **Look back again at Reading 1. How is it organized? (Hint: Look at the subtitles.)**

2. **Look at the section subtitled *Being Very Optimistic*. Number the types of information below to show the order in which they appear in that section. Then look at the other sections. Do they follow a similar organization?**

   _____ expert advice

   _____ statistics from the author's study

   _____ opinions of experts or information from other studies

3. In your notebook copy the following diagram showing the organization of the reading. Complete the boxes for points 2–5.

```
┌──────────────────────────┐        ┌──────────────────────────┐
│  Introduction to general  │───────▶│ Introduction to specific  │
│      topic of survey      │        │  points found in the survey│
└──────────────────────────┘        └──────────────────────────┘
```

POINT 1: Being very optimistic	POINT 2:	POINT 3:	POINT 4:	POINT 5:
a. Survey: 54% of readers are very optimistic, 37% somewhat optimistic	a._____	a._____	a._____	a._____
b. Study: seniors who expect to be unhealthy have more problems	b._____	b._____	b._____	b._____
c. Pessimists can unlearn negative thinking through "reframing"	c._____	c._____	c._____	c._____

Conclusion

READING STRATEGY: Using Transition Words to Predict

You've learned how to predict before you begin reading. You can also use the skill of predicting *while* you read. Good readers look for clues in the reading that will help them guess what kind of information will be coming next. If you predict as you read, you will be able to read more quickly and with greater comprehension.

There are many kinds of clues that will help you to guess what is coming next. For example, transition words are a very powerful type of clue.

Look at this example:

"If you constantly think you're about to be cheated by every person you look at, you're in a state of negative arousal, which is harmful to your body. **Alternatively**," says Dr. Billings,…

What do you think will come next? Check your guess by looking back at paragraph 18 in Reading 1.

4. Find the following transition words in the reading. Match the words with the kind of information that each one signals. Write the letters on the lines. An example has been done for you.

____ 1. alternatively   ____ 4. similarly

____ 2. in contrast   ____ 5. overall

_c_ 3. likewise

a. a conclusion made based on the information that you have just read

b. a statement that is the opposite of what you have just read

c. a statement that is the same, in some way, as what you have just read

---

READING STRATEGY: Writing Margin Notes

Many people think that reading is a receptive or inactive activity, but the best readers are very active while they are reading. In fact, they often evaluate what they think and carry on a dialogue with the writer. This ongoing dialogue may take place only in their heads, but they sometimes write their ideas as notes in the margin of the text.

Look at the text below. What does the reader think of the author's ideas?

ATTITUDES THAT MATTER MOST _____

So, what are the <u>seven positive attitudes</u> that, according to our survey, define "The Spark of Life"? Here's what we found:

1. Being very <u>optimistic</u>   *Yes!*
2. Having a strong belief in a higher power
3. Thinking of the <u>future, not</u> the <u>past</u>   *I agree!*
4. Thinking people are good
5. Being very trusting *?????*   *not so sure about this one*
6. Thinking you control your life
7. Thinking you <u>control your health</u>   *How can we do this?*

We cannot ignore the growing body of medical evidence <u>linking opti-</u> <u>mism with healthier,</u> longer lives. And, at the very least, positive people are happier and have a greater sense of well-being than their negative neighbors. So thinking positive is a goal worth striving for. The question is: Can we learn optimism? *No. Optimists are born, not made.*

What evidence do you have for this??

Are there any benefits to making margin notes such as the ones above?

---

5. **Reread Reading 1. Make margin notes about things that you agree or do not agree with.**

READING STRATEGY: More Practice with Recognizing Referents

In Unit 2, you learned to recognize referents by looking back in a reading to find the word or concept that is being referred to. Pronouns such as **they, she, their,** and so on are used as referring words. Look at this example:

Professional athletes practice meditation as part of **their** training.

6. **Complete the chart with referents from Reading 1.**

REFERRING WORD	PARAGRAPH NUMBER	LINE NUMBER	REFERS TO
1. them	7	3	_____
2. that	9	2	_____
3. she	9	3	_____
4. their	13	7	_____

F. Strategies for Unknown Vocabulary

VOCABULARY STRATEGY: Recognizing Collocations

Collocations are groups of words that usually occur together. Two- and three-word verbs such as **get used to** and **call** (someone) **up** are collocations. However, there are many collocations which are not verbs. Here are some examples:

in the **final analysis**   **examples of**   **harmful to** your body

Recognizing collocations can help you predict which words are coming. Therefore, as you are reading, you should look for them. Note that they do not always occur next to each other. Look at these examples:

compare these answers **with**

enjoyed **better** health and energy **than** those who didn't

It is helpful to learn common collocations as single vocabulary units.

Look for words in Reading 1 and complete the collocations.

1. ...according _____ our survey

2. ...a goal worth striving _____

3. ...wide _____ of...

4. ...by noticing things rather _____ just accepting...

5. ...body _____ (medical) evidence

6. ...look on the _____ side

G. Building Your Vocabulary

Use these steps to build your vocabulary with words from the reading.

1. Look back at Reading 1 and make a list of five to ten new words that you feel are important to learn.

2. Write these words in your vocabulary notebook. Group words that are similar (e.g., *belief/believers/nonbelievers, optimist/pessimist/realist*). Copy a sentence or phrase in which the word appears. Decide on the part of speech of the word and write a definition for it.

3. If you are still unsure of the meaning of this word or the part of speech, look it up in the dictionary and write the definition in your own words. For additional practice, write your own sentence.

H. Writing Your Ideas

Look at the writing topics below. Choose at least one and write about it.

1. Choose one of the seven attitudes and write about how you feel about it. Do you have it? Why or why not? If you do not, would you like to have it? How could you begin to do that? Explain.

2. The article quotes many experts in this field. Choose one or two of the pieces of advice that you think are useful and explain why you think so.

READING 2: "MAKING THE CONNECTION"

A. Pre-reading the Text

PRE-READING STRATEGY: Formulating Questions

You have learned how to preview by making predictions about the reading. Another important previewing strategy is to formulate questions. Many times previewing brings up questions that you cannot answer. Reading with these questions in your mind will help you to focus on the author's main points.

---

1. **Look at these example questions and write your own questions about Reading 2.**

Title: _What connection is being referred to here?_

Subtitle: _What is a wellness program?_

Introduction/Conclusion: _____

Author: _____

Source: _____

2. **Read the text closely. Remember to cover the margin questions the first time that you read.**

3. **Reread the text, using the margin questions to help you.**

READING 2

Making the Connection:

Students Learn to Control Emotions in Center's School Wellness Program

by Kelsey Menehan

Excerpted from "The Mind-Body Connection"

1 What is the author's purpose for telling Gwenetta's story?

1 Up until a year and a half ago, Gwenetta Neal was a notorious fighter. Whenever she got angry, she'd start hitting someone. She fought with her mother, her siblings, her teachers, her classmates. "I got suspended from school all the time for fighting," Gwenetta recalls. "I just couldn't stop."

2 Today, when Gwenetta gets angry, she goes into another room, drinks a glass of water, sits down and crosses her legs and thinks for awhile. "I focus on my breathing, and I start to feel relaxed," she explains. It's a simple technique that has made a huge difference in Gwenetta's life. She learned it through the School Wellness Program at City Lights School, sponsored by the Center for Mind-Body Medicine.

2 What information do you expect will follow this paragraph? Why?

3 Since May of 1995, at least forty students with learning, emotional and behavioral problems have been attending City Lights, an alternative high school in Philadelphia. The focus of the City Lights program is to teach these students about the mind-body connection and how to make that connection work in their favor instead of against them. Gwenetta isn't the only one who notices changes in her life.

4 Once seen as a completely unmanageable troublemaker, Michael didn't trust anyone, and so he was unable to have close relationships with people. Now, however, Michael talks about his feelings as a way of taking care of himself. He learned this through the Wellness Around the World game, created by Jane Kauffman, the Center's director of school programs. The game allows students and teachers to win points for doing things to feed their souls, such as "getting a massage," "smiling at a stranger," "saying no when appropriate," "preparing a healthy meal," "listening to someone in need," or "noticing your good and bad habits in others." Those with the most points get prizes such as a full-body massage or a CMBM T-shirt.

5   Michael told Kauffman that he had noticed behavior in other peo-
     ple that was true of himself—and he didn't like it. "I see people
     going off at their teachers and I don't like it. I don't want to do
     that." Now aware of his own behavior, he has the option to do
     things differently when he gets angry. Instead of "going off," he
     now talks through his problems.

6   For her part, Gwenetta found ways to deal with her anger through a
     movement class with dance instructor and massage therapist Kris
     O'Shee, a volunteer with the Center. "I didn't like it at first," Gwenet-
     ta recalls. "I thought it was boring until we started moving. It felt
     good to loosen my body up."

3 Do you understand
    admonish?

7   When Kris introduced the idea of healing touch through simple
     shoulder and neck massage, Gwenetta wasn't interested. She didn't
     much like people touching her. But her friend Tania admonished
     her, "Don't turn down anything that's free."

8   "There was relaxing music and you would breathe in and out along
     with the other person. It was good," Gwenetta recalls. Later, she
     agreed to have Kris give her a full body massage. "After that I was
     ready to go home and go to sleep. I never thought I could relax like
     that." Now when Gwenetta finds herself getting angry, she thinks
     about getting a massage and calms right down.

9   Gwenetta has also learned to relax by heating her hands. The Center
     provides students with bio-dots, stick-on thermal monitors that
     change color as the person's stress level lessens. "When your hands
     are cold you can't see anything. When you heat your hands, you
     relax and it turns all different colors—blue, neon, black, purple,"
     says Gwenetta. "My mom uses them, too."

10   For Gwenetta, the mind-body connection comes down to this:
     "When you're angry and frustrated, your body isn't right. I never

knew that had anything to do with my body." Gwenetta now knows that she doesn't have to keep the anger in—and then blow up and fight to get the energy out. "I can talk about what's going on and feel good after that. I can be myself and think big and look forward instead of backward, and walk away from fights. My friends talking to me helps me to think positive, too."

11   City Lights staff members are amazed by the changes in Gwenetta. "She has become a role model for the other young people here," says Andrea Conner. "I never see her hyped. She's a very positive young lady. She's telling other kids about the program and encouraging them to join in."

B. Checking Your Comprehension

Complete the chart with information from Reading 2.

Name of the program: _____

Who it serves: _____

What it does: _____

Program philosophy: _____

_____

Methods: _____

_____

Degree of success: _____

C. Making Inferences

1. **Do you think many of the students at City Lights are unwilling to cooperate with the program at first? Why?**

2. **How is Gwenetta Neal probably typical of the students in this program? How is she probably not typical?**

D. Topics for Discussion

Discuss the following questions with your classmates.

1. Do you think a program such as this one would be useful for teenagers in your country? Why or why not?

2. In your country, how do people try to help troubled teenagers?

3. Do you think any of these mind-body techniques would be useful for other people who don't have the same problems as these students? Why or why not?

E. Reading Strategies

READING STRATEGY: More on Signal Words and Phrases

You have already learned that some words and phrases help you to predict what kind of information will come next. One of these is **at first**. A writer uses the phrase **at first** to signal that the situation changed from the beginning to the end.

Look at this example from the reading:

For her part, Gwenetta found ways to deal with her anger through a movement class with dance instructor and massage therapist Kris O'Shee, a volunteer with the Center. "I didn't like it **at first**," Gwenetta recalls. "I thought it was boring until we started moving. It felt good to loosen my body up."

What change does **at first** signal in this paragraph? How did Gwenetta feel when she started the program? How did her feelings change?

Signal Word/Phrase	Meaning
at first	signals that a situation is going to change
at the start	signals that a situation is probably going to change
in the beginning	signals that a situation is probably going to change
from the start	signals that a situation is *not* going to change
first	introduces a series of steps or ideas

---

1. Look at the sentences below. Underline the signal word or phrase. Then circle the letter of the statement that logically follows.

1. At first, the students refused to cooperate,
   a. and they remained uncooperative all year.
   b. but after a month they saw the value of the activities.

2. The students were very unhappy at the start
   a. and the situation never got any better.
   b. however, the staff was soon able to change their minds.

3. In the beginning, David was very uncooperative,
   a. but by the end of first term, he was one of the most enthusiastic students.
   b. and he ended up being one of the students who made no progress.

4. First, students are recommended for the program by their teachers.
   a. But they often do not like it.
   b. Then, they are interviewed by the staff.

5. From the start, most of the staff was very optimistic.
   a. Their attitudes changed when they met the kids.
   b. That attitude helped them to make the program a success.

READING STRATEGY: Summarizing a Reading

A summary of a reading gives a very brief restatement of the most important points of a reading.

Most good summaries include:	**Most good summaries do not include:**
the author's purpose	examples
the main idea	opinions
conclusions or results	background information
recommendations	

2. Read the summaries below. What are some of the good and bad points of each one? Look at the box above for some ideas.

1. *Prevention Magazine* wanted to know which attitudes seemed to promote good health, so they surveyed their readers. They asked them questions about their health, friendships, relationships, lifestyle, and so on. From these questions they came up with a list of seven attitudes. These attitudes are:
   - Being very optimistic
   - Having a strong belief in a higher power
   - Thinking of the future, not the past
   - Thinking people are good
   - Being very trusting
   - Thinking you control your life
   - Thinking you control your health

2. This article is about a survey done by *Prevention Magazine* on attitudes that promote good health. It gives a lot of advice on how to develop healthy attitudes if you do not have them now.

3. "Thinking Yourself Healthy" gives advice on how to develop the seven attitudes that promote good health. These attitudes are things such as being very optimistic, thinking people are good, and thinking that you control your life and your health. The article also explains why it is important to have these attitudes.

3. Which of these points should be included in a summary of the article you just read (Reading 2)?

1. Gwenetta Neal used to fight a lot.

2. City Lights is a program for students with emotional problems or learning problems.

3. City Lights students sometimes get massages.

4. City Lights students learn mind-body techniques to control their emotions.

5. One teacher has developed a game called "Wellness Around the World."

6. City Lights has been very successful with students like Gwenetta and Michael.

4. On a separate piece of paper, write a summary of Reading 2.

F. Strategies for Unknown Vocabulary

VOCABULARY STRATEGY: Choosing the Right Definition

When you decide that you need to use a dictionary, you must use it carefully. Many dictionary entries give several meanings that are closely related. To choose the correct one, look back at the original context and test each meaning to see which fits best.

---

1. Look at the word *once* in these sentences. Match them with the number of the correct dictionary definition below. Write the numbers on the line.

_____ 1. *Once* seen as a completely unmanageable troublemaker, Michael didn't trust anyone and so he was unable to have close relationships with people. Now, however, Michael talks about his feelings as a way of taking care of himself.

_____ 2. *Once* Gwenetta had learned to stop fighting, she was ready to go back to a normal school program.

_____ 3. Students are encouraged to get a massage *once* a week.

> **once** [wuns] adv. **1.** at one time in the past; formerly: *a once powerful nation* **2.** a single time: *I see them once a year.* **3.** whenever; as soon as: *Once you're finished, you can leave.*

> **focus** ['fo-kes] n. **-cuses 1.** an adjustment (of the eye, camera lens, microscope etc.) to a clear picture: *I adjusted the focus of the camera to 6 feet.* **2.** an object of attention: *The focus of the news report was the state of the economy.*
> **-v. -cuses 1.** to adjust in order to get a clear picture: *A scientist focused her microscope on the bacteria.* **2.** To center one's attention on: *The Senator's speech was focused on health care reform.* **3. to be in or out of focus:** to have a clear or unclear picture: *We couldn't see their faces because the photograph was out of focus.*

2. Now choose the correct definition for the word *focus* in these sentences.

_____ 1. I *focus* on my breathing, and I start to feel relaxed...

_____ 2. The *focus* of the program is to teach them about the mind-body connection.

3. **Try to complete these collocations. Then look back at Reading 2 to check your answers. An example has been done for you.**

    1. I got suspended _from_ school

    2. I focus ____ my breathing

    3. ...sponsored ____ the Center for Mind-Body Medicine

    4. ...to teach these students ____ the mind-body connection

    5. ...to make that connection work ____ their favor instead ____ against them

4. **How can you use general knowledge to guess the meanings of these words? Complete the chart.**

WORD OR EXPRESSION	PARAGRAPH NUMBER	POSSIBLE MEANING
1. siblings	1	_____
2. suspended from school	1	_____
3. going off at	5	_____
4. massage	7	_____

G. Building Your Vocabulary

Use these steps to build your vocabulary with words from the reading.

1. Look at your reading list from Reading 1. Put a checkmark (✓) next to any words that also appeared in Reading 2. Then look back at Reading 2 and make a list of five to ten new words that you feel are important to learn.

2. Write these words in your vocabulary notebook. Group words that are similar (e.g., *emotional/behavioral, forward/backward.*) Copy a sentence or phrase in which the word appears. Decide on the part of speech of the word and write a definition for it.

3. If you are still unsure of the meaning of this word or the part of speech, look it up in the dictionary and write the definition in your own words. For additional practice, write your own sentence.

H. Writing Your Ideas

Look at the writing topics below. Choose at least one and write about it.

1. Do you think that a program such as City Lights can help troubled children? Why or why not?

2. What are some things that you do when you become angry? Which of these things are helpful? Which are not? Why?

3. Can you think of some other kinds of things people can do to control their anger? Explain.

I. Making Connections

Both Reading 2 ("Making the Connection") and Reading 1 ("Thinking Yourself Healthy") talk about the mind-body connection. How are the strategies that are mentioned in Reading 2 different from the advice given in Reading 1? How are they the same?

PART *B* FOCUS ON READING FOR A PURPOSE

When you have finished Readings 1–6, you will complete the Unit Task. Imagine that you work for the National Association for Stress Management. You have been given the task of writing a pamphlet on the mind-body connection for *one* of the following groups. This group will be your audience. Choose one of the following:

- teenagers who are about to enter college

- people who want to improve their performance (e.g., athletes, musicians, or businesspeople—choose *one*)

- senior citizens

Further details on the Unit Task can be found on page 165. Your purpose in reading the rest of Unit 3 is to gather information and ideas for the Unit Task. You will need to use the steps in reading for a purpose that you learned about and practiced in Units 1 and 2. In your own words, explain what each of these steps are:

Pre-Step: Identify the Information You Need _____

_____

Step 1: Preview _____

_____

Step 2: Read Closely _____

_____

Step 3: Note Useful Information _____

_____

Pre-Step: Identify the Information You Need

1. In order to read and collect information more efficiently, you must first identify the kind of information that you will be looking for. Work with other students who have chosen to write a pamphlet for the same group. Think about your audience. What sorts of problems do they have? How might they benefit from knowing about the mind-body connection?

2. Make a list of the group's problems in the chart below. Then look back at Readings 1 and 2. Did these readings give you any information about the problems your audience faces? Which ones? Write the reading numbers in the chart on page 140.

Group That the Pamphlet Is for: _____

Problems common to that group that can be solved through mind-body techniques.	Readings that have information to help with the problem.
_____	_____
_____	_____
_____	_____
_____	_____
_____	_____
_____	_____
_____	_____

3. Now look ahead to Readings 3–6. Which of them might discuss these problems? Write the reading numbers in the chart.

4. You also need to think about convincing your audience. How likely are they to believe in the techniques described in the readings? How much background information will they need? How much "proof" will they require?

5. Copy the chart below into your notebook. Refer back to it as you work on Readings 3–6. Every time you find useful information for the Unit Task or think of a new idea, add it to the chart. However, remember that you will not have to do the Unit Task until the end of the unit.

Problem	Information that will help (techniques, advice, etc.)	Proof/Research	Reading number(s)

READING 3: "THE MENTAL EDGE"

Step 1 : Preview

1. Look at the title and the subtitle of this reading. Are there any words that you do not understand? Where can you look for information to help you guess their meanings?

2. What do you think the reading is going to be about? Write your guess below.

_____

3. Now preview the reading to see if you were correct.

PREVIEWING STRATEGY: Scanning for Key Words

When a reading is long, it is often helpful to scan for key words when you preview. Key words are words that are related to your purpose. They help you to locate relevant sections more easily.

If you keep your key words in mind as you are reading, they can also help you to focus on the most important information.

4. Here are some key words for the Unit Task. Add others specific to the group for whom you are writing the pamphlet.

advice   helpful   improve   strategy   _____

_____   _____   _____   _____   _____

Step 2: Read Closely

1. **Look back at the charts on pages 139 and 140. Will this reading have any information to fill in the charts? Read the text closely. Remember to cover the margin questions the first time that you read.**

2. **Reread the text, using the margin questions to help you.**

READING 3

1 What does the phrase *once considered* signal here? What was the old view? What is the new view?

2 The word *CEO* is all capital letters. What does that tell you?

3 What does *for instance* signal?

4 In paragraph 4, how can parallel structure help you to understand *adept*?

![green square] **The Mental Edge:
The brain is the key to peak
performance, in sports and life**

by William F. Allman
From *U.S. News & World Report*

1   There is a new emphasis in the sports world on training athletes' minds as well as their muscles. Once considered a form of psychic voodoo, sports psychology is rapidly becoming an important part of nearly every serious athlete's normal routine, right along with weight lifting and nutrition. The new focus on the "mental game" is increasingly finding an enthusiastic audience in business, medicine and the military as well. "The implications go far beyond sports," says Brad Hatfield of the University of Maryland. "Whether it's an airline pilot, musician, surgeon or CEO, everyone's goal is achieving a peak performance."

2   The importance of controlling the power of the mind has long been part of folk wisdom. Today, scientists are revealing that such age-old wisdom has a biological basis. "Over the years, people have found that certain psychological techniques seem to work," says neurologist Marcus Raichle of Washington University in St. Louis. "Now, we're beginning to find out that there is a basic 'brain' reason why."

3   Scientists are showing, for instance, that one crucial aspect of peak performance—going into a state of intense concentration—is associated with profound changes in the brain.

The University of Maryland's Hatfield gave skilled marksmen tiny electrodes that measure the brain's electrical activity and monitored their minds as they shot at a target. He found that just before an expert shooter pulls the trigger, the left side of the brain gives off a burst of so-called alpha waves, which are characteristic of a relaxed, dreamlike state. Similar results have been found in golfers as they putt, archers releasing an arrow and basketball players shooting a free throw. This sudden change in brain waves seems to reflect a dramatic change in the athlete's mental state at the moment of peak performance, says Hatfield.

4   Neuroscientists have long known that each hemisphere, or side, of the human brain specializes in certain activities. The left brain is better at language and analytical skills and the right brain is more adept at spatial

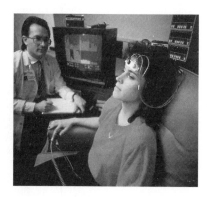

relations and pattern recognition. Hatfield's research suggests that during peak performance, the mind relaxes its analytical side and allows its right side to control the body. The result is the dreamlike "flow" state that many athletes, musicians and other people report experiencing when they are intensely engaged in an activity.

5 The ability to enter a state of deep concentration at the right moment is a key part of acquiring an athletic skill, even though people typically are not aware that they are doing it. In one new study, psychologist Dan Landers of Arizona State University monitored the brain-wave patterns of a group of novices as they underwent a 15-week training course in archery. Landers found that as the archers' skills improved, the brain-wave patterns they displayed during shooting changed, too. Toward the end of their training, the archers had improved their scores by more than 60 percent—and they had begun to show the same burst of alpha waves right before a shot that researchers find in very skilled archers.

6 So important is this flow state to peak performance that athletes can actually improve their performances by learning to control their brain waves. In one study by Landers, experienced archers were hooked up to a machine that measured the activity in either the left or right side of the brain. The brain monitor was connected to a video screen showing two bars of light that moved closer together as the subjects successfully relaxed one side of their brains. Eventually, they became adept at controlling the movement of the bars, thus learning to control their brain waves. Following this biofeedback training, those archers who had learned to control the brain waves in their left hemisphere shot significantly better, with their arrows hitting nearly an inch closer to the bull's-eye on average. Those who had trained their right hemisphere did far worse.

7 One way that psychologists train athletes to bring their minds into a flow state is by having them go through a prearranged mental routine. An archer, for example, might go through a mental checklist such as "position the feet, draw the bow, take a deep breath, focus and release the arrow." Having a fixed routine can help improve concentration and performance off the playing field, too. A lawyer might carefully arrange notes and pencils before making a final argument at a trial, for instance, just as a surgeon might go through a ritual preparing for an operation.

8 Whether the athlete is an Olympian or an amateur, a key component of preparing for a peak performance is letting the automatic processes of the mind take over to move the muscles. This "muscle memory" appears to have a basis in biological fact. In a study published this month, neurologist Scott Grafton of the University of Southern California found that the brain learns a new skill by fine-tuning the specific neural circuits that are involved in making the motion. At first, when people are learning a new task, many different areas of their brains are active simul-

5 Can you use general knowledge to understand the word *novices?*

6 In paragraph 7, what other phrases are used as synonyms for *mental checklist?*

taneously. But as people become better at a task, their brain activity becomes more focused on the brain circuits directly involved in producing the movements.

Creating mind movies _____

9　Physically moving the muscles is not the only way to practice a new skill. The brain is so powerful that merely imagining making the movement can sometimes result in a better performance. Golf great Jack Nicklaus, for instance, has said that he would "watch a movie" in his head before each shot. Peter Fox of the University of Texas at San Antonio and his colleagues did research that monitored people's brain activity as they performed various body motions and also as they imagined performing the motions. They found that the actual physical movement consistently involved the interaction of several specific areas of the brain. The researchers discovered that imagining the movement also activated those same areas of the brain. In other words, mental rehearsal of an action puts the mind through a neural workout that is similar to the real thing.

10　The power of conjuring up mental images goes beyond merely practicing a particular movement. Imagery can help people prepare for peak performances by mentally walking them through successful strategies and potential pitfalls. Experts recommend that athletes develop an "image bank" containing mental movies they can play for relaxation, for getting psyched up, and for building confidence.

Setting the right goals _____

11　The opportunity for a peak performance is sometimes lost at the starting line, psychologists believe, because people set out to achieve the wrong goals. "Focus only on those things you can control," says Shane Murphy, sports psychologist for the US Olympic team. Since it is impossible to control the judging of an event or other competitors' performances, people should concentrate on doing their best, not winning the match or getting the great new job. Psychologists also say that long-term goals, such as finishing a major project, should be divided into several short-term goals, so that the positive feedback of achieving one goal helps to propel one toward the next.

Catching the flow _____

12　At the moment of peak performance, athletes, musicians and other performers speak of being "in the zone," a state of total attention to the task at hand. One way to help reach this zone of deep concentration is to select several "focus" words to repeat to oneself while in the midst of the event. An archer, for instance, might work up to his shot by slowly reciting to himself, "Draw…breathe…aim…release," focusing on the target and leaving his mind otherwise blank.

Coping with setbacks _____

13　Unexpected occurrences such as a bad call from a judge or an unlucky bounce can derail a performance, so psychologists train athletes to devise a number of "coping strategies" to get them back on track. One of the most important is "self-talk"—the running commentary that tennis players, for example, carry on in their minds between points. One's thoughts can have a profound effect on the body. Negative thoughts can lead to anxiety or depression, changing one's breathing patterns and heart rate and wasting energy. Because the mind typically dwells on only one thing at a time, psychologists train athletes to think positively by reminding themselves of their past successes.

7　How do the next four subtitles relate to one another?

8　How does paragraph 10 build on the information in paragraph 9?

9　Does paragraph 13 serve as a conclusion for the whole article? Why or why not?

A. Checking Your Comprehension

1. Complete the chart with information from the reading.

NAME OF RESEARCHER	GROUP(S) STUDIED	RESULTS
Hatfield	archers	

2. Complete the following sentence.

In order to achieve peak performance, some things athletes can do are:

_____

_____

B. Making Inferences

Scientists believe that either the left or right hemisphere of the human brain is more dominant in most people. Which side of the brain do you think is more dominant in:

1. artists   _____

2. mathematicians   _____

3. musicians   _____

4. architects   _____

C. Topics for Discussion

Discuss the following questions with your classmates.

1. Have you ever had an experience of peak performance in sports or any other area?

2. Is this article persuasive? Do you believe what it says? Explain.

3. The article claims that these techniques are not just for athletes. Do you think that they would work as well for lawyers or businesspeople as they would for athletes or musicians? Why or why not?

4. How might you use some of these concepts to improve your own performance?

D. Additional Strategy Practice

VOCABULARY STRATEGY: Using Larger Contexts to Guess Meaning

You already know some strategies for dealing with unknown words. One of these is to look at the whole sentence and use your general knowledge to guess what that word means.

Sometimes, however, the sentence doesn't give you enough information. In this case, you should look at the sentences right before and right after the word. They may provide more clues to help you guess.

Look at the word **implications** in paragraph 1 of Reading 3. Does the sentence give you enough information to guess the meaning? Read the sentence right before and right after this sentence. Can you make a guess about the general meaning of **implications**?

Also, scan the reading to see if the word occurs again. If it does, another context might give you further information.

Sometimes you may need to look even further to understand the meaning of a word. Find the phrase **peak performance**. Where does it first appear? Do you think that it is important to understand this phrase? Why or why not? Is there enough information there for you to guess its meaning?

Scan for other occurrences of the phrase **peak performance**. In which paragraphs does it appear? Read each occurrence of this phrase until you have enough information to guess the meaning.

1. **Try to guess the meaning of these words. In each case, look beyond the sentence where the word occurs.**

WORD	PARAGRAPH NUMBER	GUESS ABOUT THE MEANING
1. folk wisdom	2	_____
2. monitored	3	_____
3. routine	7	_____

VOCABULARY STRATEGY: Deciding When to Look for Further Information

Some words are not very important for your purpose, and a very general understanding of the word may be enough. However, there are other words that are so important that you may need to look for a more complete explanation.

2. **Do you need more information about any of these words? Which ones? Scan for the words you select and reread the sections of the text they are found in. Write short definitions of each of the terms based on the information in the reading.**

   1. archery _____
   2. biofeedback _____
   3. concentration _____
   4. imagery _____
   5. focus/flow _____

3. Then read the encyclopedia definitions on page 169. Underline the information that is new to you. Did the encyclopedia definitions increase your understanding of Reading 3?

Step 3: Note Useful Information

1. Highlight and/or make margin notes in Reading 3 on information that will help you with the Unit Task, writing a pamphlet on the mind-body connection for a particular audience. Then compare your work with a classmate who is writing a pamphlet for the same audience. Did you note the same information?

2. Did this reading remind you of other problems that the readers of your pamphlet might have and techniques or advice that can help? If so, add these to your chart with the information you highlighted and/or noted in Reading 3.

E. Building Your Vocabulary

Use these steps to build your vocabulary with words from the reading.

1. Look at your reading list from Readings 1 and 2. Put a checkmark (✓) next to any words that also appeared in Reading 3. Then look back at Reading 3 and make a list of five to ten new words that you feel are important to learn.

2. Write these words in your vocabulary notebook. Group words that are similar (e.g., *psychic/psychology/psychological, dramatic/automatic*). Copy a sentence or phrase in which the word appears. Decide on the part of speech of the word and write a definition for it.

3. If you are still unsure of the meaning of this word or the part of speech, look it up in the dictionary and write the definition in your own words. For additional practice, write your own sentence.

F. Writing Your Ideas

Look at the writing topics below. Choose at least one and write about it.

1. Write about a peak performance you have had. What were you doing? How did you feel? Use the technical terms from this reading to describe your experience.

2. Interview a serious athlete, musician, or any other person who regularly performs a set routine. Talk to them about some of the concepts in this reading. Have they experienced these things? Write about their answers.

G. Making Connections

Compare the concept of self-talk in Reading 6, Unit 1 with the concept of self-talk in paragraph 13 of this reading. How are they similar?

READING 4: "THE STRESS CURE THAT'S RIGHT FOR YOU"

Step 1: Preview

1. What should you look at in this article in order to make a prediction of what it is about? _____

2. Skim the reading and write a one-sentence prediction of what it is about _____

3. Compare your prediction with the predictions of other students in your class. Do you wish to change or add to the chart you filled in on page 139?

Step 2: Read Closely

1. As you read, look for information to complete the chart on page 140. Remember to cover up the margin questions the first time that you read.

2. Reread the text using the margin questions to help you.

READING 4

1 If you are not sure of the meaning of the word *cure*, keep on reading until you get enough information to make a guess.

2 Who does *you* refer to in this paragraph?

3 Who does *our* refer to?

4 This part of the reading uses parallel organization. What is that organization?

The *STRESS CURE* that's Right for YOU

by Daryn Eller

1   A friend tells you that since she has taken up yoga, her stress has disappeared. But when you tried it, it didn't work. Stress reducers aren't cure-alls: What helps one person won't necessarily work for another. To find your method, you have to consider your personality and how you react to pressure. Our quiz and guide to the most popular techniques will help you do just that.

What's Your Stress Personality?

2   Read the following profiles, developed with the help of Julie Kembel, director of education at the Canyon Ranch Health and Fitness Resort in Tucson, Arizona, then decide which most resembles the way you respond to life's problems.

5 Does *you* refer to <u>all</u> readers here?

6 Do you have enough information to guess the meaning of *cure?*

7 Do the negative and positive examples help you to understand the word *conversely?*

The "Only When Something Bad Happens" Reactor

3   You're fairly relaxed. You don't keep an appointment book, and if someone keeps you waiting on the phone more than 45 seconds, you simply hang up. But when something goes wrong—dinner is delayed because you were late getting home, your boss wants you to redo a report—you become nervous and upset.

4   <u>Recommended Cures:</u> You need a quick and accessible solution for those times when you feel anxious. Consider aerobic exercise, sports, or an interesting leisure activity, such as crafts or computer games.

The Physical Reactor

5   You're stressed only some of the time, but when you are, you tend to feel it in your body. If someone leaves you hanging on the phone, you immediately start tapping your foot. A disagreement with a neighbor gives you a backache. Conversely, positive touch—a friend puts her hand on your arm to emphasize a point—pleases you.

6   <u>Recommended Cures:</u> Because you tend to respond to things physically, you'll benefit from stress-reduction techniques that unwind your tight muscles. Consider nonstrenuous exercise such as yoga or tai chi.

The Overreactor

7   When your presentation at work doesn't go well, you're sure you'll be fired. You try to be organized—you even note in your appointment book when you'll do the laundry—but you still feel stressed most of the time. Even small problems upset you: If you have to run to catch the bus, you have a headache or stomachache for the rest of the day.

8   <u>Recommended Cures:</u> With the level of stress you're under, you need skills you can use on a regular basis to help you reduce your tension. Consider biofeedback, meditation, or a stress-management workshop.

How Your Prescription Works

9   Stress-control techniques vary in the types of tension they relieve—and how they do it. Some may be difficult (but worthwhile for the long-term relief they bring), while others are quicker, easier, with immediate but non-lasting benefits. Here's what you can expect.

Aerobic Exercise

10   Exercising hard can have a relaxing effect. In addition, it provides a burst of pleasure, elevating your mood, explains Lewis G. Maharam, M.D., a sports medicine specialist in New York. Also, the more fit you get through aerobic exercise—an aerobics class, running, walking, using the Stair Master—the lower your heart rate will be. A lower heart rate will help you in tense situations that can raise your heart rate to stressful levels.

11   You don't have to train like Jackie Joyner Kersee to get the rewards. Short sessions reduce anxiety as much as longer ones do, reports John Raglin, Ph.D., associate professor in the department of kinesiology at Indiana University in Bloomington. But if you decide to undertake a more difficult

8 The next section of the text is also organized in a parallel way. Describe the organization.

9 Do you know who Jackie Joyner Kersee is? What can you guess about her by using your general knowledge?

workout, ask yourself whether you'll really be able to continue with it: If you can't, you'll probably end up feeling guilty. Then you're right back where you started," says Dr. Maharam.

Leisure Activities

12 Hobbies and other fun activities are often the first thing people give up when they are under pressure. That's too bad, because they're one of the most easily obtainable types of stress reduction, says Kimball. An activity that occupies the mind and the body, such as painting, ceramics, chess, or computer games, can help you to stop thinking about everyday worries.

13 So, too, can activities that involve a soothing, repetitive motion, such as knitting, woodworking, or gardening. "Anything that helps you feel more in control will make you feel better," says Kimball. If, however, you need relief from constant stress, think of such leisure-time activities as "extras" while you also pursue a more rigorous coping technique.

Yoga and Tai Chi

10 Can you guess the meaning of *martial arts?*

14 If you don't love to sweat, you may enjoy the quietness of an Eastern exercise class. In yoga, you stretch and meditate; tai chi is a gentle form of martial arts. Neither one is simple. Both require a lot of concentration. But that may be why they're so calming. Like some forms of meditation, the concentration gives your mind a brief escape from worries about your job, your family, and the hundred things you have to do. Also, Dr. Mahatma has found, light workouts like yoga provide a gentle sense of well-being that starts slowly and lasts for hours after.

If you don't love to sweat, you may enjoy tai chi.

Biofeedback

15 The name says it all: Biofeedback measures biological functions, such as muscle tension, heart rate, and blood flow, to tell you how your mental state is affecting your body. Once you're aware of your physical overreactions, you can learn to control them, explains Francine Butler, Ph.D., executive director of the Association for Applied Psychophysiology and Biofeedback. If, for example, your muscles tend to tighten under stress, you can be taught a calming technique called progressive muscle relaxation. Visualization techniques—imagining yourself in a relaxing environment—can help slow an accelerated heart rate. The technique does take work, but it is satisfying for those who like to see tangible results of their efforts.

Meditation

11 Do you need to understand the word *entail* to understand the sentence?

16 There is more than one way to meditate. Some forms—such as transcendental meditation—entail sitting quietly while paying attention to your breathing, and focusing on a single sound or phrase. If your mind wanders, you ignore any thoughts and come back to the sound or phrase. This type of meditation is designed to help you calm your breathing, relax muscles, and keep anxious thoughts away.

12 What does the phrase *at first* signal?

17 Another type of meditation, called mindfulness, does the opposite: You accept rather than ignore your mind's wanderings. Although this can make stress more acute at first, ultimately you become calmer, explains Elana Rosenbaum, a senior instructor at the Stress Reduction and Relaxation Program at the University of Massachusetts Medical Center in Worcester. "By noticing your thoughts, you often have greater ability to see how your mind affects your body, to understand what you're thinking and even change the way you think," she says.

18 Meditation does take some time to learn and requires commitment. But once you've developed the skill, you can meditate on your own for as little as five minutes. It's not, however, a good technique if you're very nervous: You may have trouble sitting quietly enough to benefit from it.

Mini Stress Managers

19 If the techniques above will not fit into your busy schedule, you can try one of these in only five minutes.

20 Self-Massage—Robin Ehrlich-Bragdon, director of Eastside Massage Therapy Center in New York, recommends this do-it-yourself method: Move your head to the right side. With your left hand, grasp the muscle that runs from your neck to your shoulder between your palm and fingers (don't use your thumb). Lift the muscle, squeeze five times; repeat on the other side.

21 Abbreviated meditation—Watching soundless motion for several minutes can help you feel better. Look out a window, focusing on the passing traffic or pedestrians.

A. Checking Your Comprehension

Write descriptions of the three stress personality types from the article in the boxes. Then write each of the five different stress control techniques in the box below the stress personality type that it fits best.

Stress personality type:	Stress personality type:	Stress personality type:
Stress control technique:	Stress control technique:	Stress control technique:

B. Making Inferences

1. Why do you think each of the following techniques can help relieve stress?

1. abbreviated meditation (p. 150)

2. self-massage (p. 150)

3. imagining yourself in a relaxing environment (p. 150)

2. Why do you think hobbies and other fun activities are often the first things people stop doing when they are stressed? (p. 149)

C. Topics for Discussion

Discuss the following questions with your classmates.

1. Which stress personality do you think you have? If your classmates know you well, do they agree?

2. What do you do to try to relieve stress?

3. Can you think of any other stress personality types that aren't mentioned in the reading?

D. Additional Strategy Practice

READING STRATEGY: Using Margin Notes to Highlight Information

In Reading 1, you learned about making margin notes to show your opinion. Margin notes can also be combined with underlining to pick out important information. Look at this example:

The Physical Reactor

5   You're ¹stressed only <u>some of the time</u>, but when you are, you tend to ²<u>feel it in your body.</u> If someone leaves you hanging on the phone, you immediately start tapping your foot. A disagreement with a neighbor gives you a backache. *characteristics* Conversely, ³positiv<u>e touch—a friend</u> puts her hand on your arm to emphasize a point—pleases you.___

6   <u>Recommended Cures:</u> Because you tend to respond to things physically, you'll benefit from stress-reduction techniques that unwind your tight muscles. Consider nonstrenuous exercise <u>such as yoga or tai chi.</u>   *yoga* *tai chi*

Use margin notes and underlining to show the important information in the paragraphs below.

The Overreactor

7   When your presentation at work doesn't go well, you're sure you'll be fired. You try to be organized—you even note in your appointment book when you'll do the laundry—but you still feel stressed most of the time. Even small <u>problems upset you: If you have to run to catch the bus,</u> you have a headache or stomachache for the rest of the day.

8   <u>Recommended Cures:</u> With the level of stress you're under, you need skills you can use on a regular basis to help you reduce your tension. Consider biofeedback, meditation, or a stress-management workshop.

Step 3: Note Important Information

1. **Did you find information relating to any of your questions? If you have not already done so, go back and underline, highlight, or write margin notes about this information.**

2. **Did you find anything useful that you didn't expect to find? If so, go back and note this information as well.**

E. Building Your Vocabulary

Use these steps to build your vocabulary with words from the reading.

1. Look at your reading list from Readings 1–3. Put a checkmark (✓) next to any words that also appeared in Reading 4. Then look back at Reading 4 and make a list of five to ten new words that you feel are important to learn.

2. Write these words in your vocabulary notebook. Group words that are similar (e.g., *reduce/reducers/reduction, nervous/anxious/rigorous*). Copy a sentence or phrase in which the word appears. Decide on the part of speech of the word and write a definition for it.

3. If you are still unsure of the meaning of this word or the part of speech, look it up in the dictionary and write the definition in your own words. For additional practice, write your own sentence.

F. Writing Your Ideas

Look at the writing topics below. Choose at least one and write about it.

1. Which stress personality profile fits you best? Describe your reactions to stress and decide which type of stress cure would suit you.

2. Do you know anyone who copes with stress very well or very badly? Describe how they react under stress and why you think it is particularly good or bad.

G. Making Connections

Are there any ideas in this reading that are related to ideas in Readings 1–3? Which ideas are they? How are they related?

READING 5: "LAUGHTER AS THERAPY"

Step 1: Preview

1. **Look at the items below. Which ones may give information about the topic? Which ones may give information about the audience? Check (✓) them.**

	TOPIC	AUDIENCE
Title	_____	_____
Subtitles	_____	_____
Author	_____	_____
Source	_____	_____
Format	_____	_____
Introduction	_____	_____
Conclusion	_____	_____

2. **Scan Reading 5 for the items in column 1 of the chart above. What predictions can you make about:**

   1. topic _____

   2. intended audience _____

   3. any problem that you might have with this reading

   _____

3. **Do you have any questions about Reading 5? If so, write them in your notebook.**

Step 2: Read Closely

1. **Reading 5 is highly technical, so read selectively and strategically. Keep the points below in mind as you read.**

   Reading an article that was written for people who have a lot more knowledge in a subject area than you have can be very difficult. The writer assumes that the reader has a good understanding of basic principles and is familiar with the technical vocabulary of that field. Previewing is particularly important in this situation because it helps you to anticipate problems and locate the sections that are likely to be more helpful or easier to read than others.

   Things to remember as you are reading difficult technical material:

   • <u>Do not</u> try to understand every idea.

- Keep your purpose in mind and look for the parts that are relevant.

- Write down a few key words that will help you to find relevant information more easily.

- Do not give up immediately. Think of the reading as a challenging puzzle.

- Be prepared to stop reading if you get too frustrated. You can come back to difficult sections later if necessary.

2. **As you read, look for information to complete the chart on page 140. Read the text closely. Remember to cover the margin questions the first time that you read.**

3. **Reread the text, using the margin questions to help you.**

READING 5

LAUGHTER AS THERAPY

From *Pulmonary Rehabilitation: Guidelines to Success*, Patty Wooten, RN BSN CCRN

"A merry heart does good like a medicine, but a broken spirit dries the bones"
—Proverbs 17:22

1 Laughter can be a powerful therapy for both the patient and the caregiver. This chapter will examine the beneficial effect of humor and laughter on the body, mind, and spirit; for the patient during recovery from illness; and for the health professional during delivery of care.

1 Is *or* used to give a definition here?

2 Most experienced caregivers have discovered that attention to only the physical body during treatment will produce a partial or temporary recovery. The patient's emotional responses, belief system, support network, etc. can all affect agreement to treatment and the ability to cope with fear, pain, and loss.

3 The ability to laugh at a situation or problem gives us a feeling of superiority and power. Humor and laughter can cultivate a positive and hopeful attitude. We are less likely to succumb to feelings of depression and helplessness if we are able to laugh at what is troubling us. Humor gives us a sense of perspective on our problems.

2 What may help you to understand the phrase *succumb to feelings of depression?*

4 Laughter provides an opportunity for the release of those uncomfortable emotions which, if held inside, may create biochemical changes that are harmful to the body. For thousands of years, the human race has praised the health benefits of laughter. Current research by Lefcourt, Guillemin, and Fry in the areas of psychology, physiology, and psychoneuroimmunology has defined the specific changes effected by laughter.

5 Therapy is defined as "an activity or treatment intended to alleviate an undesirable condition." With that in mind, let's explore the therapeutic benefit of laughter for the body, mind, and spirit.

LAUGHTER SUPPORTS RECOVERY FROM ILLNESS

3 What is the purpose of this section?

6 Norman Cousins, former editor of the magazine *Saturday Review*, first brought the attention of the medical community to the possibility that laughter might aid healing. In 1964, Cousins was diagnosed with ankylosing spondylitis, a progressive degenerative disease of the collagen tissue. His physicians gave him little hope for recovery, indicating that a possible cause of his illness was due to heavy-metal poisoning.

7 When he thought about his activities in the month before his symptoms began, he remembered frequent exposure to diesel exhaust fumes during his travel in Russia. From his reading of Hans Selye's 1956 book about the body's response to stress, Cousins recalled that research had shown that negative emotions could create chemical changes which would eventually lead to adrenal exhaustion. He suspected that this condition weakened his ability to tolerate the toxic exposure. He wondered if positive emotions (such as faith, hope, confidence, and joy) might create changes within the body which would help him recover. He decided to find out.

4 Do you understand *adrenal exhaustion*?

5 What is the important idea in this paragraph?

8 Since laughing tends to make people feel positive emotions, Cousins began viewing movies that made him laugh. After each laughing episode he noted that he could sleep comfortably without the need for medication. He also discovered that laughter stimulated a decrease in his sedimentation rate, indicating a reversal of the inflammatory response. Contrary to the predictions of the entire medical establishment, Cousins made a complete recovery.

9 After his recovery, he spent the last ten years of his life as an adjunct professor at U.C.L.A. Medical School where he established a Humor Task Force to coordinate and support clinical research. Today, more than 25 years after Cousins' experience, we have the scientific research to explain the specific physiological changes which his experience suggested. Laughter does affect the body, mind, and spirit.

PHYSIOLOGICAL RESPONSE

6 Are any of your key words in this paragraph? What should you do?

10 Humor is a perceptual process while laughter is a behavioral response. This behavior creates predictable physiological changes within the body. As with other exercise, we see two stages of the body's response, the arousal phase when the physiological parameters such as heart rate increase, and the resolution phase when they return to resting rate or lower. With vigorous sustained laughter, the heart rate is stimulated, sometimes reaching rates of above 120 bpm (beats per minute); the normal respiratory pattern becomes chaotic; respiratory rate and depth are increased while residual volume is decreased. Coughing and hiccups are often triggered due to phrenic nerve irritation or the dislodging of mucus plugs. Oxygen saturation of peripheral

blood does not significantly change during the increased ventilation occurring with laughter. Conditions such as asthma or bronchitis may be irritated by vigorous laughter. Peripheral vascular flow is increased due to vasodilitation. A variety of muscle groups become active during laughter—diaphragm, abdominal, intercostal, respiratory accessory, facial, and occasionally muscles in the arms, legs, and back.

7 Are any of your key words in this paragraph? What should you do?

8 Underline the technical words. Is it time to stop reading?

11 Some of the most exciting research exploring the potential healing value of laughter is in the area of psychoneuroimmunology, the area of research which explores the connections among the nervous system, the endocrine system, and the immune system. Loma Linda University Medical Center has recently completed research showing that the neuroendocrine system is affected during the experience of mirthful laughter. This work by Lee Berk and Stanley Tan has shown that serum cortisol levels decreased with laughter. Also, the experimental group demonstrated a lower baseline epinephrine level than the control group (possibly due to their relaxed status in anticipation of the laughter experience). Levels of cortisol and epinephrine (known to be immunosuppressive) are elevated during the stress response. Therefore, Berk and Tan conclude that by decreasing these levels we can diminish the suppression of the respective immune components. Other research has demonstrated that mirthful laughter increases the spontaneous lymphoycyte blastogenesis and the natural killer cell activity. Natural killer cells are a type of lymphocyte that have a spontaneous cytolytic activity against tumor cells.

A. Checking Your Comprehension

Read each exercise below. Then reread the article for the answers.

1. Explain how Norman Cousins investigated the relationship between laughter and health.

2. Sir William Osler said, "It is more important to know what sort of patient has the disease, than what sort of disease the patient has." Would the writer of Reading 5 agree with this quotation? Why or why not?

B. Making Inferences

1. What kind of person was Norman Cousins?

2. What might make you believe that Cousins' theories were accepted by the medical community?

3. Why might the information in this reading be more persuasive than information in some of the other readings?

C. Topics for Discussion

Discuss the following questions with your classmates.

1. Are you surprised by the connection between good health and laughter? Why or why not?

2. Do doctors and nurses that you know seem to be aware of the connection between humor and good health?

Step 3: Note Useful Information

Did this reading give you as much information as Readings 1–4? Why or why not? Was any of the information useful? Which parts? What ideas may be important for the Unit Task?

D. Building Your Vocabulary

Use these steps to build your vocabulary with words from the reading.

1. This reading contains many technical words. What can you say about how you read this article? If you stopped before the end of the article, how did you feel about that? Was it a good decision? Why or why not? If you read selectively, how did you decide which parts of the reading to read carefully and which to skim over?

2. Because there is so much technical vocabulary in this reading, when you choose words that may be useful to you, you probably will not want to include these words. Which parts of the reading should you look at to find new words that will be the most useful?

3. Now look at the list of words from Readings 1–4. Put a checkmark (✓) next to any words that also appeared in Reading 5. Then look at Reading 5 again. Choose three to five more words that you think will be the most useful to learn.

4. Write these words in your vocabulary notebook. Group words that are similar (e.g., *laugh/laughter/laughing, therapy/therapeutic*). Copy a sentence or phrase in which the word appears. Decide on the part of speech of the word and write a definition for it.

5. If you are still unsure of the meaning of this word or the part of speech, look it up in the dictionary and write the definition in your own words. For additional practice, write your own sentence.

E. Writing Your Ideas

Look at the writing topics below. Choose at least one and write about it.

1. Summarize the story of Norman Cousins.

2. Can you think of any time that laughing made you feel better about a bad situation? Explain.

3. Talk to someone who works in health care. Ask them about the role of humor in promoting good health. Do they believe that it can be helpful? Do they know of any specific cases in which humor aided a patient's recovery? Write a summary of their responses.

F. Making Connections

1. **Would the writer of this article agree with the information in Readings 1–4? Why or why not?**

2. **How does the article differ from Readings 1–4? What new information, if any, does it add?**

READING 6: "HEALING WORDS"

Step 1: Preview

1. **Look at the way parts of this reading are printed. What differences do you notice about them? What purpose do these differences serve?**

2. **How is this reading different from all the others so far? How might this difference affect how you preview the reading?**

3. **Preview the reading to make predictions about topic and audience.**

4. **Preview the reading for your key words. How useful will it be for the Unit Task? Are there any sections that seem more useful than others?**

5. **Write three or four questions that you expect this reading will answer.**

Step 2: Read Closely

1. **This reading contains some very controversial ideas. As you are reading, make your own margin notes about ideas that you agree with and do not agree with. However, do not look at the printed margin questions the first time that you read.**

2. **Read the text closely. Remember to look for your key words and any information you may still need for your chart (from page 140).**

3. **Reread the text, using the margin questions to help you.**

Healing Words

©1995 Daniel Redwood, DC

1 *Mainstream* is used twice in this paragraph. Can you guess its meaning?

1 Larry Dossey still finds that his transition from mainstream physician to unorthodox medical philosopher is something of a mystery. He began by practicing standard Western medicine and then became interested in patients who experienced "miracle cures" that mainstream medicine could not explain. Searching for an understanding of the interaction between mind, body and spirit, he developed a biofeedback department at the Dallas Diagnostic Association, and started to study religion, philosophy, meditation, oriental literature, parapsychology and quantum physics. Dr. Dossey is the author of *Space, Time and Medicine; Beyond Illness; Recovering the Soul*; and *Healing Words*. He was the first physician ever invited to deliver the Annual Mahatma Gandhi Peace Foundation Memorial Lecture in New Delhi, India. Dossey has retired from active medical practice and devotes his time to writing and lecturing. He is the editor of the journal *Alternative Therapies in Health and Medicine*. He lives in New Mexico.

2 In this interview with Dr. Daniel Redwood, Dr. Dossey discusses fascinating medical research which demonstrates the healing effects of prayer.

3 **DR: What would you say was the major turning point in your medical career, or in your life?**

4 LARRY DOSSEY: I don't think there was one key turning point. It was a gradual development of a different way of seeing, and a different way of being. When I got out of medical school, I was as typical and orthodox a person as you could find.

5 Then I discovered a body of knowledge in Eastern thought which affected me tremendously. I was greatly influenced by Buddhism, particularly Zen. I also discovered the mystical traditions of Christianity, and the medieval mystics, who are very similar to the Zen masters. I also had a difficult health problem, migraine headaches. When conventional medicine did not help me, I turned to biofeedback therapy in the early 1970's. From a philosophical, spiritual and a personal level there were many influences in my life which pushed me in these directions, but no one specific wake-up call or single event.

6 **DR: In your books you talk about different eras or periods in medicine. Could you define what you call Era III Medicine, and how it differs from Eras I and II?**

7 LARRY DOSSEY: Era I is normal mechanical medicine, technical orthodox medicine. Drugs, surgery and radiation. Era II is involved any time we talk about mind/body events within the person. My mind affecting my brain, affecting my body, for good or ill. It's confined to the present moment, it's "here and now" medicine, it's local. Era III is mind/body medicine from a different perspective. It's a collective mind, a mind not localized to the brain or the body. It's mind possibly affecting many bodies, across space and across time. Mind that is not localized to the present moment, breaking time barriers, as in the recent study where people received

2 What does *Eastern* refer to in paragraph 5?

3 In paragraph 6, are these Eras in medicine generally accepted or are they specific to Dr. Dossey?

a message three days before it was sent. Temporal or time nonlocality.

8 **DR: Could you tell us about that study?**

9 LARRY DOSSEY: Sure. Era III is nonlocal medicine, with "nonlocal" meaning that minds are not confined to points in space (such as brains or bodies), or time (such as the present moment.) At the Princeton Engineering Anomalies Research Laboratory studies have been conducted for a decade by the ex-Dean of Engineering Dr. Robert Jahn and his colleague Brenda Dunne. There were many experiments, but the ones that show this nonlocality of the mind are their remote-sensing experiments. The experiment was done like this: They had one person in Princeton attempting to mentally send a computer-selected image to a person 6000 miles away. Frequently, the receiver not only got the message in great detail, but received it in many instances up to three days before it was even sent! This is an example of a mind operating outside of space and time. Minds seemingly united, not totally confined to brains. This means it's broken through space and time with this inversion of the future and the present.

10 There is absolutely no way you can explain this with a local definition of the mind/brain/body relationship. So you are forced, if you believe it, to make a model of reality and mind that explains it. The only model that fits is a nonlocal model.

11 **DR: How would a mainstream scientist, one who would deny the possibility of nonlocality, reply to data like that?**

12 LARRY DOSSEY: Let me tell you why I picked the term "nonlocality." It is an accepted term in modern physics. There are books written in that field explaining that the nature of the world, at rock bottom, is nonlocal. Nick Herbert's book *Quantum Reality* clearly shows that whatever model you make of the world has to be a fundamentally nonlocal model. So physicists have accepted this already.

13 **DR: So, is the mainstream medical community ready to accept this data?**

14 LARRY DOSSEY: There's a tremendous battle line being drawn within orthodox science. There's a famous statement from one scientist: "This is the sort of thing I wouldn't believe in even if it were true." So even though these new studies are scientific, their implications for reality are so incredible that many orthodox scientists won't have anything to do with them. But it's data, it's good data, and it's not going to go away.

15 **DR: You tell an amazing story about a study in which prayer seemed to affect medical outcomes. What are the implications of that study?**

16 LARRY DOSSEY: I'm not as enthusiastic about this study as I was when I first discovered it, but it's still worth mentioning. It was done by Randolph Byrd, in the cardiac care unit at the San Francisco General Hospital. It involved about 400 patients. Half were treated with routine standard care, as was the other half, but in addition the patients in the second half were prayed for. Their names were given to various prayer groups.

17 Nobody among the nurses and doctors knew who was and who wasn't being prayed for. This prevented them from unconsciously giving preferential treatment to the prayed-for group. When the results were in, it appeared as if the group that was being prayed for had been given some kind of miracle drug. There were no deaths in the prayed-for group, while there were three deaths in the other group. Twelve people in the group not being prayed for had heart attacks and had to have CPR, or needed a mechanical ventilator, an artificial breathing machine. None of the prayed-for group had to have that

done. Twelve to zero—those are pretty good odds. The late Dr. William Knowland, a very orthodox physician said, "It appears on the basis of this study that we physicians… should be writing orders that say 'Pray for my patient three times daily.'"

18 Still, this wasn't the best study in the world. At most, what you could say about the study is that it is very strongly suggestive that prayer has an effect, that it has a life-and-death influence on people, even when they do not know they are being prayed for.

19 **DR: What problems are there with this study?**

20 LARRY DOSSEY: One of the weak points was that we don't really know the details on how often the praying people prayed, or whether in fact they did their job. Also, we don't know how often the people who were sick prayed for themselves. We can't control that. It's also possible that the "unprayed-for" group had relatives praying for them, unknown to the sci-entists doing the study. This gets really tricky once you think about it. At first, I thought that it was a really clean study, but the more I thought about it, that's not entirely true.

21 **DR: How long will it be before the mainstream medical community will really start believing in spiritual therapies such as prayer?**

22 LARRY DOSSEY: Change never comes as fast as we want it to. It seems agonizingly slow, but if you look back over the past ten to twenty years since I've been writing about this, the change seems immense. But when you come down right on the moment, you can't see the change happening.

Daniel Redwood is a chiropractor, writer and musician who lives in Virginia Beach, Virginia. He is the author of *A Time to Heal: How to Reap the Benefits of Holistic Health* (A.R.E. Press) and is a member of the editorial board of the Journal of Alternative and Complementary Medicine.

4 What does *this* refer to in paragraph 20?

5 What does *clean* probably mean here?

A. Checking Your Comprehension

1. **In your notebook, write a description of Dr. Dossey's three eras in medicine.**

   1. Give each era a name based on the descriptions in the text.

   2. What era are most doctors in?

   3. What era is Dr. Dossey in?

   4. What era does biofeedback belong to?

2. **Complete the information about the two studies mentioned in the article.**

   Researcher 1: _Robert Jahn and Brenda Dunne_____

   Place of research: _____

   Purpose of study: _____

   Methodology: _____

   Results: _____

Researcher 2: __Randolph Byrd__

Place of research: _____

Purpose of study: _____

Methodology: _____

Results: _____

B. Making Inferences

1. Do you believe that the interviewer agrees with Dr. Dossey's opinions? Why or why not?

2. Is there any part of the interview that makes Dr. Dossey seem more credible (believable)? less credible?

C. Topics for Discussion

Discuss the following questions with your classmates.

1. Do you personally agree with Dr. Dossey? Why or why not?

2. Would Dr. Dossey's ideas be controversial in your culture? Why or why not?

3. Do you know anyone who has ever experienced a "miracle cure"? What happened?

Step 3: Note Useful Information

1. Were any of the questions you formulated in the previewing section answered? If so, go back and underline, highlight, or make margin notes of the answers, if you have not already done so. Add this information to the chart on page 140.

2. Did you find any other information that might be helpful for the Unit Task? If so, go back and note these sections.

D. Building Your Vocabulary

Use these steps to build your vocabulary with words from the reading.

1. Look at your list of words from Readings 1–5. Put a checkmark (✓) next to any words that also appeared in Reading 6. Look at Reading 6 again. Choose five to ten more words that you think will be the most useful to learn.

2. Write these words in your vocabulary notebook. Group words that are similar (e.g., *mystical/spiritual, local/localized*). Copy a sentence or phrase in which the word appears. Decide on the part of speech of the word and write a definition for it.

3. If you are still unsure of the meaning of this word or the part of speech, look it up in the dictionary and write the definition in your own words. For additional practice, write your own sentence.

E. Writing Your Ideas

Look at the writing topics below. Choose at least one and write about it.

1. Have you ever prayed for someone or something? What happened? Do you believe in the power of prayer?

2. Do you believe that people can affect the physical world with their minds? Why or why not? What would it mean if we could do this? How might the world be different?

F. Making Connections

Ideas similar to Dr. Dossey's were mentioned in another reading. Which one was it?

PART C   DOING THE UNIT TASK

Building Your Vocabulary: Summary

Prepare for the Unit Task by reviewing the most important vocabulary from this unit. Look at your list of words from Readings 1–6. Are there any words that are related? For example:

benefit-beneficial

optimist-optimistic

respond-respondent

Write these words in a separate list.

Look at the first list again. Can you think of any other words that are related to the words on the list? Think of word beginnings (prefixes) such as *un-, non-, in-,* and *dis-*. Also think about word endings (suffixes) such as *-ion, -ly, -ial,* and *-ness.*

believer-nonbeliever

encourage-discourage

helpless-helplessness

Add these words to your second list.

Look again at your first list, which contains the vocabulary for the entire unit. How many words have checkmarks (✓)? What can you say about these words?

Now think about the Unit Task, writing a pamphlet on the mind-body connection. Are there any words that you will probably need that are not in your second list? If so, add them.

You now have a new list of words that are probably the most useful words for you to learn. In general, it is useful to study:

words that can easily be related to other words (e.g., *benefit-beneficial*)

words that appear frequently in the reading

words that will be useful for your task.

You should also be able to understand all the other words in the first list, but you do not have to use them in speech or writing.

Learning Words in Groups

One way to learn new words is to put them in similar groups. A useful way is to put the words in groups according to their part of speech. In your notebook, make a chart like the one below. If you are not sure of the part of speech, look in the dictionary. Remember that some words can be used as more than one part of speech.

NOUNS	VERBS	ADJECTIVES	ADVERBS
benefit	benefit	beneficial	beneficially
_____	_____	_____	_____
_____	_____	_____	_____
_____	_____	_____	_____

UNIT TASK:
Reporting on the Mind-Body Connection

Write a pamphlet on the mind-body connection. The information in your pamphlet should be aimed at one of these three groups:

- teenagers who are about to enter college
- people who want to improve their performance (e.g., athletes, musicians, or businesspeople—*choose one*)
- senior citizens

---

1. Look back at the sections of Readings 1–6 that you underlined or highlighted and make a list of the information that you think is the most important.

2. You will need to organize the information into categories. Think about what categories would make sense. The purpose of

informational pamphlets such as these is to provide complex information in a simplified form for the general public. This means that:

- the organization should be simple and easy to follow.

- the information should be divided into small "chunks" so that it is easy to understand.

If possible, find one or two pamphlets to use as models. These can often be found at health clinics or government offices. You might also think about using parallel organization.

3. Discuss your answers to questions 1 and 2 with your group. Your group should be composed of students who have chosen to write for the same audience.

4. With your group, look at the additional readings for this unit and choose one which you think will be most useful for your purpose. Each person in the group should read it and make notes of useful information.

5. Compare your notes on the additional readings. Then add the information to the list you made in question 2.

6. Write your pamphlet. Ask each person in the group to write a different section.

7. After you are done with the first draft of your section, ask other members of your group to read it and give you suggestions for ways to improve it. Revise it.

8. Combine all the sections of your pamphlet together to make the final product.

9. If possible, make several copies of your pamphlet, so that your classmates can see what you have done.

PART D EXPANSION ACTIVITIES

Applying Your Knowledge

1. Find a doctor or a coach who knows about mind-body issues. Invite that person to come to your class for a discussion, or interview him or her outside of the class. Write up the class discussion, or report to your class on the outside interview.

2. Look for news items that are related to the mind-body connection. Summarize them for your class.

The Electronic Link

1. Look on the Internet to find more information about the mind-body connection. Some possible key words to search for are:

   biofeedback

   mind-body connection

   sports psychology

   meditation

2. Find a Web site that has an e-mail address to ask specific questions. Formulate one or two questions and ask them. Report to your class on the answers.

   Name of the Web site _____

   _____

   URL (Web address) _____

   _____

   Your question _____

   _____

   Their answer _____

For More Information

Institute for Noetic Sciences
475 Gate Five Road
Suite 300
Sausalito, CA 94965
www.noetic.org

 See Additional Readings for this unit on pages 226–231.

Essay Questions

Choose one of the topics below and write an essay about it.

1. If you were a physician, how would you use the information you have read about in this unit? Would you use any of the techniques? Which ones? When?

2. Do you agree with Dr. Dossey's description of the three eras in medicine? Why or why not?

3. Compare the health-care establishment in your country to what is described in this unit. Are healthcare professionals generally more or less accepting of unorthodox treatments? Do they use any other treatments not mentioned in these readings?

Evaluating Your Progress

**Think about the skills and strategies that you used in this unit.
Check (✔) the boxes that apply to you.**

	NEVER	SOMETIMES	OFTEN	ALWAYS
1. I was able to find the author's important points.	☐	☐	☐	☐
2. When I scanned, I was able to find my key words.	☐	☐	☐	☐
3. When I skimmed, I was able to get a general idea of the reading.	☐	☐	☐	☐
4. I formulated questions before I read.	☐	☐	☐	☐
5. I used transition words and phrases to predict.	☐	☐	☐	☐
6. I made margin notes as I read.	☐	☐	☐	☐
7. I was able to write effective summaries.	☐	☐	☐	☐
8. I used prefixes and suffixes to help me to guess the meaning of unknown words.	☐	☐	☐	☐
9. I looked for collocations as I read.	☐	☐	☐	☐
10. I was not frustrated by technical vocabulary.	☐	☐	☐	☐

Setting Your Reading Goals

Choose three items from the list above that you would like to improve. Write them below.

Goal #1: _____

Goal #2: _____

Goal #3: _____

Encyclopedia definitions from Exercise 3, page 146.

Biofeedback is a method of learning to regulate body processes that occur involuntarily. In biofeedback, electronic instruments are used to monitor such body functions as heartbeat, brain waves, and muscle tension, and the information is simultaneously "fed back" to the individual by sound or visual signals. Once a person becomes aware of the thoughts and feelings that produce changes in these functions, he may learn to alter these functions at will.

Focus is complete attention to the execution of a skill. **Flow** is the state of being completely involved in the execution of a performance to the exclusion of everything else. Flow has several qualities. The first is that all attention is focused either on the skills or routine being performed or on the input from senses relevant to the activity. In addition, a person in flow is not aware of this focus, does not evaluate performance, and is not concerned with distractions such as results, audiences, or other people's expectations. Finally, a person in flow does not make any conscious decisions or reason with words. A human body in flow has been compared to an airplane on automatic pilot.

Imagery is the process by which a person can create, modify, or strengthen pathways important to the coordination of muscles, by training purely within the mind. Imagination is the driving force of imagery. It is possible to exercise these parts of the brain with inputs from the imagination rather than from the senses: the parts of the brain that are trained with imagery experience imagined and real inputs similarly, with the real input being merely more vividly experienced.

N THIS UNIT

Reading Strategies

- Making global inferences
- Finding main ideas
- Using organization to identify main ideas
- Understanding complicated sentences
- Using transition words

Strategies for Unknown Vocabulary

- Combining vocabulary strategies
- Using synonyms in paraphrasing
- Using larger contexts to guess meaning
- Deciding when words are not important
- Using a vocabulary decision tree

The World of Work

Think About It

*I*n a survey asking what people felt it meant to be successful in their work, the responses were:

Personal satisfaction from doing a good job	52%
Earning the respect or recognition of supervisors and/or peers	30%
Getting ahead or advancing in job or career	22%
Making a good income	21%
Feeling that my work is important	12%
Having control over work content and schedule	6%

From *The Practical Guide to Practically Everything,*
Peter Bernstein and Christopher Ma

Discuss these questions with your classmates.

1. Which of these statistics do you find most surprising? least surprising?

2. These statistics are the result of a survey in the United States. Do you think that a survey in another country would give the same results? Why or why not?

3. Do you think there is any factor that isn't listed but should have been included?

4. What do *you* think being successful in your work means? Do you think this will change for you ten years from now? If so, in what ways?

Looking Ahead in Unit Four

Look through the unit quickly and answer these questions.

1. Find the titles and page numbers of the readings.

READING	PAGE NUMBER
1. _Jobs to Die For_	_173_
2. _____	_____
3. _____	_____
4. _____	_____
5. _____	_____
6. _____	_____

2. Find one reading that is written from the point of view of an employer and one that is written from the point of view of an employee. Write their titles on the lines.

   _____

   _____

3. In this unit, you will have a choice of three different Unit Tasks. What page can you find them on? Write their titles below.

   page number: _____

   _____

   _____

   _____

PART *A*   FOCUS ON SKILLS

READING 1: "JOBS TO DIE FOR"

A. Pre-reading the Text

1. **Pre-read the text and complete the predictions below by filling in the blanks and circling the correct words.**

   Title: This reading will tell me about _____.

   Genre: This reading is probably from a _____.

   It <u>is/is not</u> a news item. It is a _____.

   Introduction: The reading is written in a very <u>formal/informal</u> style. Therefore, I should expect to find <u>technical vocabulary/casual language</u>.

The information in the reading came from _____.

Subtitles: The reading discusses _____ different jobs.

2. **Use your general knowledge. Brainstorm this question with your class: What makes people love their jobs?**

3. **Read the text closely. Check your predictions in questions 1 and 2. Remember not to look at the margin questions the first time that you read.**

4. **Reread the text, using the margin questions to help you.**

READING 1

1 How is this reading organized?

2 How did the author choose the people that he interviewed? What kind of information was he looking for?

3 How can you tell when the writer is talking and when Ms. Sallee is talking?

JOBS TO DIE FOR

From skydiving instructors to matchmakers, some folks just love their jobs.

1   Yes, some people love their jobs. Whether they serve mankind, help others with self-improvement or just want to feel the rush of pure adrenaline, they're out there. When I asked our readers to tell me about their dream jobs, I got hundreds of responses. I chose to profile workers who make enough money to live on and have a strong sense of accomplishment. None of them are attracted to their jobs for the money. In fact, many said they would do it for nothing. (Just don't tell their bosses.) Here are four who are in enviable positions.

Shelly Sallee, 31, skydiving instructor.

2   "I have a job with an incredible view. It's high-speed and full of fun," says Sallee, an instructor for Front Range Skydivers in California and an examiner for the US Parachute Association.

3   "Every time I jump, I get another adrenaline rush. After 2,500 jumps, it's still an exciting experience. I have the most exhilarating job in the world." But her real thrill is for her students.

4   "I love seeing a student on their first jump all nervous and excited beforehand. Then, when they get to the ground, they're completely exhilarated. They can't wait to get to a phone to call everyone they know and tell them they've just jumped out of an airplane," Sallee says. "Later, they learn to turn and fly forward. Then, they realize they're not just flying rocks. They're birds. They can fly!"

5   "The air can't hurt you. Only the ground can," she says with a smile. Despite all her jumps, Sallee has had only three malfunctions in which she had to depend on a second, reserve chute.

"That's pretty good odds," she says. "You have more chance of getting hurt in a traffic accident than you do skydiving."

6   Requirements for a skydiving instructor are six hours of free fall, the equivalent of about 1,000 jumps and up to two years of training. Only about half of the candidates meet the instructors' rigid requirements. Entry-level pay for a full-time instructor is $15,000.

Sheila Osburn, 37, emergency medical technician.

7   Osburn is an EMT with a big heart. "Every day is different and it doesn't feel like a job. I enjoy it so much. I never know what to expect when I go to work," she says. When someone calls an ambulance, Osburn is there to help with everything from moving an elderly patient from the hospital to a nursing home, to helping a child hurt and scared on the playground. She sees life and sometimes she sees death. "I put my whole heart and soul into this job," Osburn says.

4 Why didn't the author comment on this example?

8   "I encountered one elderly patient last week who had to move to a nursing home from her home of 50 years," Osburn says. "All of her control had been taken away. I told her someday I would be where she was and I admired her. I feel deeply for these people. I think it takes a great amount of strength for them because in a lot of ways, their choices have been taken away and it takes strength to accept their new environment."

Greg Marshall, 46, potter.

5 What two phrases refer to the kind of work that Marshall does?

9   "I have a great job. I get to play in the mud every day. Who could ask for more?" says Marshall of Manitou Springs, Colorado. It took Marshall a while to discover his labor of love. He was an education major in college when one semester he took a pottery class, "…because I needed another class to be a full-time student." It was there that he discovered his heavenly handicraft. A former art student-teacher and a wrestling coach, Marshall now specializes in functional pottery: mugs, bowls, and plates. He says, "It's great for people to appreciate something so much that they're willing to pay for it and have it be a part of their lives and in their homes. Everything I make I feel like there's a part of me in it. It feels good when other people like it too."

6 What does this list illustrate?

Donna Shugrue, 49, matchmaker.

7 What information do you expect in this section?

10   "People always tell me I have the most fun job in the world, and I do!" says Shugrue, a matchmaker with unmatched enthusiasm. Her matchmaking has led to 60 marriages and 50 engagements since she started her own company 20 years ago. "That doesn't say anything about the people dating and having fun and making friends," says Shugrue, co-owner of "Perfectly Matched."

8 There are two lists in this paragraph. What does each one illustrate?

11   Shugrue starts her clients with a compatibility profile, a written test of 46 questions in which they must rate themselves on a scale of one to five on parameters such as attitude toward life, sociability, religion and financial status. Then, she matches people with similar interests and long-term goals. "And of course there has to be a physical attraction," she says. She also considers height, weight, age, occupation, smoking, drinking, children, education, and race when getting couples together. "I can't imagine a job that's much more gratifying than when someone calls and says, 'Yes, it worked!' One couple stopped by from the hospital with their new baby three months ago. It still gives me chills to think about it."

Knight-Ridder News Service

B. Checking Your Comprehension

Complete the chart with information from the reading. An example has been done for you.

JOB TITLE	JOB DESCRIPTION
1. Matchmaker	Helps people find someone to marry
2.	
3.	
4.	

C. Making Inferences

Reread the section on each job. List the personality characteristics one should have in order to enjoy the different jobs.

JOB TITLE	PERSONALITY CHARACTERISTICS
1.	
2.	
3.	
4.	

D. Topics for Discussion

Discuss the following questions with your classmates.

1. If you had to have one of these jobs, which one would you choose? Why?

2. Do you know anyone who loves his or her job? What does he or she love about it?

3. What are some ways to discover what kinds of jobs you would like?

E. Reading Strategies

> ## READING STRATEGY: Making Global Inferences
>
> You learned earlier about local inferences. Those are inferences based on the information in specific parts of a reading. Global inferences are based on information from several different parts of a reading. To make a global inference, you need to combine various statements to see the bigger picture. Then, you need to relate this to your general knowledge to come up with a general unstated point. For example, you might try to infer from this reading which aspects of work give people the greatest satisfaction.
>
> One possibility might be "Being able to help other people." This is not specifically stated, but both the emergency medical technician and the matchmaker seem to get great enjoyment from helping people. Therefore, it is a reasonable global inference.

1. **Look at these statements about what creates job satisfaction. Put a checkmark (✓) next to the ones that are supported by the reading. Be prepared to defend your choices.**

   People feel satisfied with their work when they:

   ____ 1. get a good salary.

   ____ 2. make other people happy.

   ____ 3. enjoy the activity.

   ____ 4. get ahead in their career.

   ____ 5. are able to do a variety of tasks.

   ____ 6. produce a great amount in a short time.

   ____ 7. are in a position of authority.

   ____ 8. make or do something useful.

> ## READING STRATEGY: Finding Main Ideas
>
> Sometimes main ideas are not stated directly. In that case, we need to use inferences to find the author's intended meaning. For example, this reading is almost entirely made up of examples, so you may have to infer a more general point from specific examples.
>
> What was the author's purpose in writing this article?
>
> 1. to describe four very different jobs
> 2. to prove that some people love their jobs
> 3. to illustrate the characteristics of a good job
>
> How did the writer choose to achieve his purpose?

2. **Look back at the exercise for Making Global Inferences on page 176. Complete this sentence about the author's main idea.**

The author believes that to have job satisfaction you must have:

_____

F. Strategies for Unknown Vocabulary

VOCABULARY STRATEGY: Combining Vocabulary Strategies

One strategy does not always give you enough information to enable you to guess the meaning of a word. Often, you have to combine several strategies.

For example, look back at the word **malfunctions** in this sentence:

Despite all her jumps, Sallee has had only three malfunctions in which she had to depend on a second, reserve chute.

You might try to figure out this word in this way:

1. General knowledge: When does a person have to use a second chute? Probably in an emergency, or when something goes wrong.

2. List of examples: I don't see any examples here. This strategy is not useful here.

3. Grammar: It says "three ___s." That means it is a noun—something that she has had three times.

4. Synonyms: I don't see any synonyms. This strategy doesn't help here.

---

1. **Look at the underlined words and decide what combination of clues can help you guess the meaning.**

   1. "That's pretty good <u>odds</u>," she says." You have more chance of getting hurt in a traffic accident than you do skydiving."

      Meaning: _____

      Clues: _____

   2. Marshall now specializes in <u>functional</u> pottery: mugs, bowls, and plates.

      Meaning: _____

      Clues: _____

   3. It's great for people to <u>appreciate</u> something so much that they're willing to pay for it and have it be a part of their lives and in their homes.

      Meaning: _____

      Clues: _____

4. "After 2,500 jumps, it's still an exciting experience. I have the most <u>exhilarating</u> job in the world."

Meaning: _____

Clues: _____

5. "But her real <u>thrill</u> is for her students. I love seeing a student on their first jump all nervous and excited beforehand. Then, when they get to the ground, they're completely exhilarated."

Meaning: _____

Clues: _____

6. "I can't imagine a job that's much more <u>gratifying</u> than when someone calls and says 'Yes, it worked!'"

Meaning: _____

Clues: _____

VOCABULARY STRATEGY: Using Synonyms in Paraphrasing

When you discuss a reading or write a summary, you often need to paraphrase. When you paraphrase, you change the author's words but not his or her ideas. Sometimes you paraphrase to shorten the ideas. Sometimes you just do not want to quote the author directly.

Synonyms are one of the main building blocks of paraphrasing. For example, if you were going to paraphrase this statement:

"After 2,500 jumps it's still an exciting experience. I have the most **exhilarating** job in the world."

You might write:

Even though she has jumped more than 2,500 times, she still thinks it's thrilling. In fact, she believes that she has one of the most exciting jobs in the world.

Analyze the original statement and the paraphrase. Which synonyms were used? What other changes were made?

---

2. **Write in your notebook a paraphrase of what the four people in the reading like about their jobs. (Hint: You may want to reread the exercises for Making Global Inferences and Finding Main Ideas on page 176.)**

3. **You probably had to use clues from more than one or two sentences in order to guess the meaning of the four jobs mentioned in the reading. Look back at the reading and think about the clues you used to guess the meanings of the following words. Write them on the lines.**

    1. skydiver _____

    2. Emergency Medical Technician _____

    3. potter _____

    4. matchmaker _____

G. Building Your Vocabulary

Use these steps to build your vocabulary with words from the reading.

1. Look at Reading 1 again. Choose five to ten words that you think will be the most useful to learn.

2. Write these words in your vocabulary notebook. Group words that are similar (e.g., *accomplishment/improvement, sociability/compatibility*). Copy a sentence or phrase from the reading in which the word appears. Decide on the part of speech of the word and write a definition for it.

3. If you are still unsure of the meaning of this word, look it up in the dictionary and write the definition in your own words. For additional practice, write your own sentence.

H. Writing Your Ideas

Look at the writing topics below. Choose at least one and write about it.

1. Describe your ideal job. What would you do? Where would you work? Would you work alone or with other people?

2. Write about a job that you had. Was it enjoyable? What parts did you like? What parts didn't you like? Why?

3. Write about a job that you think is unpleasant. Why is it unpleasant? Explain. Why would you *not* want to do that job? Can you think of any reasons why a different person might *like* this job?

READING 2: "GET INTO THE FLOW"

A. Pre-reading the Text

1. **Work through the chart below to guess the meaning of *flow*.**

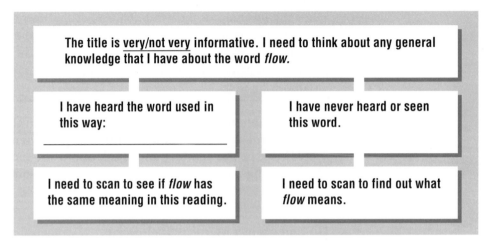

> The title is <u>very/not very</u> informative. I need to think about any general knowledge that I have about the word *flow*.
>
> | I have heard the word used in this way: _____ | I have never heard or seen this word. |
> | I need to scan to see if *flow* has the same meaning in this reading. | I need to scan to find out what *flow* means. |

2. **Scan for the word *flow*. As you are scanning, think about these questions:**

   1. Is the word *flow* very important in this reading? Why or why not?

   2. Can you find a definition, explanation, or example of *flow*?

3. **Now read the text closely and look for advice on how to "get into flow." Remember not to look at the margin questions the first time that you read.**

4. **Reread the text, using the margin questions to help you.**

READING 2

1 Is Joe's workspace pleasant or unpleasant? How do you know?

Get Into the Flow
Hippocrates, Inc.

1   Joe Huggins, who is 44, works 12 hours a day, up to six days a week in the cramped, windowless baker's corner which is in the kitchen at Belia's Garden restaurant in western North Carolina. Each day he turns out more than a hundred loaves of bread, 400 or so rolls, several batches of granola, plus dozens of cakes, pies, muffins, cobblers and cookies. Many of his customers are tourists who have come to go canoeing, biking and hiking along

the Nantahala River—things Joe rarely has time to do.

2 Can you guess the meaning of *ivory-tower scholar?* What may help you?

3 What is a synonym for *research?*

4 The second sentence in paragraph 9 compares two things. What are they?

5 Which strategy is referred to in paragraph 10?

2   So, on a Thursday morning at the crack of dawn you might expect to find Joe complaining or a least looking dour now and again. Instead, he's full of enthusiasm, one moment sliding bread into the oven, the next elbow-deep in a bowl of biscuit dough. Under his blue baseball cap, the wrinkles around his brown eyes deepen, and he smiles.

3   In this age when managers, blue-collar and clerical workers all find it more and more difficult to meet the demands of their jobs, Joe Huggins is rare. He's a person who manages not only to survive, but thrive in a job that's stressful, unglamorous and repetitive. "I love coming to work," he says. "Sometimes the work has a rhythm to it, a music. There are all these little dance steps I do. I forget about time."

4   What's with this guy? Psychologist Mihaly Csikszentmihalyi (chik-sent-me-hi) of the University of Chicago would say he's developed a talent for "flow." Over the past 30 years, Csikszentmihalyi and his colleagues have interviewed more than 8,000 people around the world, seeking an answer to the elusive question: What makes people happy?

5   Csikszentmihalyi is no ivory-tower scholar. He does much more than just think about this question. He has taken his research into practical everyday life. In his studies, participants wear beepers that go off randomly throughout the day. When they hear the beep, they fill out detailed questionnaires describing what they're doing and whether they feel challenged, bored or anxious.

6   The results have been remarkably consistent. Across cultures and occupations—from Italian farmers to American executives—people describe the same state of mind when they talk about their most enjoyable experiences. It's what Csikszentmihalyi has named "flow"—complete absorption in the activity at hand, a deep sense of exhilaration and clarity and a feeling that there is nothing else one would rather be doing. It's what a tennis player experiences when she is playing against an opponent of equal ability and both mind and body are stretched to their limits. Musicians feel it when suddenly they can no longer tell whether they are playing the music or the music is playing them.

7   Creating flow requires some work. Hardly anyone experiences it during passive activities like watching television. In fact, one of the best places to experience flow is at work. Csikszentmihalyi has found that even though most of us say we'd like to work less and spend more time in leisure, we actually report more positive experiences at work than during our free time. In one study, people reported being in flow 54% of the time while working, but only 18% of the time during leisure.

8   Csikszentmihalyi says that anyone can develop a talent for creating flow experiences on the job. Joe Huggins is a good model of this principle. "When I first did restaurant work, I just sat down and cried sometimes," Joe says. "Just the overload of it—all the rush and remember details. I'm really not a rush and remember kind of guy." But he was determined to find a way to manage the stresses of his job. "If you're not enjoying your work, you're not enjoying your life. For me, it's a constant test to see if I can find the happiness in it."

9   Those who are able to make their jobs enjoyable, Csikszentmihalyi says, are less likely to find work stressful. In one study of executives, he found that those who were in flow most often at work were less stressed out and took fewer sick days than did colleagues who had the same work load but couldn't get into flow. If Csikszentmihalyi is right, one way to cope with job stress may be to become more, rather than less involved with work.

10   To Joe Huggins this strategy makes perfect sense. It's something Joe has learned himself over the years by trial and error. He has his own thumbnail description of what flow is all about. "Energy generates energy," he says. "The more you use, the more you have."

11 It is about six in the evening, and Joe's long stainless-steel baker's table is lightly dusted with flour; butter, eggs, mixing bowls and a whisk lie scattered about. Joe has been on the job since 5:30 this morning and is starting to slow down. But everyone else is revving up for the busy dinner hour, and there is still a lot of work to do.

12 As Joe butters bread pans, the pastry brush clacking furiously, a worried waiter rushes back and puts a stack of dessert dishes onto the bakery table. "Joe, we need twelve more cobblers for the group upstairs."

13 As soon as Joe has finished spooning out the cherry cobbler, the kitchen manager, Daisy Serle, comes in looking upset. "Heather just dropped a whole chocolate pie—should we take it off the menu?"

14 "Oh no, we've got lots more," Joe says, slapping dough out on the counter, cutting pieces to roll into loaves, his hands in constant motion. He looks up and laughs at a couple of kitchen workers eating hunks of broken pie. "I think that waitress was tripped," he says.

15 It's Joe's determination to enjoy himself in the middle of all of this confusion that explains how he can handle the stresses of his job. "When things get crazy, he remains calm," says waitress Debbie Brown. "People look to him to gain a sense of peace in the midst of whatever chaos is going on."

16 Whether you are washing dishes or balancing spreadsheets, Csikszentmihalyi says, stay focused on the task. It keeps you alert to subtle details that help you experience familiar tasks in a new way. People who are easily distracted are cut off from the flow experience.

17 Research psychologist Jean A. Hamilton of Duke University suggests that high-flow people like Joe may actually use their brains differently from people who rarely get into flow. When college students who said they hardly ever experience flow were asked to concentrate on a series of flashes or tones, Hamilton found that they used more mental energy than their typical baseline level. But high-flow students actually used less mental energy than usual when asked to focus their attention.

18 For many of us, the biggest obstacle to flow is simple self-consciousness. In Hamilton's research, students who were constantly worrying about how others perceived them—How am I doing? What do they think of me?—found it difficult to achieve flow. She and Csikszentmihalyi have discovered that people who learn to focus attention not on themselves, but on what's happened around them, can transform stress into an opportunity to learn.

19 Approaching your work more as a game than a job is another way to start creating flow. Joe, for instance, is constantly inventing tricks to make his work more interesting. When the bakery work starts to feel repetitive or boring, he reminds himself that no matter how many times he's baked bread or pie, if he looks hard enough, he can find a new, better way to do familiar tasks.

20 "There ought to be one day a week when you don't do anything the way you're used to," Joe says. "You discover things." For instance, when he noticed how easy it was to lose track of the number of ingredients he'd put into a mixing bowl, he began creating visual patterns to help him remember. Now, instead of just putting each tablespoon of cinnamon in one after the other, he arranges them in a circle on top of the batter. When he's created a flower with seven petals of cinnamon, he knows he's got the seven tablespoons he needs.

21 It's early in the evening, and Joe has headed home. Like most of us, Joe doesn't get into flow as easily during his time off. Or so he says. However, even at home the evidence of his ability to make an ordinary activity into something special is everywhere. He's covered his trailer home with wood shingles so it looks like a cozy cabin. He's planted trees along the east edge of his property and built a wall with rocks. "Even when you're playing, you're usually working at something," he says. "There's enough out there to find interest and challenge in almost any situation you find yourself in."

6 Do you understand the phrase *balancing spreadsheets?*

7 In paragraph 18, what is the purpose of the questions between the dashes?

8 In paragraph 19, what does the phrase *for instance* introduce?

9 How does paragraph 20 relate to the one before it?

B. Checking Your Comprehension

1. Answer the questions.

1. What would be a suitable subtitle for this article?
   a. The best place to buy baked goods in North Carolina
   b. Working conditions make all the difference
   c. How to work harder and enjoy it more
2. What kind of environment does Joe work in?
3. What kind of attitude does Joe have about his work?
4. What is Joe able to do that many workers cannot?
5. What has Joe learned about his work that helps him enjoy it?

2. Complete the information about the two studies that are mentioned in the article.

Researcher 1: _Mihaly Csikszentmihalyi_

Area of study: _____ University: _____

Purpose of study: _____

Research methods: _____

_____

Conclusions: _____

_____

_____

Researcher 2: _Jean A. Hamilton_

Area of study: _____ University: _____

Purpose of study: _____

Research methods: _____

_____

Conclusions: _____

_____

_____

3. Write a one-paragraph summary of each study.

C. Making Inferences

1. How does the writer think most people would feel about Joe's job?

2. Why is flow more common at work than during leisure time?

D. Topics for Discussion

Discuss the following questions with your classmates.

1. Have you ever experienced flow? When? How did it feel?

2. Do you think that you are a high-flow person? Why or why not?

3. Do you know any high flow people? What are they like?

4. Do you think people can work to increase their flow? Why or why not? If so, how?

E. Reading Strategies

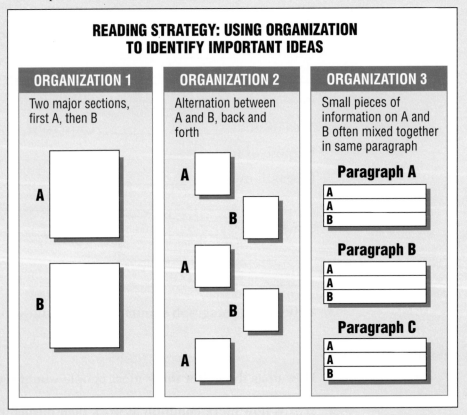

READING STRATEGY: Using Organization to Identify Main Ideas

Analyzing the organization of a reading can help you decide on the author's main ideas. Reading 2 contains two different kinds of information. One is about Joe, the baker. What is the other?

1. _Joe, the baker_

2. _____

When there is more than one kind of information in a reading, it can be organized in different ways. The following three are the most common. (A and B each represent a kind of information.)

READING STRATEGY: USING ORGANIZATION TO IDENTIFY IMPORTANT IDEAS

ORGANIZATION 1

Two major sections, first A, then B

A

B

ORGANIZATION 2

Alternation between A and B, back and forth

A

B

A

B

A

ORGANIZATION 3

Small pieces of information on A and B often mixed together in same paragraph

Paragraph A
A
A
B

Paragraph B
A
A
B

Paragraph C
A
A
B

1. **Complete the sentences about purpose. Write the answers to these questions in each box. (Each box represents a paragraph.) Who or what is this paragraph about? Is this a general point or a detail?**

Section 1

The purpose of this section is:
_____
_____
_____

1.
_____

2.
_____

3.
_____

4.
_____

Section 2

The purpose of this section is:
_____
_____
_____

5.
_____

6.
_____

7.
_____

8.
_____

9.
_____

2. **Look for the three additional sections in the rest of the reading.**

1. First identify these sections. Then, on your own paper, continue the diagram above. Remember to answer these questions:

   Who or what is this paragraph about?

   Is it a general point or a detail?

   What is the purpose of each section?

2. After you have finished the diagram, look back at the three types of organization. Which type of organization does this reading have?

3. Now think about the author's purpose in writing this article. (Did he probably start out to write an article about Joe, the baker, or about psychological research?) Which sections are most related to that purpose? Where are you likely to find the author's important ideas?

4. If you are reading for a specific purpose, will the author's important ideas always be the most important information for you to note? Why or why not?

READING STRATEGY: Understanding Complicated Sentences

Many long, complicated sentences contain relative clauses. Most relative clauses begin with a relative pronoun. The most common relative pronouns are: **that, which, who, when, where,** and **whose.** You can sometimes make the sentence easier to understand by omitting the relative clause.

Relative clauses between commas can always be omitted. Other relative clauses may contain important information. One good strategy is to read the sentence twice. The first time, read the sentence *without* the relative clause to get the basic meaning. Then read it again *with* the relative clause for the complete information.

Underline the relative clause in this sentence. Is the information in the relative clause important or not?

When college students who said they hardly ever experience flow were asked to concentrate on a series of flashes or tones, Hamilton found that they used more mental energy than their typical baseline level.

---

3. **Look at these sentences and underline the relative clauses. Does the relative clause contain important information?**

   1. Joe Huggins, who is 44, works 12 hours a day, up to six days a week in the cramped, windowless baker's corner which is in the kitchen at Belia's Garden restaurant in western North Carolina.

   2. In one study of executives, he found that those who were in flow most often at work were less stressed out and took fewer sick days than did colleagues who had the same work load but couldn't get into flow.

   3. In this age when managers, blue-collar and clerical workers all find it more and more difficult to meet the demands of their jobs, Joe Huggins is rare.

   4. In Hamilton's research, students who were constantly worrying about how others perceived them—How am I doing? What do they think of me?—found it difficult to achieve flow.

READING STRATEGY: More Practice with Using Transition Words

In Units 1 and 3 you practiced using transition words to predict what information would come later. As you encounter transition words in your reading, you should be sure that you understand what they mean and what function they have in the reading.

4. Look back at the text and answer these questions.

1. What two ideas does *instead* connect? (paragraph 2)

2. What is the function of *not only..., but...* in this paragraph? (paragraph 3)

3. What two ideas does *even though* connect? (paragraph 7)

4. What two ideas does *but* connect? How does it help you to guess the meaning of *revving up*? (paragraph 11)

F. Strategies for Unknown Vocabulary

VOCABULARY STRATEGY: Deciding When Words Are Not Important

There are different ways to decide on the importance of an unknown word. One way that you have already learned is to see if the word is used several times in the reading. Another way is to see if the word occurs in an important section of the reading. To do this, you must see which parts of the reading contain the author's important points and which are examples.

1. Read these sentences. They contain many unknown words. Which part of the reading do they come from? Should you spend a lot of time trying to understand all these words? Why or why not?

1. As Joe butters bread pans, the pastry brush clacking furiously, a worried waiter rushes back and puts a stack of dessert dishes onto the bakery table. "Joe, we need twelve more cobblers for the group upstairs."

2. As soon as Joe has finished spooning out the cherry cobbler, the kitchen manager, Daisy Serle, comes in looking upset." Heather just dropped a whole chocolate pie—should we take it off the menu?"

3. "Oh no, we've got lots more," Joe says, slapping dough out on the counter, cutting pieces to roll into loaves, his hands in constant motion.

VOCABULARY STRATEGY: Using a Vocabulary Decision Tree

By now you have learned many different ways of dealing with unknown vocabulary. One possible way of putting them in a logical order is to use a vocabulary decision tree like the one below.

Do I need to understand this word?

Does it occur several times in a reading?

Does it occur in an important section?

If yes, it's probably important. Try to guess the meaning by using:

If no, it may not be important. Continue reading.

word analysis and parts of speech

using a larger context

examples

looking for general meaning

lists

using punctuation cues

internal definitions

recognizing technical words

synonyms or antonyms

using parallelism

my general knowledge

If these strategies do not work:

Look in a dictionary

Underline it or write it down and come back to it later

Ask someone else

Other?

2. Use the vocabulary decision tree to decide how to deal with these words and phrases. Write your decisions on the lines.

	PARAGRAPH NUMBER	DECISION
1. dour	2	_____
2. blue-collar	3	_____
3. ivory-tower scholar	5	_____
4. opponent	6	_____
5. thumbnail	10	_____
6. clacking	12	_____
7. determination	15	_____
8. chaos	15	_____
9. balancing spreadsheets	16	_____
10. perceived	18	_____

G. Building Your Vocabulary

One more step could be added to the vocabulary decision tree above: deciding which words you want to add to your vocabulary notebook. How might you make this decision?

Use these steps to build your vocabulary with words from the reading.

1. Look back at the list of words you wrote after Reading 1. Do any of these words occur in Reading 2? Put a checkmark (✓) next to them. Then look at Reading 2 again. Choose five to ten words that seem important.

2. Write these words in your vocabulary notebook. Group words that are similar (e.g., *repetitive/elusive/passive, overload/thumbnail*). Copy a sentence or phrase from the reading in which the word appears. Decide on the part of speech of the word and write a definition for it.

3. If you are still unsure of the meaning of this word, look it up in the dictionary and write the definition in your own words. For additional practice, write your own sentence.

H. Writing Your Ideas

Look at the writing topics below. Choose at least one and write about it.

1. Try to get into the flow of a task. Then write about this experience. Were you able to do it? Why or why not?

2. Think about something you do regularly (e.g., reading, studying, etc.). How could you develop flow while doing that activity? Describe what you would do.

3. Find someone that you think is "in the flow." Describe how that person works in this condition.

4. Compare two kinds of activities that you do. Choose one in which you usually achieve flow and one in which you usually do not. Use one of the types of organizations on page 184 to write your essay.

I. Making Connections

1. **Compare the description of flow in this reading with the description given in Unit 3, Reading 3. How are they the same? How are they different?**

2. **Which of the two readings on flow would be more useful for someone who wanted to learn to "get into the flow"?**

3. **How much of Joe's flow is related to his attitude about his work? How might attitude and flow be related to attitude and health as described in Reading 1 of Unit 3 ("Thinking Yourself Healthy")?**

PART **B** FOCUS ON READING FOR A PURPOSE

When you have finished Readings 1–6, you will complete one of the Unit Tasks described below. Further information on the Unit Task can be found on page 214. Your purpose in reading the rest of Unit 4 is to gather information and ideas for your chosen Unit Task.

What are the steps that you will follow in order to do this? Write them on the lines.

_____

_____

_____

In this unit, there are three possible Unit Tasks. You need to choose only one. Read the options below and then answer the questions that follow. These questions will help you choose which Unit Task to do.

Unit Task 1: Job Satisfaction Survey

In groups, create a survey about job satisfaction. Give the survey to as many people outside of your class as possible. Then tabulate the results and make a presentation to your class.

In order to conduct the survey, you will need to do the following:

1. identify the factors that create job satisfaction

2. write a questionnaire that contains items that focus on these factors

For an example of an opinion survey, see the first Additional Reading for this unit on page 231.

Unit Task 2: Careers Pamphlet

With a group of students or individually, use ideas from the readings to write a pamphlet to help graduating college seniors in their job search. This pamphlet will help them make informed decisions about choosing a career and give them advice on what to look for in a company.

In order to write the pamphlet, you will need to do the following:

1. decide which ideas in the readings are the most important to job satisfaction

2. turn those ideas into practical suggestions

Unit Task 3: Presentation on Finding Good Employees

In groups or individually, prepare a presentation for employers on what characteristics they should look for in employees. Make suggestions for general characteristics as well as essential qualities for certain jobs.

1. Does one of these options seem more interesting than the others? Which one? Why?

2. Is there a Unit Task that you would definitely not like to do? Which one? Why?

3. Is there a Unit Task that seems particularly suited to you (e.g., you prefer to work alone, you like to conduct surveys)? Which one? Why?

Pre-Step: Identify the Information You Need

Choose a Unit Task. If you are working on a group task, do the following activities with your group. If you are working alone, do the following activities and discuss the results with a classmate or your teacher.

1. Think of three to five questions that you will need to find the answers to in order to do the Unit Task. Write them in your notebook.

2. Look back to Readings 1 and 2. Was there any information in those readings that is relevant to the questions you wrote above? Underline, highlight, or make margin notes about the information.

3. Now look ahead to Readings 3–6. Which of your questions do you think these readings might address? Write your answers in the chart.

READING NUMBER	TITLE	QUESTIONS THAT THE READING MIGHT ADDRESS
3	How to Hire Employees	_____
4	The First 100 Days	_____
5	What It Takes	_____
6	Make Your Resume Do the Work	_____

4. Now continue on to Readings 3–6, keeping in mind the Unit Task that you have chosen. Remember, you will not have to do the Unit Task until the end of the unit.

READING 3: "HOW TO HIRE EMPLOYEES"

Step 1: Preview

1. **Preview this reading and make predictions based on these features.**

FEATURE	PREDICTION
Title	_____
Source	_____
Format	_____
Author	_____
Introduction/Conclusion	_____

2. **Were all the features equally helpful? Which ones were not helpful?**

3. **What general knowledge do you already have about the topic of this reading?**

4. **What information might this reading contain that would be relevant to your task?**

1. **Think about your predictions in Step 1. What are you going to be looking for as you read this selection?**

2. **Read the text closely. Remember not to look at the margin questions the first time that you read.**

3. **Reread the text, using the margin questions to help you.**

READING 3

How to Hire Employees

by Joshua Hyatt
Inc. Magazine

Tom Melohn judges job candidates by their values

1 What is the purpose of the information between the dashes? Is it essential to the sentence?

1   Thomas Melohn, the president and co-owner of North American Tool & Die Inc., contends that his employee-oriented management style—which begins with a comprehensive hiring process in which Melohn selects two employees from three hundred candidates—makes money, and lots of it. Since he and a partner bought the San Leandro, California company in 1978, sales have risen from about $2 million to more than $20 million.

2   At the same time, Melohn has cut turnover from 27% to less than 4%, and virtually eliminated absenteeism from its 10% high. The numbers, Melohn says, reflect the fact that "we truly care. I don't think most companies are concerned about employees."

3   After spending 24 years in corporate America, the 58-year-old Melohn says he felt disillusioned and looked for a better way to manage people. He believes that the most important thing is to give your company a set of values and then "make sure you find people who have those values and can work together." It's not easy, but Melohn contends that hiring should be the chief executive's top priority. "Without good people, you're dead."

APPLICATIONS

Apply yourself and you'll learn a lot

2 What does the word *first* signal?

3 What is the next signal word?

4   About 90% of candidates can be eliminated by examining job applications, Melohn contends. He first looks at how much time they have spent in previous jobs. He doesn't interview most candidates who have spent less than a year with any one employer. Then he looks at their salary level. And if their previous salary amounts to 20% more than what Melohn can offer, he passes. Such people, he insists, probably won't stay long. They will always be looking for a better-paying job.

Questions to ponder while reading applications

4 Why are there questions at the beginning of paragraphs 5–8?

5   Is it neat? Your first-grade teacher was right, after all. Neatness counts, especially if you are hiring someone for a highly technical job. "Neatness means there's a caring person," says Melohn.

6   Is it complete? If not, observes Melohn, "it's an indication that the person doesn't follow instructions very well."

Singing in a choir is an activity that says, "I give, I belong."

7   What about outside interests? Coaching soccer or singing in a church choir are "activities that say, 'I give. I belong,' " says Melohn. A candidate who lists nothing—or thinks it is nobody's business—should make an employer think twice. "I don't need someone like that," says Melohn.

8   Is there any relevant experience? Skills can be taught to the right person. But in Melohn's case, the "right" person probably worked in a factory before. He doesn't want people who are afraid of machines or who cannot stand loud noise.

5 Look quickly at the section called "Recruiting." What is it a list of?

RECRUITING

Read all about it: newspaper ads

9   Run ads only in neighborhood newspapers. An unduly long commute—any trip that takes more than 45 minutes—will encourage people to continue to look for jobs closer to home.

10   Design an ad that will be noticed. Small ads will be missed by anyone who blinks. Melohn tries to get his ads at the top of a category listing, and runs them for ten straight days.

11   Choose words that communicate your company's values. Melohn uses such language as "caring about people," "fun," "super," and "neat."

12   Resist the standard appeal for résumés and references. Melohn's ads for salespeople ask candidates to "write me a short note explaining why your background fits." Their notes give Melohn early insight into their values and communications skills. He asks production workers to come down and fill out an application. "It's an interesting way to see if they can find their way down here," he notes. "It shows how well they follow instructions."

THE PERFECT INTERVIEW

A timetable

6 What are the important points in this section?

13   Melohn's job interviews last 30 minutes. Here's a breakdown of how he spends that time:

14   Small talk (two minutes): "Can I get you something to drink?" Melohn begins. He gets the drinks himself because he wants to show that his employees aren't his slaves. During this time he chats about the weather or sports, anything that will make the candidate feel comfortable.

15   Housekeeping details (two minutes): Melohn almost never hires on the spot; he tells the interviewee that outright. "Knowing the schedule makes the interview much less stressful. It takes the pressure off them," he says.

16   Answering questions (seven to fifteen minutes): "A job interview is a two-way street," Melohn tells applicants. "So tell me, what kinds of questions do you have?" He then shuts up. If they don't have any questions, Melohn prods, and they usually open up. What's the pay? Can you tell me the vacation policy? Such questions reveal someone who just wants a job. Melohn prefers to hear genuine curiosity. What do you manufacture here? Can I tour the plant?

17   Start selling/cut it off (ten to twelve minutes): If Melohn likes what he hears, he starts selling candidates on coming to North American Tool & Die. He'll mention, for example, that medical benefits begin on day one of employment. Then he starts asking them about which shift they

A job interview is a two-way street.

prefer or the machine that most interests them. If Melohn isn't interested in the person, he'll bring the interview to a close.

The warning signs

18 An interviewee is probably stretching the truth when…

- he or she leans forward and says, "Let me be honest with you."
- everything is "my" this or "my" that.

The last step

19 When he's hiring someone for a skilled job, Melohn's final test involves having them come in for a paid day-long or half-day trial.

7 What are the examples of tasks?

20 Melohn's managers ask the candidates to perform certain tasks: set up that machine, come up with a quote from this blueprint. "It's not only how they do, but it's the questions they ask along the way," he notes. "You can't fake it." Sometimes the tryout can be quite decisive. One candidate left and called in his withdrawal from a nearby pay phone.

21 Once hired, a new employee must still go through what Melohn calls "a 30-day honeymoon." During that period, says Melohn, "we see if we like him and he likes us." New hires get progress updates every Friday from department heads. Few fail.

8 What part of speech is *hires?* How do you know?

9 What does *few* refer to?

22 "If you lower your standards, you deserve everything you get. You should hire temps to get through a shortage, if you have to. But don't lower your standards. You should know the price of one bad apple."

Melohn's final test involves having job candidates come in for a paid day-long or half-day trial.

23 When it comes time to negotiate compensation, Melohn offers a radical proposal: be totally honest. With production workers, he simply pulls out a sheet listing the salary range for each job. "Given your skills," he'll say, "I think you fall about here."

24 Melohn tries to avoid paying less than what the candidate currently makes. On the other hand, he won't meet high demands. "It's not fair to the people who are here," he says. "Plus, if you meet that demand, you have to wonder what the next demand will be: a corner office? Time off? A title?"

25 "One guy during an interview said, 'I love to dance.' I asked him why. He said, 'Because I enjoy the teamwork of it, the coordination with a partner.' I liked his honesty. For a man to admit that he loved to dance wasn't easy. And that he enjoyed teamwork would serve well here, I thought."

You've probably found a good employee when…

26 Someone is candid enough to admit they were fired from their last job. Or to say, "I didn't like my last job." Of course, honesty is relative. "If someone says, 'I need the job to buy drugs,' that's the truth," notes Melohn. "But it's not the right motivation to work here."

Hello, I must be going

27 Once, during a promising interview, the prospect got up and announced that he had to leave. "I've got tickets to the Oakland A's baseball game this afternoon," the man explained. Right then and there, Melohn decided against him. But not because of his priorities. "He didn't plan ahead," says Melohn, "and that's not good."

28 Then there's the woman who brought her seven-year-old son to an interview and left him outside in the waiting room. Bring the lad in, Melohn suggested. "Watching them interact was a good way to see her values," he says. He liked what he saw, so he hired her.

How to make your interview questions more effective

by Bruce Posner

Deciding whether someone is right for a job is always a little confusing. It's rare for a manager to have all the information he or she needs to make well-informed decisions. But knowing how to ask good questions can make a world of difference. The secret, says psychologist and personnel consultant Kurt Einstein, is understanding the difference between open-ended and closed-ended questions.

The problem with closed-ended questions is that they encourage limited, yes/no answers. Either that or they'll signal to the interviewee what you're hoping to hear. Open-ended questions make no prejudgments—and provide greater insights into the candidate. Here are some examples of each:

Closed-ended questions

Can you learn quickly under pressure?
Can you accept criticism easily?
Are you ambitious?
Have you ever thought of doing any other type of work?
Did you get along with your previous supervisor?

Open-ended questions

Under what kinds of conditions do you learn best?
Give some examples of times you've been criticized. How did you react, and why?
What is your interpretation of success?
If you could structure the perfect job for yourself, what would you do, and why?
How would you describe your previous supervisor? How were you alike, and how were you different?

A. Checking Your Comprehension

List four of the values and qualities that Melohn is looking for in his potential employees.

1. _____

2. _____

3. _____

4. _____

B. Making Inferences

1. **An inference is a guess. But not all guesses are equal. Some are reasonable; that is, they seem logical and probably true. Some are not. Put a checkmark (✓) next to the reasonable inferences and an X next to the unreasonable ones. Explain your answers to a partner.**

   ____ 1. The author believes Melohn is a good boss.

_____ 2. Melohn spends a lot of time hiring new employees.

_____ 3. Melohn's employees are satisfied.

_____ 4. Melohn's employees are well-paid.

_____ 5. Many of the qualities Melohn looks for relate to a person's character.

2. **Sometimes an inference can be made from just one statement. Read what Tom Melohn says. Then write what a successful job applicant would have to do.**

1. "Neatness counts, especially if you are hiring someone for a highly technical job."

_____

2. "What about outside interests?"

_____

3. "It's not only how they do, but it's the questions they ask..."

_____

4. "A job interview is a two-way street."

_____

5. "I liked his honesty. For a man to admit that he loved to dance wasn't easy."

_____

6. "It shows how well they follow instructions."

_____

C. Topics for Discussion

Discuss the following questions with your classmates.

1. Would you like to work for a boss like Melohn? Why or why not?

2. Do you disagree with any of Melohn's opinions?

3. What do you think of his ways of questioning? Do you think they are fair? Why or why not?

4. Can you think of two more pairs of open-ended and closed-ended questions for a job interview?

5. Should all employers look for the qualities that Melohn looks for? Why or why not?

D. Additional Strategy Practice

Use the vocabulary decision tree to decide how to deal with the words below. Write your decisions on the lines.

	PARAGRAPH NUMBER	DECISION
1. turnover	2	_____
2. disillusioned	3	_____
3. relevant	8	_____
4. values	12	_____
5. small talk	14	_____
6. interviewee	15	_____
7. two-way street	16	_____
8. negotiate	23	_____
9. compensation	23	_____
10. candid	26	_____

Step 3: Note Useful Information

1. **What is the author's purpose in writing this article? Is his point of view the same as yours in your chosen Unit Task? Who is your intended audience?**

2. **If the author's point of view is different from yours, is it still possible for you to get useful information from this reading? How?**

3. **Reread and highlight, underline, make margin notes, and/or make notes in your notebook on the useful information for your Unit Task.**

E. Building Your Vocabulary

Use these steps to build your vocabulary with words from the reading.

1. Look back at the list of words you wrote after Readings 1 and 2. Do any of these words occur in Reading 3? Put a checkmark (✓) next to them. Then look at Reading 3 again. Choose five to ten words that seem important.

2. Write these words in your vocabulary notebook. Group words that are similar (e.g., *apply/applicant/application, open-ended/close-ended*). Copy a sentence or phrase from the reading in which the word appears. Decide on the part of speech of the word and write a definition for it.

3. If you are still unsure of the meaning of the word, look it up in the dictionary and write the definition in your own words. For additional practice, write your own sentence.

F. Writing Your Ideas

Look at the writing topics below. Choose at least one and write about it.

1. Have you ever been to a job interview? What happened? What was the atmosphere like? Did you feel nervous or relaxed? How long was the interview? What kinds of questions were you asked? What kinds of questions did you ask?

2. What are the most important qualifications for the job you want? Which ones are the same as the ones Melohn looks for? Which are different? Which qualifications relate to personality and character? Which relate to education and work experience?

3. If you were going to have a job interview soon, how would you prepare for it? Describe what you would do.

READING 4: "THE FIRST 100 DAYS"

Step 1: Preview

1. **Preview this reading and make predictions based on the information in these sections of the text.**

SECTION	PREDICTION
Title	_____
Source	_____
Format	_____
Author	_____
Introduction	_____

2. **What information might this reading contain that would be relevant to your task?**

Step 2: Read Closely

1. **Read the article and check the predictions that you made above in question 1. Remember to cover up the margin questions the first time that you read.**

2. **After you have read the text once, read it again, using the margin questions to help you.**

READING 4

By Patricia Kitchen
Newsday, 11/26/98

The First 100 Days

1. HOWARD FERO puts it this way: "This is a whole new world. A new way of life. I don't have a syllabus. I make my own, and set my own objectives. I'm pushing myself. It's me working to put money in my own pocket."

2. Fero, a Hofstra University graduate, is one of thousands of young people who recently received degrees, found work or created their own, and have now been on the job at least 100 days. That's traditionally a time for evaluation so Fero and three other young people have agreed to examine their recent transitions from school to work.

3. Fero, like others, sees a decrease in personal time, a big adjustment by all accounts. Once masters of their own schedules, these newcomers to work are now governed by alarm clocks that go off about 6 a.m., five days a week. Besides the technical aspects of their jobs, they also have to master the more shadowy features. "They have to learn [bosses' or customers'] expectations, corporate customs, the best sources for internal information, and how to fit in," says Pamela Lennox, director of professional experience and placement at the C.W. Post Campus of Long Island University.

4. And, especially in today's workplace, they need to learn how to work as part of a team. "Schoolwork can be an independent activity. In the workplace, success is based on being collaborative," Lennox says. "A team succeeds."

Monica Bahamonde

5. MONICA BAHAMONDE remembers the good old days. Scheduling her own classes. Home from a part-time job by 4:30 p.m. Parties. An occasional nap.

6. Now, she's up at 6:30 a.m. She runs for the two subway trains that get her to her job at a Manhattan public relations firm by 8:45 a.m. If she's lucky, she gets home again by 7 p.m. She eats dinner. And hits the sack.

7. Welcome to the world of work, where time is no longer your own. "I find it much harder now to do the things I used to do. On weekends I catch up on errands, washing clothes and cleaning my room," she says. And her social life is on hold until, as she puts it, "I'm used to my job and what I'm doing."

8. She sees a real difference, too, in the way time is spent during the workday. "In college you finish something and wait for instructions," she says. But now, the pressure is on to take initiative. "You have more responsibility. Clients pay money to see publicity," she says, and they measure success by how many times they're mentioned in the media.

9. This means a more serious tone. "No joking around," she says. So, she's learning to have more businesslike conversations with colleagues and clients. "You have to talk different. No more 'yes' and 'no' answers. You need to explain yourself more," she says.

10. Despite the pressure, Bahamonde is finding great reward from her job. She really likes getting steady feedback. "My boss reads everything line by line and gives comments. He tells you when you do a good job," she says, adding that most professors weren't as attentive in that way.

11. She also enjoys all the phone work she does. "I'm a phone person," she says, but admits it was hard at first when her jobless friends called in the summer to invite her to skip work and go to the beach. "I don't even want to think about it," she says.

Howard Fero

12. HOWARD FERO works 12 hours a day at Lifeline Worldwide Services, Inc. He calls on customers. He makes sales. He monitors operations and billing. When one of the trucks breaks down, he takes to the road and delivers the package himself. "When the phone rings—that's my job, too," Fero says. That's because he's not an employee, but one of the company's owners.

Margin questions:

1 Which paragraph in the introduction gives you the most information about the article?

2 Does the context give you a general idea of the meaning of *collaborative*? What is it contrasted with?

3 Are these complete sentences? Why did the author choose to write in this way?

4 Can you guess the meaning of *take initiative* in paragraph 8? What is it contrasted with?

5 Paragraph 10 begins with *Despite*. What does that word signal?

13　"I'm the hardest boss I could possibly have. I'm doing this for myself," he says. "School was much more relaxing. You'd have three or four classes a day. And then a test. Now I have a test every time I answer the phone. You never know who's on the other end," he says. "I can be dealing with the president of a corporation one minute and someone from mail services the next," he says.

14　His studies in marketing and industrial psychology were good preparation for running his own business. And, he met his now-partner, the owner of a messenger service, by working as his intern. The two put their heads together and came up with the idea for a new, expanded courier business.

15　As for this partnership, "It's like a marriage," Fero says. "I'm more married to him than to my fiancée. I spend 12 hours a day with him and then call him on the phone to discuss more business."

16　His advice to today's future business owners on college campuses: Find out about internships as soon as you can. "Take as many as you can during your four years in college," he says. "You'll learn about all the different aspects of running a business." And, of course, small businesses always need the help. Fero, in fact, has brought on board two young women interns—both college freshmen.

Mary Jacob

17　WHEN SHE WAS a marketing student at Hofstra University, Mary Jacob's thinking on the origin of money was like that of many students. "When I was low, I called home to say, 'I'm outta money,'" she says.

18　But now, with a steady paycheck of her own coming in—along with a steady stream of bills for rent, insurance, a van, school loans, and credit cards—she's learning some important lessons in money management. "I wonder, 'How can I be getting paid, and still have no money?' Things never seemed expensive before. Now everything is expensive. I even complain about the price of cereal."

19　So, she's learning the advantage of bringing her lunch, skipping the $200 shoes in favor of $40 pairs, and as for a new leather jacket? "Forget it," she says. But, thankfully, the time she spends earning that paycheck is not as frustrating. "I'm doing what I like to do and applying what I learned in college," says Jacob, who is a marketing information assistant at Manhattan East Suite Hotels in Manhattan.

20　She credits the ease of her transition to two internships and a three-month training program she went through when she was hired. Those experiences, she says, gave her self-confidence. However, she does admit she finds relating to executives more frightening than to professors. Her tips for speaking with busy execs: "Be specific and come to the point. Anticipate what's most important for them to hear. They don't have time for long speeches."

21　Though she says she's no public speaker, she's learning that skill too. Jacob, who is in a wheel-chair, just received an award from the agency that helped her find her job—Just One Break Inc., a nonprofit employment service in Manhattan that helps people with disabilities find positions.

22　She had to give an acceptance speech to an audience of more than 300 people, including company presidents and CEOs. "It wasn't as bad as I thought," she says. "The applause helped."

William Arias

23　"AS STUDENTS we listen. We take information in, and don't ask enough questions. We are not taking initiative other than doing our homework," William Arias says. He's finding all that's different in the work world. "There's no book or professor telling me now," says Arias, who works with young people ages 10 to 18. He says his job now is to "express myself and educate others."

24　Arias, who is a community organizer/youth worker at United Community Centers in Brooklyn, really gets a kick out of the results he sees. "In school you put in hard work, but don't see the real payoff…Your payment was a grade." Now he has a sense of making a difference. He sees a "more immediate reimbursement of effort."

25　One example is the camping trip to a lake near Bear Mountain that he helped set up. Most of the 15 young people who went had never been out of their neighborhood. "All they know are violent streets, prostitutes, drugs on the corner," says Arias, who was amazed by their reaction to things in nature he has seen many times.

26　"The first morning they woke up they saw the sunrise above the lake. They said it was really awesome. They said, 'We never knew that happened,'" Arias says. "It was really powerful."

27　A professor once told him the benefits of getting an education <u>start</u> when you go to work—that all the schooling pays off. "I didn't realize how valuable getting an education is," he says. For some, it's just getting a piece of paper. But for him, the real value has been the self-confidence that comes from knowing what he's talking about. "It's a big asset," he says.

---

6 Can you use your general knowledge and context to guess the meaning of the idiom *put their heads together?*

7 What are the items in this list examples of?

8 Did you figure out the meaning of *take initiative* in paragraph 8? Does your definition fit the context in paragraph 23?

A. Checking Your Comprehension

Complete the first two lines below about each of the people in the reading.

1. Name: _____

   Job: _____

   Lesson(s) learned: _____

2. Name: _____

   Job: _____

   Lesson(s) learned: _____

3. Name: _____

   Job: _____

   Lesson(s) learned: _____

4. Name: _____

   Job: _____

   Lesson(s) learned: _____

B. Making Inferences

Look at the information above, then look back at the reading. What do you think the four people would say were the lessons they learned from working? Write your ideas on the last lines above. Compare your answers with your classmates'.

C. Topics for Discussion

Discuss the following questions with your classmates.

1. Do you think these people are good employees? Why or why not?

2. Which of the profiles was the most useful to you? Why?

3. If you are already employed, are there any other things that you have learned since you began working?

Step 3: Note Useful Information

1. What kind of information does this article provide that may be useful for the Unit Task?

2. Is there any information that you think is irrelevant?

3. Reread and highlight, underline, and/or make margin notes on the important information for the Unit Task.

D. Building Your Vocabulary

Use these steps to build your vocabulary with words from the reading.

1. Look at your reading list from Readings 1–3. Put a checkmark (✓) next to any words that also appeared in Reading 4. Then look back at Reading 4 and make a list of five to ten new words that you feel are important to learn.

2. Write these words in your vocabulary notebook. Group words that are similar (e.g., *partner/partnership, adjustment/reimbursement*). Copy a sentence or phrase in which the word appears. Identify the part of speech of the word and write a definition for it.

3. If you are still unsure of the meaning of this word or the part of speech, look it up in the dictionary and write the definition in your own words. For additional practice, write your own sentence.

E. Writing Your Ideas

Look at the writing topics below. Choose at least one and write about it.

1. Choose one of the lessons that the people in the article mentioned. Which of these lessons do you need to learn? Explain why you think it may be difficult for you to learn.

2. Interview someone who has recently started working. Write about what he or she has learned and how his or her life has changed.

READING 5: "WHAT IT TAKES"

Step 1: Preview

1. **Where will you look to preview this reading? Make two predictions about what you expect to find. Write them on the lines.**

   _____

   _____

2. **Do you think this reading will be useful for your chosen Unit Task?**

Step 2: Read Closely

1. **Read the text closely and check your predictions. Use the reading and vocabulary strategies that you have learned as you are reading. Remember not to look at the margin questions the first time you read.**

2. **Reread the text, using the margin questions to help you.**

WHAT IT TAKES

From *Inc. Magazine*, Brokaw, Murphy & Seglin

1 What is the purpose of this paragraph?

1 *Here, in their own words, is how some of the country's most innovative and ambitious people managers are trying to build the perfect workplace. To report this story, we spoke with dozens of company owners and managers across the country. Each had his or her own view about the best ways to take care of employees. Here is what some of them said.*

ENVIRONMENTAL ACTIVISM
Dahlin Smith White

2 Who is speaking here?

2 *John Dahlin, Darrell Smith, and Jon White started the advertising agency that bears their names only six years ago. "We wanted to build the company that we'd always wanted to work for," recalls president Dahlin. "Someplace rewarding, stimulating, fun." Ninety people later, Dahlin Smith White, in Salt Lake City, is a $60-million agency. Dahlin explains their company philosophy.*

3 Who is speaking here? How do you know?

4 What is the purpose of these *if* sentences?

3 "In this business, we have to have an environment that's a little loose if we're going to cultivate creativity, new ideas, and great advertising. That means being flexible about how and when people work. If people want to play music or dance in the hallways, they can. If they want to go skiing or go to a movie in the middle of the day, they can. If they want to play pool, we have a poolroom right here. It sounds crazy, but that kind of craziness is actually essential to our business. We want people to have fun, to be stimulated, to do something wild.

5 What *environment* does this section refer to? Is this company working to save endangered species?

4 Even the physical environment—our office space—was designed to encourage that. None of the walls are straight; they tilt or angle in. There are two or three different door sizes and different windows. A yellow metal-and-glass staircase lights up and greets you as you enter. We want people to be stimulated as soon as they walk in. By the time I hit my desk, I'm already jazzed. Even customers respond to it. They might not know whether they like it or hate it, but they have a reaction to it. Isn't that what good advertising is supposed to do?

6 Can you guess the general meaning of *eclectic*?

7 Whose rules are these?

5 All employees get an art budget of $100 to $200 each to decorate their offices, which makes the decor totally eclectic: Indian tapestries, sculpted glass heads, gigantic light bulbs. We want people to be real, to be themselves. The motto here is "Do Something Wild." We can all do something wild, push ourselves, test our limits. We try to break as many rules as we can without losing our basic stability as a company.

6 There are lots of dinners, movies, retreats. We go mountain climbing, horseback riding, snowmobiling. We counted forty parties last year—Friday the

8 What is the information between the dashes?

13th, an April Fools' bowling party—most of them pretty spontaneous because we hate to plan ahead. We keep people thinking there might be something coming to them at any moment. But it's not predictable. It would get boring if there weren't some uncertainty with incentives.

7   What's the reward for working so hard to create this kind of environment? It's simple: better advertising. We get a more innovative, more energetic, more stimulated staff. When people are having fun, they're encouraged to work harder. If we get people to work one more hour a day because they enjoy their work and like the environment, that's 12.5% more output.

8   Every day I think about the environment we provide and our employees. I let my partners take care of the clients. I worry whether the staff are happy. Are they motivated and compensated well enough to create great advertising for our clients? To create unique advertising, we need people who are having fun.

FAMILY VALUES
Rhino Foods

9 What do you predict this company's program focuses on?

9   *In the past two years, Rhino has grown from 13 people to 70 with more than $5 million in annual sales. Rhino Foods has a company "list of purposes," which declares among other things that "Rhino Foods is a vehicle for people to get what they want." Ted Castle, the founder and president, was determined that the business wouldn't run him, that he'd still have time for sailing, golf, and mountain-climbing. And he figured that if the business would serve him, he wanted it to serve the other employees. Maybe that's radical, but that's the kind of company he wanted.*

10   "One of our projects is called Focus on Families. A group meets every Thursday to oversee programs for employees and for community groups. The meetings last about half an hour, on company time, with anywhere from 7 to 25 people attending. We're about to start something called the Nurturing Program, a 15-weekend program that works with parents and kids to develop better parenting skills.

10 What are some examples of *difficult backgrounds?*

11   Many people in our work force come from difficult backgrounds—broken homes or terrible childhood experiences. Many of the mothers here are single mothers or have a mate who's not the father of their kids. We sent six people from our company to an educators' conference on children recently, They reported back to the Focus on Families group on what they'd heard and they also got a lot of self-esteem. They were really proud because they were representatives of their business. That sort of stuff works. We see people coming to work now with incredibly great attitudes, people who are working hard, who feel they're getting something back for it. And people here work very hard; production work is not easy. It's physical; you're on your feet all the time; it's fast.

11 *On the other hand introduces a contrasting idea. What two ideas are being contrasted?*

12 On the other hand, this is still an amazingly levelheaded organization. We don't think this way out of charity; there are some very logical reasons for these programs. We view the things we're doing as good business. You have lower turnover; you have fewer sick days; you have people who are excited about coming to work. It makes sense that people will be more productive if they're happier at home. It's the idea of thinking globally but acting locally: for us, "locally" is right inside this company."

BASIC TRAINING

White Storage and Retrieval Systems

12 *What kinds of programs do you think this company offers its employees?*

13 *When Donald Weiss became CEO of White Storage in 1975, the company, an offshoot of a now-46-year-old family business, had $4 million in sales. Seventeen years and thousands of training hours later, Weiss's company, which is based in Kenilworth, N.J., employs 400 people and reports $50 million in annual revenues.*

14 I remember attending a seminar on quality back in 1988 and being completely inspired by it. But I took one look around at our work force and realized it would be impossible to teach the concept of quality to people who didn't even have basic language or math skills. So many had never been properly trained or educated. More than a hundred barely understood the language. We were going to have to start at the beginning—with basic English.

13 *What does the expression after-hours mean?*

14 *What are the differences between the first two years and after that?*

15 I began by paying a couple of teachers to come in for two hours a week. Employees volunteered their time and came in after-hours. We had about forty in the beginning. For about two years, the first classes were held for two hours a day, two days a week. Then, we got state and federal money to help pay for a complete workplace-literacy program. We got teacher salaries covered and started offering the classes during working hours. Soon we had 100 students in five levels of English classes. And training started to take hold in the entire company. By 1991 we were offering 7,000 hours of training, everything from English as a Second Language, to how to use small tools.

15 *Start looking for the ways the company has benefited.*

16 We've seen the benefits in a number of ways. The most significant benefit is the sense of dignity people have. The training programs literally changed the company culture. People appreciate the opportunity to educate themselves and improve their skills, and they feel more confident and secure in their jobs.

17 Turnover used to be above 25%; now it's below 10%. We've seen tremendous improvement in safety. In 1988 we had 180 reported accidents. This year it'll be just over thirty. And productivity is up. In one year alone we saw the turn-around time on orders drop from seven days to one.

16 What is Weiss going
to talk about in this
paragraph?

18 As for costs, the program has been surprisingly inexpensive. We get a return on everything we spend. We get more productive people. We get better ideas out of them, better performance. Plus we get better relationships with people. The power of the people who work for you is incredible if you choose to use it.

19 I don't think of this as some kind of heroic effort. It's a necessity. Most of our competition comes from foreign companies. And they don't have the education or language problems we have. In Japan and Germany, workers tend to be better educated. Many enlightened companies are doing what we're doing. This is the direction all companies will have to take in the future.

A. Checking Your Comprehension

1. Complete the information from Reading 5.

1. Name of company: _____

   Principles from the company philosophy: _____

   _____

   Innovative programs: _____

   _____

   Benefits to company: _____

   _____

2. Name of company: _____

   Principles from the company philosophy: _____

   _____

   Innovative programs: _____

   _____

   Benefits to company: _____

   _____

3. Name of company: _____

   Principles from the company philosophy: _____

   _____

   Innovative programs: _____

   _____

   Benefits to company: _____

   _____

2. Whose viewpoint is shown in this reading, the employer's or the employee's?

B. Making Inferences

1. What can you say about the employees of each company by looking at what benefits their employers offer? Think about their level of education, values, and so on.

2. How are these companies the same? How are they different?

C. Topics for Discussion

Discuss the following questions with your classmates.

1. Would you like to work for these companies? Why or why not?

2. Do you know about similar company philosophies?

3. How much do you believe that one's working environment (for example, tilted walls) influences one's work? Explain.

4. Do you think that these ways of running businesses work? Explain.

5. Why are there so few companies like these? Explain.

Step 3: Note Useful Information

1. Look at the information in Checking Your Comprehension. Do any of those ideas suit your chosen Unit Task?

2. Look back at the reading. Is there any other information that might be useful? Highlight, underline, and/or make margin notes about it.

3. Look at your list of questions on page 191. Now that you have more information, are there any questions you would like to add?

D. Building Your Vocabulary

Use these steps to build your vocabulary with words from the reading.

1. Look back at the list of words you wrote after Readings 1–4. Do any of these words occur in Reading 5? Put a checkmark (✓) next to them. Then look at Reading 5 again. Choose five to ten words that seem important.

2. Write these words in your vocabulary notebook. Group words that are similar (e.g., *productive/productivity, dignity/safety*). Copy a sentence or phrase from the reading in which the word appeared. Decide on the part of speech of the word and write a definition for it.

3. If you are still unsure of the meaning of this word, look it up in the dictionary and write the definition in your own words. For additional practice, write your own sentence.

E. Writing Your Ideas

Look at the writing topics below. Choose at least one and write about it.

1. Pretend that you are the president of a company. What would your company philosophy be? Would you have employee-friendly policies and programs? If so, what would they be?

2. If you have a job, what could your employer do to make his or her employees happier? Give specific suggestions and explain how they would benefit both the employees and the company.

F. Making Connections

1. **Do you think people who work at these companies would say that they have a "job to die for"? Why or why not?**

2. **Would Tom Melohn be in agreement with the company presidents who are profiled here? Why or why not?**

READING 6: "MAKE YOUR RESUME DO THE WORK"

Step 1: Preview

1. **Preview this reading and make predictions about what you expect to find. Write your answers on the lines.**

2. **Explain your predictions to a classmate.**

Read closely and check the predictions you made above in question 1. Notice that there are no margin questions in this reading. Try to think of your own questions as you read, and write them in the margin.

READING 6

Make Your Resume Do the Work

Timothy D. Haft claims his tips will keep your resume on a potential employer's desk, not thrown in a trash basket.

by Carla Wheeler
Gannet News Service, 6/15/95

1 It's a dog-eat-dog job market. Finding a job can be like fighting for a bone, especially when unemployment rates are up and many companies have laid off many workers.

2 Prestigious, high-paying jobs demand education and experience. And every year, a fresh group of college graduates enters the job market. They get some of the available jobs, but they also face plenty of challenges in the job market, just like everybody else.

3 The Bureau of Labor Statistics reports that the number of college graduates working as street vendors increased from 57,000 in 1983 to 75,000 in 1990.

4 It's a statistic to chew on from "Trashproof Resumes" (Random House, $9.95), a new book that teaches the art of writing eye-catching, memorable resumes that will snag job interviews.

5 Author Timothy D. Haft, a career counselor for students at the University of New York, claims his tips will keep your resume on a potential employer's desk, not thrown in a trash basket. "Many employers skim resumes rather quickly, and if nothing piques their curiosity right away, they might not bother reading the rest," says Haft, who aims his book at college graduates. "Your resume must sell you."

6 Haft says research for "Trashproof Resumes" showed that some employers spend less than a minute looking over a resume, so a person's qualifications should jump off the page quickly. "They want to know about your skills. What you can do for them."

7 Haft says, "One employer admitted she spends five seconds (reading) before she puts a resume into a 'yes' or 'no' file. She looks fast at the education and job titles the person has held." So never beat around the bush. List schooling or job experience most relevant to the job you want first, says Haft, 34, who teaches resume writing workshops and has written, edited or critiqued more than 5,000 resumes.

8 College graduates often use their resumes to talk about hobbies or jobs that have absolutely nothing to do with the job they're applying for, Haft says.

9 "I was working with a student who was a fashion designer and a third of her resume was devoted to hotel and restaurant jobs," says Haft. "I told her, 'We are not advertising your waitressing skills, we are advertising your design skills.'" So the student rewrote her resume, putting her design education and last projects first, Haft says.

10 People can list their unrelated jobs, if they want to show they worked their way through school and have a strong work ethic, he says. But add the information at the end of the resume. "Put it in a brief bullet under your education," Haft says.

11 Here are several other recommendations from "Trashproof Resumes":

–Before putting ink to the resume, play detective. Investigate what skills and qualifications the employer wants from the person they're seeking for the job.

–Tailor the resume for each job you apply for in a different field. If you want work as an accountant, list your college business major high up in the resume. But if you're applying for another job—for example as a photographer—write another resume that first lists the three years you spent taking photographs for a newspaper. "For each position, you want to stress different skills on your resume," Haft says.

–Keep the resume to one page, especially if you've just graduated from college.

–Be conceited but truthful. Never lie on a resume, but feel free to brag about your accomplishments and grades. "Because the competition is so stiff, you've got to toot your own horn," Haft says.

–Keep resume language simple. Say "met with" instead of "interfaced."

–At the top of the resume, list your name. Never include vital statistics such as height, weight and race, unless you want work as a model or actress.

–Use power verbs to describe skills. If you want to work as a White House press secretary, say you "briefed reporters at the United Nations about the famine in Somalia."

–Mail 50 to 100 resumes during your job search because five to 10 resumes may produce no results.

12 Haft cautions people not to rely on a wonderful resume to do the job of finding a job. "No resume gets a job offer. You do," Haft says. "A resume does not speak for you, dress you suitably, shake hands firmly for you or teach you body language techniques. Looking great on paper is important, but it mostly serves to set the tone for the main act—the interview."

A. Checking Your Comprehension

Read each question below. Then look back at the article for the answers.

1. Why is it important that your resume be well written?

2. What should you do before you write your resume?

3. What kinds of information should a resume include?

4. What kinds of information should a resume probably leave out?

5. According to the author, what are some other characteristics of a good resume?

6. What can't a good resume do for you?

B. Making Inferences

1. Who is the primary audience for this article? Why do you think so?

2. Why did the author choose this quotation?

"The Bureau of Labor Statistics reports that the number of college graduates working as street vendors increased from 57,000 in 1983 to 75,000 in 1990."

C. Topics for Discussion

Read these situations and give each person advice on what to keep and what to change on his or her resume.

1. Pedro is an engineer. He graduated from college one year ago. His resume is four pages long. It begins with his education. It then lists all his jobs going back through high school.

2. Karen has been working as a secretary in a law office in New York. She would like to get a job as a guide for tourists who come to New York City. Her resume is only one page long. It lists her education in secretarial school. It also says that she is fluent in Spanish, French, and German. Actually, her Spanish is good, but she only speaks a little French and German.

3. Ted graduated from college with a degree in business administration. However, he has been interested in journalism since he won a prize for newspaper writing when he was in college. He has worked at various office jobs since he graduated from college three years ago. Now he would like to work as a reporter for a newspaper. His resume is one page long. It lists his education and his post-college work experience.

Step 3: Note Useful Information

1. **Was your original prediction about the usefulness of this article correct? Why or why not?**

2. **Was your purpose for reading the article the same as the author's purpose for writing it? How might that make a difference when you are looking for useful information?**

3. **Look back and highlight, underline, and/or make margin notes on the points that are useful for the Unit Task.**

D. Building Your Vocabulary

Use these steps to build your vocabulary with words from the reading.

1. Look at your reading list from Readings 1–5. Put a checkmark (✓) next to any words that also appeared in Reading 6. Then look back at Reading 6 and make a list of five to ten new words that you feel are important to learn.

2. Write these words in your vocabulary notebook. Group words that are similar (e.g., *employer/unemployment, recommendation/qualification*). Copy a sentence or phrase in which the word appears. Identify the part of speech of the word and write a definition for it.

3. If you are still unsure of the meaning of this word or the part of speech, look it up in the dictionary and write the definition in your own words. For additional practice, write your own sentence.

E. Writing Your Ideas

Look at the writing topics below. Choose either topic 1, or both topics, to write about.

1. Imagine that you are applying for a specific job. Think about your education and experience and write a resume for that job.

2. Exchange the resume you wrote in question 1 with another student and give each other suggestions on how to improve it.

F. Making Connections

1. **Compare this reading to Reading 3 ("How to Hire Employees"). Would Tom Melohn agree with the advice in this article? Why or why not?**

2. **Compare the information in this reading to the process of preparing a resume in your own country. How is the process the same or different? What kinds of information are you expected to include on your resume? How is it the same or different from what the writer of this article suggests?**

Building Your Vocabulary: Summary

Prepare for the Unit Task by reviewing the most important vocabulary from this unit. Look again at your vocabulary list for all six readings. Make a list of all the words that:

> have checkmarks (✓)
>
> are similar to other words
>
> will be important for your task

You now have a list of words that are probably the most useful words for you to learn.

Show your list to a classmate. How many words do you have in common? How many words are different?

In Unit 3, you grouped words according to parts of speech. In this unit, you will put the new words into just two categories: words that are directly related to the topic of work, and words that are important but not restricted to the topic of work.

Compare your lists with a classmate. Do you agree which group each word belongs to?

UNIT TASK:
Survey, Pamphlet, or Presentation

Unit Task 1: Write a job satisfaction survey. In order to do this you must first decide on the factors that create job satisfaction. Next, create questions that will ask about those factors.

Unit Task 2: Construct a pamphlet with career advice for graduating college seniors. The pamphlet should include suggestions on choosing a career and a company. It should also give tips on interviewing techniques and how to write an effective resume.

Unit Task 3: Imagine that your classmates are employers. Prepare an oral presentation for them on the characteristics they should look for when hiring new employees.

Do the following activities in groups or pairs to develop your ideas for the task.

---

1. Look back at your list of questions on page 191. Which ones did you find information about? Write your questions on the lines below.

_____

_____

_____

_____

2. Look back at the readings and your notes. Which ones contain useful information for your chosen Unit Task?

3. Decide how you are going to organize the information in your report. If you are doing Unit Task 1, the survey, you may want to group the questions according to their content. For Unit Tasks 2 and 3, you will need to make an outline or an organizational plan for the report or the presentation. The questions that you wrote may help you to organize the information.

4. If you feel that you need more information, you can do research in secondary sources. You could:

Look at the additional readings for this unit on pages 231–237. Preview each reading. Begin to read those that you predict will be useful. Stop reading if you find out that they are not useful.

Do research on the Internet. Do a key word search. Be careful to check the sources. A lot of information on the Internet looks factual, but is not.

Look in current newspapers, magazines or books for information on your topic.

5. Now prepare your survey, pamphlet, or presentation. Use the information and ideas from your discussion. If you have written a survey, find a few people outside of your class to take it. Report your findings to the class. If you have prepared a pamphlet, make enough copies to share with the class. If you have prepared a presentation, give it for your classmates.

Applying Your Knowledge

1. Interview the owner or the manager of a small business. Ask him or her about the business's philosophy and values. Then ask whether the company has employee-centered programs. Is the philosophy reflected in the programs? Report your findings.

2. Plan a career day at school. Invite people from different careers to come to speak to the students. Ask speakers to talk about why they love their jobs.

3. Interview the human resources (personnel) director of a company. Find out what general qualities he or she looks for in a job applicant. Report your findings to the class.

4. Watch a television program that features people in a specific career (police officers, doctors, lawyers, etc.). Make notes about what they do in a typical day. Then interview a person with that job. Is the job the same as it is portrayed on television? If not, how is it different?

The Electronic Link

1. Look on the Internet to find more information about working and job satisfaction. These sites will be helpful:

   http://www.careerbuilder.com/

   http://www.jobs-career.com/

   http://www.brookfieldct.org/JobCaree.htm

2. Do a search for a company on the Internet that gives information about its personnel relations. Answer these questions.

   Name of the company _____

   URL (Web address) _____

   Brief description of the company _____

   _____

Personnel policies _____

_____

_____

_____

_____

_____

Do you think you would like to work for this company? Why or why not?

_____

_____

_____

_____

For More Information

The Best Work of Your Life, Pat Alea & Patricia Ann Mullins. New York: Putnam Publishing Group, 1998.

Change Your Job, Change Your Life: High Impact Strategies for Finding Great Jobs in the 21st Century (6th Ed.). Ronald L. Krannich & Caryl R. Krannich, Manassas Park, VA: Impact Publications, 1996.

What Color Is Your Parachute? A Practical Manual for Job-Hunters and Career Changers. Richard Nelson Bolles, Berkeley, CA: Ten Speed Press, 1998.

100 Best Careers for the 21st Century. Shelly Field, New York: Macmillan, 1995.

 See See Additional Readings for this unit on pages 231–237.

Essay Questions

Choose one of the topics below and write an essay about it.

1. Compare the employee-friendly companies you read about in this unit with other workplaces that you know about. How are they the same? How are they different?

2. Who is responsible for job satisfaction: the employee, the employer, or both? Explain and give examples.

3. What does an employee owe his or her employer? What does the employer owe the employee? Write a descriptive list of the rights and responsibilities of employers and employees. Give reasons for each item.

4. What is the general attitude about work in your country? How do people choose what work they are going to do? Do some jobs have higher prestige than others? Which ones? Do you agree with these attitudes?

Evaluating Your Progress

Think about the skills and strategies that you used in this unit. Check (✔) the boxes that apply to you.

	NEVER	SOMETIMES	OFTEN	ALWAYS
1. I was able to find the author's important points.	☐	☐	☐	☐
2. I scanned for key words.	☐	☐	☐	☐
3. I made accurate predictions when I previewed.	☐	☐	☐	☐
4. I understood complicated sentences by breaking them down.	☐	☐	☐	☐
5. I used the organization of the reading to help me to locate important information.	☐	☐	☐	☐
6. I thought about the strength of the author's argument as I read.	☐	☐	☐	☐
7. My underlining/highlighting/margin notes helped me to find useful information quickly.	☐	☐	☐	☐
8. I was able to combine vocabulary strategies to guess meaning.	☐	☐	☐	☐
9. I felt confident deciding that some words were not as important as other words.	☐	☐	☐	☐
10. I was able to make reasonable inferences.	☐	☐	☐	☐

Setting Your Reading Goals

Choose three items from the list above that you would like to improve. Write them below.

Goal #1: _____

Goal #2: _____

Goal #3: _____

1. CONSUMER WATCHDOG GROUP ANNOUNCES 1997 DECEPTIVE AD "WINNERS"

New York—The National Center for Consumer Education (NCCE) yesterday announced their 1997 Deceptive Ad Awards. These awards are given by the group every year for those advertisements that they consider to be the most dishonest. The awards are given in nine different categories. These categories refer to the most common advertising techniques or gimmicks. "Our aim is to educate the public about advertising," said NCCE head, Jane Donaldson. "Consumers need to understand how advertisers use psychological appeals to make them buy things that they do not need. For example, all of us want to be attractive. That's why advertisers use sex appeal to sell everything from cigarettes and gasoline to paint and pens. It's disgraceful how advertisers deceive consumers. Believe me, if consumers were well-educated, advertising would change completely."

When asked about the list, Philip Sage, head of the American Organization of Advertising Agencies (AOAA) said, "The advertising industry is essential to American business. We create need, that's true. However, that need creates jobs. People who criticize advertising should think about that."

Here are the 1997 Deceptive Ad Winners in the following categories:

1. Sex Appeal: The consumer will be more attractive to the opposite sex if they use this product.

The Montgomery Cigarette Company, for their series of ads featuring handsome men offering cigarettes to beautiful women.

2. Snob Appeal: The consumer will become more like the rich if they use this product.

Fancy Flavor cat food, for an ad showing cats eating out of crystal dishes.

3. Appeal to Tradition: The manufacturer says to the consumer, "We have made the best product for over one hundred years." Experience is the key. This may also include appeal to patriotism, "Buy American."

Sellmart Stores, for their ad that suggested that shopping at other stores was un-American.

4. Appeal to Authority: The advertiser uses a famous spokesperson, a television star, or a well-known athlete to sell the item. The ad implies that if you use this product, you will be as wealthy, famous, talented, or beautiful as this person.

Health Aid vitamins, for a series of ads with Olympic athletes that give the impression that these athletes achieved greatness by taking these vitamins.

5. Bandwagon: Everyone else has one, so if you don't have one, you will be different from everyone else.

Hamburger Hut Restaurants, for their ads that encouraged young children to make their parents take them to Hamburger Hut in order to become members of the Hamburger Hut Cool Kids Club.

6. Plain Folks: The advertiser says that the product is good for ordinary people. For example, a cereal manufacturer shows an ordinary family sitting down to breakfast and enjoying their product.

Simpson Soups, for their ads talking about the simple, homecooked flavor of their soups, which actually contain many chemical preservatives and artificial flavors.

7. Magic Ingredients: This gimmick says that the product has a secret ingredient that its competitors do not have.

Madox Pain Reliever, for ads that imply that their product contains a secret ingredient that other pain relievers do not have.

8. Transfer: The manufacturer uses illustrations and/or situations to make people feel good (or cool, warm, relaxed, etc.) and then connects this feeling with their product.

Acme Automobiles, for their ads that show

beautiful scenery totally unconnected to automobiles, which everyone knows often contribute to the destruction of lovely, unspoiled areas.

9. Wit and Humor: This technique makes the consumer smile and then connects the product with this good feeling.

Babble Baby Food, for their ads showing healthy, happy babies and their mothers but giving no information about the product.

2. CONSUMER REPORTS: SELLING TO SCHOOL KIDS

This report looks at selling to school kids, and includes sections on hard sells, the harm in the hard sell, mandatory TV watching, schoolhouse as billboard and recommendations.

HARD SELLS

Businesses, trade associations and other organizations target no less than 30,000 commercial messages to kids every single day. And those are just the ads on TV, radio, billboards and the like. Perhaps the most invasive advertising to children occurs in the nation's schools. In Colorado Springs, for instance, kids ride to class in school buses emblazoned with an ad for 7-Up soft drink. In some 400 schools nationwide, kids walk corridors filled with the sounds of pop music and commercials. In a growing number of schools, ads hang on the bathroom walls.

Once kids are in class, many of the study sheets, workbooks, audio-visuals and other instructional materials come with a message from a sponsor, and it's often a highly biased or manipulative message. For example:

• Eating meat makes people taller, according to study materials from the National Live Stock and Meat Board.

• Clear-cut logging (stripping entire hillsides of trees) is good for the environment, said materials from Procter & Gamble.

• Kellogg's Rice Krispies Treats is a snack food to choose "more often," according to a Kellogg

cereal guide that's supposed to help fourth- to sixth-graders learn "how to choose healthful foods."

• There are no endangered species, maintains the Council for Wildlife Conservation and Education, which turns out to be affiliated with the National Shooting Sports Foundation, an organization that has the same address as the Council for Wildlife Conservation and Education.

• Proving that Prego spaghetti sauce is thicker than Ragu is presented by Prego as a legitimate experiment.

THE HARM IN THE HARD SELL

Teachers, facing declining budgets, are often eager to use the free materials from businesses and trade associations. But such materials may teach kids the wrong lessons.

First, commercially sponsored activities and materials blur the line between education and propaganda. Unless these materials are handled with care by a skilled teacher who can show students how to recognize and discount the commercial content, they make it harder for students to discriminate between news and advertising, between the infomercial and the independent report, or between fact and fancy. Many of the sponsored materials on political or social issues fail to present differing points of view, to reveal who financed studies that support the sponsor's viewpoint, or to disclose information that reflects on the accuracy of the materials. The result is a distorted picture of the issues these materials cover.

Many school systems have voluntary guidelines and standards designed to protect students against biased, incomplete, discriminatory or blatantly commercial educational programming. Sponsored classroom materials often bypass any formal review process. Most are distributed free or at a nominal cost. Teachers also obtain materials directly or receive them unsolicited, sometimes supplied with professional journals or included in shipments of classroom magazines.

Financial pressures can easily make teachers

more dependent on "free" educational materials. Textbook catalogs show prices like $36.93 for a history text and $99 for a software program for teaching algebra. Yet in 1993, public-school spending for textbooks averaged only $45.91 per student. Businesses argue that their classroom materials and promotional programs augment tight school budgets, either by saving schools money or by giving them income from advertising. And some schools welcome the helping hand.

Some proponents argue that they can offer better-quality supplies or information not typically available in schools. Some suggest that in-school commercialism is a natural part of the movement to build closer partnerships between schools and the business community. And many teachers explain that they can and do evaluate incoming materials and serve as gatekeepers against excessive classroom commercialism.

Many parents and educators believe that commercialism cheapens education. As Alex Molnar, professor of education at the University of Wisconsin/Milwaukee, puts it: "The fundamental difference in the priorities of marketers and teachers distorts teaching as surely as a fun house mirror distorts the image of anyone who looks into it." Other critics point to the threat of a "shadow" curriculum, one that comes into the school through the back door, rather than through formal curriculum review.

Even more serious is the potential to compromise the teacher's ethics. When a teacher uses a commercially sponsored teaching aid, he or she is implicitly endorsing the sponsor or its product. And they do so before a captive audience of students who have been trained to trust what the teacher says.

MANDATORY TV WATCHING

In 1989, Whittle Communications inaugurated Channel One, a daily news program broadcast "free" to any school system that would promise to make it a mandatory part of the curriculum. The incentive: free use of the satellite dish, VCRs and classroom monitors needed to show the program.

Channel One is now viewed five days a week in 350,000 classrooms across the country. Two minutes of each daily 12-minute program are devoted to paid commercials from such sponsors as Snickers, Rold Gold pretzels, CareFree bubble gum, Pepsi and Reebok.

Each participating school signs a three-year contract in which it promises to show Channel One on 90% of all school days and in 80% of all classrooms. Channel One Communications owns the TV sets and other equipment, maintains them, insures them, and takes them back if the school drops its contract. Schools can use the equipment for more than Channel One programming. To the schools, everything is "free." They just have to deliver the audience of youngsters to the waiting advertisers.

Channel One reportedly reaches 38% of students in grades 6–12, about 8 million kids. It finds its largest audiences in South Central, Mountain and South Atlantic states, and has the smallest audiences in schools in New England and the Pacific states. A few states and a number of school districts forbid subscribing, and the number may be growing. The program is disproportionately shown in schools located in poor communities, where education money is most lacking, according to a University of Massachusetts study. Schools in wealthy communities are least likely to subscribe.

Channel One's stated purpose is as follows: To "use news and current-events information as a tool to educate and engage young adults in world happenings; make the daily news accessible, relevant, and exciting to younger viewers; promote awareness of the relationship between national and world events and every teen's individual life; encourage young people to become productive and active adult citizens by proving to them that they are participants in history, not just witnesses to it."

The fact that students are forced to watch this programming, and the commercials, is a major concern to its critics. "The teacher is no longer the driving force," former California Superintendent of

Public Instruction Bill Honig says. "They can't decide when and how to show the program."

Although the battle over Channel One has been triggered and fueled by its advertising and the outside control of the curriculum, the network's representatives have focused much of their defense on the educational value of the nonadvertising portion of the program. In 1990, Channel One commissioned a three-year study of the program's effectiveness in helping kids become more informed about national and world events. During the first two years of the study, the researchers found that students who watched Channel One did only slightly (about 3%) better on current-events tests than students who did not watch it. They found "a consistent advantage" for viewers in the third year, when they focused only on schools where the teachers made a special effort to integrate Channel One into class discussions. But the gains were fairly small: 5% for high school students and 8% for middle school students.

SCHOOLHOUSE AS BILLBOARD

Direct advertising, in which the school itself becomes the medium, has mushroomed in recent years, as marketers come up with ever more ingenious ways to tempt needy school districts. Some districts, hungry for funds, sell advertising space on the sides of school buses. Other districts might do the same if it weren't for state restrictions. In California, the Highway Patrol blocked the Fremont Unified School District's plan for school-bus ads, arguing that the buses had to be painted bright yellow for the sake of safety and visibility.

By filling a school's hallways, lobby and lunchroom with rock music and commercials, some administrators bring in up to $20,000 a year in extra cash. That is the pitch used by Star Broadcasting of St. Paul, Minnesota, which is now broadcasting Top 50 music and commercials into 400 school cafeterias across the country. For the 1994–1995 year, Youthtalk Advertising Agency in Salt Lake City has placed wallboards in 42 high schools in 10 of the state's school districts. An estimated 80,000 students saw the ads while sitting in stalls and standing at urinals.

Sports scoreboards probably get more attention than any other school surface. A logo or ad on a scoreboard receives the equivalent of prime-time exposure throughout the sports season. Advertising revenue can be significant, and many schools avail themselves of the opportunity. Soft-drink bottlers and distributors are among the leading supporters. Trouble is, direct advertising can put a school's hallways at the same level as an airport concourse, chockablock with ads and filled with the sounds of piped-in music. The billboards also carry the school's implied endorsement.

CONSUMER REPORTS RECOMMENDATIONS

CR believes schools should be ad-free zones, where young people can pursue learning without inappropriate commercial influences and pressures. But until that ideal can be attained, it's essential to control what's allowed to enter the schools. That's especially true for classroom materials provided by businesses. Information targeted to kids must meet higher standards than information aimed at adults. It should not exploit kids' inexperience, vulnerabilities and trust in those who teach them.

Corporate materials should receive searching critical evaluation from educators. Students need to be taught to critically evaluate sales pressures and to resist them. Educators and businesses need to work under a strict code for materials provided to schools. The code CR proposes is similar to guidelines prepared by the multinational organization Consumers International, and by the Society of Consumer Affairs Professionals in Business.

Corporate-sponsored materials in the schools should be:

• Accurate-consistent with established fact or prevailing expert opinion.

• Objective-a balanced representation of points of view.

• Complete-so they don't deceive or mislead students, either directly or by omission.

- Nondiscriminatory-free of content that could be considered derogatory toward a particular group.

- Noncommercial-with the corporate name or logo used only for identification. Educational materials should neither contain ads nor be veiled ads themselves.

PPENDIX: ADDITIONAL READINGS UNIT 2

1. ARRANGED MARRIAGE

In Japan there are two types of marriage: the so-called love marriage and the arranged marriage. The love marriage is the type we are familiar with in the West, where the couple meet independently without the assistance of a go-between or match-maker. Although the arranged marriage was pre-dominant in the past, the majority of Japanese marriages today are love marriages. Estimates vary, placing the proportion of arranged marriages at anywhere from 25 to 50 percent.

The modern system of arranged marriage is somewhat similar to blind dating in the United States. When a young woman reaches marriage-able age (now about 25 for a Japanese woman), she and her parents compile a packet of information about her, including a photograph of her in kimono and descriptions of her family back-ground, education, hobbies, accomplishments, and interests. Her parents then inquire among their friends and acquaintances to see if anyone knows a man who would be a suitable husband for her. The person who does becomes the go-between, showing the packet to the potential bridegroom and, if both parties are interested, arranging a meeting between them. (The man provides a pho-tograph and information as well.) Such meetings often take place in the restaurant of a posh hotel. The go-between is present, usually along with rep-resentatives from both families. If the young couple feel inclined, they will begin dating, with marriage as a possible—but not inevitable—result. It is not uncommon for a woman to have ten or more such introductions before she finds the man she wants to marry.

The young man and woman make the final decision about marriage between themselves, though they seek the advice and approval of their parents and their go-between. Some Japanese feel that romantic love is not the most important ingre-dient in a successful marriage; perhaps this belief is borne out by the fact that the divorce rate in Japan generally is lower than that in the United States. The divorce rate for arranged marriages in Japan is lower than for love marriages.

From the Asia Society's Video Letter from Japan: My Family, 1988, p. 36-37

2. THE CHEMISTRY OF LOVE

The violent emotional disturbance that we call infatuation (or attraction) may begin with a small molecule called phenylethylamine, or PEA. Known as the excitant amine, PEA is a substance in the brain that causes feelings of elation, exhilara-tion, and euphoria. But to understand exactly how PEA might contribute to attraction, you need to know a few things about the inside of your head.

The human brain is about the size of a grape-fruit, weighing approximately three pounds, with an average volume of about 1,400 cubic centime-ters. It is about three times larger than those of our closest relatives, chimpanzees and gorillas, whose average brain volumes are approximately 400 and 500 cubic centimeters, respectively.

In the 1970s neuroscientist Paul MacLean postulated that the brain is divided into three general sections. Actually, it is a good deal more complex than this, but MacLean's perspective is still useful as an overview. The most primitive section surrounds the final bulb at the end of the spinal cord. This area, which deserves its reputation as the "reptilian brain," governs instinctual behaviors such as aggression, territoriality, ritual, and the establishment of social hierarchies. We probably use this area of the brain in courtship when we "instinctively" strut, preen, and flirt.

Above and surrounding the reptilian brain is a group of structures in the middle of the head known collectively as the limbic system. These structures govern the basic emotions—fear, rage, joy, sadness, disgust, love, and hate. So when you are overcome with happiness, paralyzed with fright, infuriated, revolted, or despondent, it is portions of the limbic system that are producing electrical and chemical disturbances. The storm of infatuation almost certainly has its physical origin here.

Overlaying the limbic system (and separated by a large layer of white matter that communicates between brain parts) is the cortex, a gray, convoluted rind of spongy matter that lies directly below the skull. The cortex processes basic functions like sight, hearing, speech, and mathematical and musical abilities. Most important, the cortex integrates your emotions with your thoughts. It is this section of the brain that *thinks* about "him" or "her."

Here, then, is how PEA (and probably other neurochemicals, such as norepinephrine and dopamine) may play a role. Within and connecting the three basic parts of the brain are neurons, or nerve cells; there are at least one hundred billion of them. Impulses travel through one neuron and jump across a gap—a synapse—to the next nerve cell. This way they gambol along the neuronal highways of the mind.

PEA lies at the end of some nerve cells and helps the impulse jump from one neuron to the next. Equally important, PEA is a natural amphetamine; it revs up the brain. So psychiatrist Michael Liebowitz of the New York State Psychiatric Institute speculates that we feel infatuation when neurons in the limbic system, our emotional core, become saturated or sensitized by PEA and/or other brain chemicals—and stimulate the brain.

No wonder lovers can stay awake all night talking. No wonder they become so absentminded, so giddy, so optimistic, so gregarious, so full of life. Naturally occurring amphetamines have pooled in the emotional centers of their brains; they are high on natural "speed" or amphetamines, heightening the infatuation high.

PEA seems to have a powerful effect on nonhuman creatures as well as people. When mice are injected with PEA, they jump and squeal, a display of mouse exhilaration known in laboratory jargon as "popcorn behavior." Rhesus monkeys injected with PEA-like chemicals make pleasure calls and smack their lips, a courting gesture, and baboons press levers in their cages more than 160 times in a three-hour period to obtain supplements that maintain a PEA high.

Auden and Mencken probably described romantic attraction astutely. The feeling of infatuation may result from a deluge of PEA and/or other natural stimulants that saturate the brain, transforming the senses, altering reality.

But infatuation is more than exhilaration. It is part of love, a deep, "mystical" devotion to another human being. Is this complex sensation due solely to natural stimulants in the brain? Not at all. In fact, PEA may give us no more than a generalized sense of awakeness, alertness, excitement, and an elevated mood, as Sabelli suggests. Sabelli measured the amount of PEA released in the urine of parachute jumpers before and after a jump. During free-fall, PEA levels soared. A divorcing couple also experienced a PEA high during court proceedings. It appears, then, that PEA gives us no more than a shot of exhilaration and apprehension—a chemical high that accompanies a range of experiences, including infatuation.

By Helen Fisher
From *The Anatomy of Love*

1. STRESSSSSSSSSSSSS

"If I had my life to live over, I'd dare to make more mistakes next time. I'd relax. I'd limber up. I would be sillier than I have been this trip. I would take fewer things seriously. I'd try to have…just moments, one after another, instead of living so many years ahead of each day."
—Nadine Stair, age 85

We hear a lot about stress these days. But do we really give it the focus it deserves? Ongoing stress can exact a heavy price on our physical and mental well-being. We can't avoid stress; we must learn how to control our reaction to it.

Dr. Hans Selye defined stress in the 1950s as the "nonspecific response of the organism to any pressure or demand." Stress is the total response of your mind and body to the stressors you experience. It includes everyday wear and tear, both "good" (a promotion) and "bad" (fight with a friend) stressors. The stress reaction in itself is neither good nor bad. It can result in a feeling of exhilaration and eagerness. Without this in our lives, things would be pretty flat. However, the stress reaction is a process of mobilizing the body's resources and, if allowed to become ongoing, can deplete those resources, resulting in illness.

The major sources of stress are the environment, our bodies, and our minds. Negative stress begins with our appraisal of a situation. Feelings aren't caused by events, but by our beliefs about them. If we determine the event is dangerous, our stress reactions will kick in. Therefore, our perceptions are very important in how much stress we feel. Internalized stress keeps the mind agitated and throws the nervous system out of balance. It interferes with the immune response and produces stress-related disorders.

BIOCHEMISTRY OF STRESS

Stress has been recognized as an important factor in health. While we might perceive it as merely a nuisance, it can be very dangerous. It's been linked to everything from the common cold and insomnia to chronic conditions such as ulcers, asthma, diabetes, cancer, and cardiovascular disease. Unfortunately, our life styles have made stress nearly unavoidable. We often take pride in being too busy and in working punishingly long hours. The result can be an addiction to stress. Chronic stress can lead to premature aging and poor health.

Our bodies are constantly trying to maintain a balanced state (homeostasis). They react to any disturbance by trying to bring the body back into balance. If any of our homeostatic systems break down, we end up with illness. In the case of stress, the body tries to bring itself back to a pre-stressed state through biochemical changes.

Stress causes the adrenal glands to secret hormones. Among them are epinephrine and norepinephrine. They help the body cope with stress by preparing it to react in a decisive, physical way:

- muscles tense
- pupils dilate
- heartbeat quickens
- reflexes sharpen
- liver releases glucose
- blood clotting ability increases
- digestive system shuts down

In addition, increased cortisol breaks down lean tissue for sugar and blocks the removal of acids from the blood. Clearly, these are primitive reactions that would help us confront a bear, but aren't much help in coping with a public speech.

If the stress is initiated by a single, frightening event such as a fall, the body replenishes its energy and returns to balance. However, for most of us, the stress is ongoing and ill-defined. Since it doesn't end, our bodies never have an opportunity to rebuild energy. After long periods of trying to resist stress, our bodies simply become exhausted.

WHAT CAN WE DO?

Studies have identified attitudes that seem to protect people from the ill effects of stress. One of these is the approach we take to change. If we see it as a challenge rather than a threat, the stress response doesn't come into play. If change is viewed as an opportunity for growth and excitement, the physiological responses we just discussed don't occur. Our view of our past performances is a critical piece in this process. If we're constantly deriding ourselves for not doing well in the past, each new challenge is just another threat to our self-esteem. Perfectionism is deadly! We must be able to view our past efforts realistically and then let them go.

Establish Realistic Expectations

Try to look at your daily agenda differently. Set honest priorities—decide what you must get done today and what can be left for another day. We often get caught up in responding to urgent requests, but the urgent isn't always what's important. Stress can result when we don't get the important things done. Allow time for interruptions and distractions. If you can accept their inevitability, the time you spend dealing with them will be much less stressful.

Social Support

There's less illness and higher performance among those working with a strong, mutual goal. Seeking that type of work environment can go a long way toward reducing your stress, whether it's your job or volunteer and community work. Social support has also been related to increased coping skills and immune function.

Social ties and life satisfaction contribute to an attitude of acceptance rather than resistance to life events. If we can accept what life hands us, we'll have fewer stressful situations to deal with—it's prevention rather than coping.

Learn to Relax

Our Sympathetic Nervous System reacts to stress even before our feelings are aroused and we know what's happening. An opposite system, the Parasympathetic, has the role of returning the body to homeostasis. This system can be activated through relaxation techniques and is often referred to as the "relaxation response."

By learning how to activate this system we reduce wear and tear on the body. It also provides us with the self control to decide how to handle a situation and *act* on it, not *react* to it. By making changes in how we view our lives and learning how to activate our relaxation response, we can find joy in dealing with a rapidly changing world.

Relaxation Exercises

Relaxation exercises are wonderful tools to get your focus out of your head and into your body. Our constant logical planning and thinking are what keep stress levels high. Relaxation techniques that focus on breathing are especially good because this triggers other parts of the body to relax. By getting in touch with that part of your body that produces the opposite of the stress response, you'll eventually be able to call upon it at will.

Dr. Herbert Benson of the Harvard Medical School found the physiological effects of mental relaxation techniques produce biochemical changes that counteract the body's biochemical stress response. They can bring about the deep relaxation that's necessary for stress recovery.

Most experts on stress encourage deep, conscious breathing as a means to trigger the relaxation response. Many of us would be surprised at how shallowly we normally breathe. By concentrating on your breath, it is possible to clear the chatter from your mind and find some serenity.

Through practice it's possible to scan your body for tension, focus on it, relax, let go, and breathe it out. Some of these exercises can be done at any time. Think how much healthier it would be to stand in a long line (it's always the slowest one, right?) and focus on your breathing, finding tension, and relaxing it rather than getting frustrated, angry, and tense. You can't change the line, but you can change your response to it.

Listening to soothing music and concentrating on it, or your breathing, can be very relaxing. Massages are wonderful! Other useful exercises are imagery and visualization, meditation, yoga, t'ai chi, thought stopping, and hypnosis. Some people take classes, others use audio or video tapes to help them learn these skills. Whatever approach you choose, remember not to make this another task—have fun with it!

Assertiveness training can be helpful to those who face recurring anger. Time management may help the stressed realize what's important and be more realistic, resulting in more manageable expectations and a rational work process.

Make Time for Fun

A balanced life is critical to good health. Work, play, laughter, and love are all important. It's been shown that loneliness itself is a major form of stress. Join an organization to pursue a sport or hobby, take a class, find a support group, or start a book group.

Don't sit all day at your desk or load yourself down with drudgery. Eat lunch someplace new with a friend, go out to the movies, do something enjoyable and interesting each week, and don't sacrifice it to "practical" demands. Your good health is important, therefore, fun is important. Put it high on your list, make it count.

Physical Exercise

Don't forget physical activity! Think about the fun you had as a child when you were just "playing around" outside. If we go back far enough, most women will be able to find pleasurable memories. It's also true that many women never developed their athletic skills and may be hesitant at midlife to become physically active.

Regardless of your current physical conditioning there are many choices of activity available. A good brisk walk will definitely improve your men-

tal outlook and will have other health benefits as well, including cardiovascular fitness and stress reduction. Don't overlook new challenges. Taking tennis lessons, learning to golf or ski, or becoming a runner may be very viable options. Some women also try competition for the first time in midlife and find it's a real high.

Don't start an exercise program to reduce stress if it adds another "thing to do" to an already hectic schedule. Do take time to experience your environment, see, smell, hear, get away from your mental efforts and into your body. It can be as good as any relaxation program.

Sleep

We can't force ourselves to sleep. Many of us try too hard and thus make it impossible. Like relaxation, we must let go and let sleep come over us. Strenuous exercise (but not just before bedtime) often helps us achieve a sound sleep. But if it simply won't come and you can't shut down your busy mind, try to invoke the "relaxation response" (see page 000) or get up and do something else until you feel sleepy. A missed night's sleep is seldom the catastrophe we make it out to be when we're having trouble sleeping.

Eat Right!

You've heard this advice before—avoid smoking, caffeine, and sugar. In addition, many professionals recommend vitamin and mineral supplements to combat stress. Although a well-balanced diet should supply what you need, the quality of our food these days and the kinds of things we eat can result in deficiencies. When you're under stress, your need for these critical nutrients increases.

As with all dietary issues, it's wise to discuss your particular needs and sensitivities with your health care professional.

From Midlife Woman

2. EMOTION: THE KEY TO THE MIND'S INFLUENCE ON HEALTH

Candace Pert, one of the most respected researchers in the area of mind/body medicine, noted in Bill Moyers' Healing and the Mind television series that emotions registered and stored in the body in the form of chemical messages are the best candidates for the key to the health connection between mind and body. It is through the emotions you experience in connection with your thoughts and daily attitudes—actually, through the neurochemical changes that accompany these emotions—that your mind acquires the power to influence whether you get sick or remain well.

The key, according to Pert, is found in complex molecules called neuropeptides. "A peptide is made up of amino acids, which are the building blocks of protein. There are twenty-three different amino acids. Peptides are amino acids strung together very much like pearls strung along in a necklace." Peptides are found throughout the body, including the brain and immune system. The brain contains about 60 different neuropeptides, including endorphins. Neuropeptides are the means by which all cells in the body communicate with each other. This includes brain-to-brain messages, brain-to-body messages, body-to-body messages, and body-to-brain messages.

Individual cells, including brain cells, immune cells, and other body cells, have receptor sites that receive neuropeptides. The kinds of neuropeptides available to cells are constantly changing, reflecting variations in your emotions throughout the day. The exact combinations of neuropeptides released during different emotional states has not yet been determined.

The kind and number of emotion-linked neuropeptides available at receptor sites of cells influence your probability of staying well or getting sick. "Viruses use these same receptors to enter into a cell, and depending on how much of the natural peptide for that receptor is around, the virus will have an easier or harder time getting into the cell. So our emotional state will affect whether we'll get sick from the same loading dose of a virus."

This kind of conclusion from a researcher at the cutting edge of research on the mind/body connection should give you all the motivation you need to undertake the 8-Step Humor Development Training Program. Your sense of humor helps assure that these chemical messages are working for you, not against you. "The chemicals that are running our body and our brain are the same chemicals that are involved in emotion. And that says to me that... we'd better pay more attention to emotions with respect to health," says Candace Pert.

It was noted earlier that preliminary research suggests that humor/laughter stimulates the production of helper T-cells, the cells attacked by the AIDS virus. If humor was to help the body battle AIDS (there is presently no evidence that it does—or does not), it probably wouldn't be as a mere result of the production of more helper T-cells, since there would be every reason to expect these new cells to also be invaded by the virus. Rather, it would probably be due to the neuropeptides produced by the positive emotional state that goes along with humor and laughter.

Along these lines, Pert has noted that "The AIDS virus uses a receptor that is normally used by a neuropeptide. So whether an AIDS virus will be able to enter a cell or not depends on how much of this natural peptide is around, which would be a function of what state of emotional expression the organism is in."

This research will not be exhaustively reviewed here, but some of the major studies will be presented to show you that there is no longer any doubt that your daily mood or frame of mind makes a significant contribution to your health—especially when the same mood or emotional state persists day after day, year after year. Anything you can do to sustain a more positive, upbeat frame of mind in dealing with the daily hassles and problems in your life contributes to your physical health at the same time that it helps you cope with stress and be more effective on the job.

Your sense of humor is one of the most powerful tools you have to make certain that your daily mood and emotional state support good health, instead of working against it. Humor also helps you maintain a healthy lifestyle in general, a practice that is increasingly being recommended by health care professionals as the country shifts toward an emphasis on preventive medicine.

Excerpt from Chapter 1, Health, Healing and the Amuse System: Humor as Survival Training By Paul E. McGhee, Ph.D.

3. ZEN AND THE OLYMPICS

Sometimes a perfect body isn't enough. At the top, whether you win or lose may depend on how you think about the game.

Here's how Rebecca Snyder remembers it: she was walking past the other air-gun shooters to take her place on the firing range. At stake was a spot on the national team and, perhaps, an Olympic berth. She felt good, strong—almost cocky. Her mouth was filled with a chunk of watermelon bubble gum. She sighted down the barrel of her gun and started firing. A solid 90 out of 100. Then a 92, a 93 and a 96. In the finals, where they count tenths, a near-perfect 98.1. "Every time I put the gun up I expected to shoot a bull's-eye," she says. "I was telling myself, 'This is so easy, it's just there today'."

Every athlete knows the feeling. The ball looks bigger. The game slows down. They have different names for it, of course: the zone, flow, harmony, the Zen moment. At the Olympics, the physical condition of the athletes is as close to perfect as human beings can get. The difference between a trip to the medal stand and a quiet plane ride home may be all in the mind.

A mind "in flow" can make an athlete seem invincible, but getting there isn't easy. "It seems to be the result of total concentration on a doable task, which can be physical, intellectual or even emotional," says Mihaly Cshikszentmihalyi, a psychologist at the University of Chicago and author of "Flow: The Psychology of Optimal Experience."

Chsikszentmihalyi started calling this state of mind "flow" 25 years ago as part of his research on happiness. But sports psychologists soon recognized that athletes describing how they felt when they were at their best sounded very much as if they'd been in flow. So why should a blissed-out state of mind enhance performance? The key is the type and amount of attention an athlete pays to the task. In a series of studies, sports scientists at Arizona State University have looked at the brain waves of archers, shooters, and golfers in the seconds before they release a motion. The researchers found decreases in activity in the left hemisphere of the brain, the hemisphere thought to handle rational thought. The decline in left-hemisphere activity represents less attention to the mechanics of the action and more on how it feels. And only certain ratios of left-to-right-hemisphere activity correlate with peak performance, suggesting that there is an ideal frame of mind.

Fear factor: Olympians have practiced their events much of their lives, but repetition guarantees only know-how. Psychological factors such as stress or fear can intervene, throwing execution off. Almost every sport now consults psychologists to help athletes integrate mental focus with physical ability. Visualization, self-hypnosis, even tapes of simulated competitions with the voices of the Olympic announcers all hone the mind-body link. Foil fencer Felicia Zimmermann repeats key words to keep herself focused. Backstroker Tripp Schwenk envisions every stroke of a race.

The athletes want to connect mind with body because performing perfectly requires the synchronization of literally millions of neural and muscular events. Visualization may cue the body to launch that optimal set of movements. A high-definition mental TV is especially important in events like weight lifting, where lifters have no way of knowing what a record weight will actually feel like, or canoe/kayak, where the paddlers don't get to try out their course. Says Dragomir Cioroslan, coach of the U.S. Weightlifting team: "We train for imagery just as we train for muscles and technique."

Though the psychologists might not be sure what's going on in flow, they know a few things about how to get there. In a beautiful irony, the harder athletes try to win, the less likely they are to find their zone. "Any time you get into that state where you're thinking about the result instead of what you're doing, you're pretty much screwed, to use a scientific term," says Shane Murphy, a sports psychologist and consultant. That's an ancient notion—since the 13th century, students of kyudo,

Japanese Zen archery, have been forbidden to even aim at a target until they perfect their drawing and firing. Even today, says Janet Dykman, a U.S. archer, "I try to have no emotion about what happens to the arrow. I just concentrate on my form." And the arrow lands smack in the bull's-eye of harmony.

By Adam Rogers with Peter Burkholder
From *Newsweek*

APPENDIX: ADDITIONAL READINGS UNIT 4

1. AMERICANS AT WORK
THE INC./GALLUP SURVEY

This year's news: workers in the United States say that times are good (still), that local businesspeople are heroes, and that the global marketplace is very scary (though they think the economy benefits when we do business abroad). The survey also reveals that one out of eight full-time employees moonlights; that youth is still wasted on the young (Generation X-ers claim the most job security but the least satisfaction); and that when it comes to praise in the workplace, women like it in writing, boomers like it more than they get it, and small companies are quickest to hand it out.

Those are among the findings of the second annual Inc./Gallup survey of American workers. You'll read about those and other discoveries in the comments annotating the survey results, below. And you'll see reflected in those notes two unmistakable patterns: when it comes to job satisfaction, Americans in smaller workplaces have it better, but Americans who own their workplaces have it best.

1997 SURVEY*

1. On a 5-point scale, where 1 is extremely dissatisfied and 5 is extremely satisfied, how satisfied are you with your place of employment?

*Percentages do not add up to 100% for some questions because of rounding and "don't know" responses.

5	35%
4	37%
3	18%
2	6%
1	4%

2. At work, do you have the opportunity every day to do what you do best?

Yes	82%
No	17%

3. Does your supervisor or someone at work seem to care about you as a person?

Yes	82%
No	14%

4. In the past seven days, have you received recognition or praise for good work?

Yes	60%
No	40%

5. Do you know what is expected of you at work?

Yes	97%
No	3%

6. At work, do your opinions seem to count?

Yes	82%
No	17%

7. Is there someone at work who encourages your development?

Yes	70%
No	29%

8. In the past six months, has someone at work talked to you about your progress?

    Yes   62%
    No   38%

9. This past year, have you had opportunities at work to learn and grow?

    Yes   84%
    No   15%

10. Are your associates (fellow employees) committed to doing quality work?

    Yes   86%
    No   12%

11. Does the mission of your employer make you feel that your job is important?

    Yes   85%
    No   14%

12. Do you have the materials and equipment you need to do your work right?

    Yes   87%
    No   13%

13. Do you have a best friend at work?

    Yes   57%
    No   43%

14. Do you believe you will continue with your current company until you retire?

    Yes   55%
    No   39%
    Don't know   6%

15. Do you feel that you have been recognized fairly by your employer for your contributions?

    Yes   74%
    No   25%

16. Are you more secure or less secure in your job than you were a year ago?

    More secure   61%
    About the same   19%
    Less secure   20%

17. From your most objective viewpoint, have you been compensated fairly this past year?

    Yes   19%
    No   30%

18. Which of the following is the most effective way an employer can recognize you as an employee?

An annual performance evaluation   6%
A cost-of-living raise   11%
A raise that is tied your performance   44%
Public recognition in front of
all employees   9%
A personal note from your manager or
supervisor recognizing your achievements 14%
A promotion or higher title   10%
More benefits   0%
Bonus   0%
Other   1%

19. Do you currently work at a second job?

    Yes   13%
    No   86%

20. Is this second job a business of your own, or someone else's?

    Own   44%
    Someone else's   53%

21. Do you expect this second job to be your primary source of income in the future?

    Yes   23%
    No   77%

22. How long have you been working at your second job?

    Less than 1 year   21%
    1 year to less than 3 years   23%
    3 years to less than 5 years   16%
    5 years to less than 10 years   12%
    10 years or more   26%

23. Have you ever owned your own business?

    Yes   30%
    No   70%

24. Do you still own that business?

    Yes   55%
    No   45%

25. Would you ever consider starting your own business?

    Yes   64%
    No   35%

26. Have you taken steps to start your own business?

    Yes   19%
    No   81%

27. Do you plan to go into business for yourself in the next two years?

    Yes   15%
    No   83%

28. Thinking about the next ten years, which one of the following best describes what is most likely to happen with regard to your present job?

    You will stay with current employer   42%
    You will be forced to change jobs
    because of job termination   4%
    You will voluntarily choose to
    change jobs   36%
    You will leave the labor force
    permanently   12%
    You will leave the labor force temporarily   4%
    Don't know/refused to answer   2%

How the Inc./Gallup survey was conducted: In January 1997, the Gallup Organization conducted a nationwide survey for Inc. magazine. All participants were required to be at least 18 years old and employed at least 30 hours a week. With the survey methods used and a sample of 801 respondents, the resulting maximum expected error range, at a 95% confidence level, is plus or minus 3%.

By Michael Hopkins and Jeffrey L. Seglin
From *Inc. Magazine*

2. WORKING HARD AT FINDING WORK

We've all heard reports that the current economy has been murder on the job market. But unemployment statistics aside, are your chances of securing gainful employment really dead?

Not at all—if you're willing to apply yourself.

Whether you've been laid off by a company forced to cut payroll or you're merely determined to find a more fulfilling position, discouraging economic figures do mean that finding another job may be more difficult now than before the recession. But let those same figures be the inspiration you need to approach your search in a more vigorous and organized fashion.

The days of merely answering want ads or sending out resumes, and then waiting for the perfect job offer to come to you-have definitely passed. Today, you'll need a thorough strategy, lots of bravado and a telephone.

STEPS TO A SUCCESSFUL SEARCH

Begin with a plan. To prepare yourself, find a book that can provide some novel techniques and concrete ideas on where to start and exactly how to proceed. *Find the Job You've Always Wanted in Half the Time with Half the Effort*, (Contemporary Books) by Jeffrey J. Mayer, offers advice on streamlining and modernizing job search strategies. Take some time to think about what kind of job you really want. What tasks did you enjoy in previous positions? Pinpoint skills and talents by remembering what things came easily and assessing notable accomplishments.

In other words, determine exactly what keeps you happy and motivates you to perform at your best. Mayer suggests taking the time to make detailed lists in all these areas, and then refining them down to discover your specific job target.

Use unconventional ways to scout out potential employers. Since many jobs are never advertised, it's important to keep in contact with as many business professionals as possible. Include family members, business associates such as your lawyer or banker, and former co-workers when formulating a list of contacts.

Add names from industry journals and business magazines to the list. Don't forget that becoming active in social clubs and community organizations can also open up opportunities. In short, create a network of relationships to extend the range of your search.

Make contact with these professionals by calling them regularly. Be as bold and persistent as you can, because the fact is that most important people are extremely busy. If you get through, don't waste their time—explain your connection immediately and take advantage of the opportunity to sell yourself.

Always keep in mind the purpose of your call—attaining an interview.

RULES OF THE RESUME

A resume—approximately two pages of written information summarizing your skills and work history—may be the only thing standing between you and a job interview. And if a resume was not required prior to the interview, you'll need to leave one upon its completion. For this reason, writing an effective resume should be a high priority.

Simplicity is the key to a standout resume. A short and concise write-up of your career objectives, qualifications, education or training and employment history is all you really need to include. You may also list any professional or civic group affiliations you feel are relevant. Don't add unnecessary information such as marital status, and never submit a photo.

With each submission, include a cover letter that states the position you're applying for and how your skills would benefit that particular company. The cover letter can be an important tool for tailoring your resume to match the needs of the employer.

Make a good first impression by submitting a resume as flawless and professional as possible. Print it out with a computer on heavy white or ivory cotton and linen paper, or have it printed by a service.

Don't underestimate the importance of this short but telling document. A little extra effort could keep it out of the circular file and get you a promising interview.

INTERVIEWING CONFIDENTLY

You've worked so hard to get to this point, and theoretically it should be the easiest part. After all, you've been answering questions your whole life with few hang-ups. But why, why do you feel this way? Panic is looking over your shoulder and you'll do anything to keep it from answering for you.

Control your fear by preparing and practicing. Read up on how to make the best impression.

Sweaty Palms: The Neglected Art of Being Interviewed, by H. Anthony Medley (Ten Speed Press), or *Hire Me! Secrets of Job Interviewing*, by *Patricia Noel Drain* (Price, Stern, Sloan), offer a wealth of confidence-building advice.

Experts agree that a neat appearance is very important when it comes to making a favorable first impression. Stylish but conservative dress is considered professional. Apply any make-up tastefully, and pay attention to body language like fidgeting that can reveal your nervousness.

Show some foresight by reading up on the company. It will help you relate to the interviewer. Practice before the interview with a list of potential questions. Both of the above books provide such a list to work with. However, resist the temptation to offer "canned" answers during the actual interview. Be honest and give real, thoughtful replies.

Finally, be optimistic and enthusiastic. Convince the interviewer that not only your skills, but your attitude as well, would be a valuable addition to their workplace.

By Jennifer Plantier
From Ethnic NewsWatch
© SoftLine Information, Inc., Stamford, CT

3. DREAMS: A WORK IN PROGRESS

LOOK OUT, WORLD. Ruby Gary is on her way.

Now a volunteer coordinator from Hempstead, she had gotten the word early on from a high school guidance counselor that "black kids from poor families could not become fashion designers."

"Ruby," she remembers him saying, "you should go to school for something that a black person could get a job doing."

But Gary, 40, got more encouraging advice this year. That word—that people of any race and age can realize their career dreams—spurred her on to develop fashion workshops for plus-size women. "I feel more powerful and confident," she said. "I wouldn't tolerate someone saying that to me now."

That's what meeting twice with Barbara Sher did for her. Sher is a therapist, career counselor and author of several books, including *Live the Life You Love—In Ten Easy Step-by-Step Lessons* (Dell, $9.95), which won this year's Books for a Better Life award given by the New York City Chapter of the Multiple Sclerosis Society in conjunction with a committee of book executives.

Sher said people often don't act on their career dreams, not out of laziness or weakness, but because of internal resistance, which she says is nature's way of protecting us from risk. To outwit it, she says, you have to start with actions so small they "sneak beneath the radar of your resistance."

Actually, relatively few people—around 25 percent—select satisfying careers to begin with, says Juliet Miller, executive director of the National Career Development Association in Alexandria, Va. Another 50 percent may not have trained for work they find rewarding, but are able to "self-correct" along the way, finding a niche that works for them. And 25 percent are unhappy and just plain stuck, needing more help and support in righting themselves, she says.

Sher met with five *Newsday* readers who had written in telling of their blocked career dreams. Instead of a traditional office meeting, Sher suggested an "idea party" at some casual setting like an Italian restaurant in Greenwich Village. So the group headed to the Minetta Tavern, first in January, then later for a follow-up.

Sher is not an advocate of the positive-thinking approach. In fact, over antipasto she said to the group, "Everybody talks about positive thinking, and it's great if you feel that way that day. But if you don't, you have to live anyway…and nobody's ever accomplished anything in this world in one mood."

What followed was a frank, freeing and sometimes painful discussion. One by one, she coaxed out each person's dream and his or her obstacles to moving ahead. She then gave each a brief strategy for getting unstuck and asked each to make a "temporary permanent commitment" to pursue that dream. Such a commitment can last for two minutes, an hour, two weeks or a month, she says. And it allows you temporarily to silence that internal "should I or shouldn't I?" debate.

The participants' reactions? Gratitude, hope, disappointment, and pain. One shed tears at confronting her unfulfilled dreams. But all came back to the second meeting, most having made progress or experiencing greater insight into their roadblocks and future paths. Here are their stories.

A DREAM IN ACTION

With her hopes of becoming a fashion designer dashed, Gary went to business school and now works as coordinator of volunteer resources for the American Red Cross in Nassau County. She finds her job rewarding, but still, that vision of working in fashion has persisted.

"I have a good eye for design," she wrote in a letter to *Newsday*. "I can look at a piece of fabric and feel it. I can see it on the body. I can see it in my head and visualize it moving along the lines of a person's frame."

However, she has not actually done any designing or sewing, so Sher's first advice was for Gary to get her hands on fabric immediately by volunteering as an assistant costume designer for an amateur theater group. That didn't feel quite right to Gary, so Sher suggested instead that she visit other members of the group and pull together outfits from their closets.

"Nothing big ever came of something that didn't start small," Sher said. "You haven't had your hands on fabric. You've got to do that first…the most important thing is doing it as soon as possible. Not going to college and getting a degree to do it, but doing it."

So Gary followed through and came to the second session with fresh insight—the idea to develop a side-profession as an image/fashion consultant to plus-size women, women who she says need to hear they are "sexy and fashionable and great." From there, who knows? A book? A video? Appearances on Oprah? All seem possible to Gary now.

Said Sher, "You were dreaming before and not doing anything. Can you see the difference between dreaming and any action—even low-risk things like going through peoples' closets? Suddenly it gets real."

Gary agrees. She grew confident when near-strangers heeded her advice about coordinating clothes and accessories. "I felt I could make changes in my life," she says. "I was ecstatic to hear Barbara Sher say, 'You were born to do this.' "

OVERCOMING INERTIA

Like many people stuck in safe but unfulfilling jobs, Michael Frisch, a machinist helper for the City of New York, returns to his home in Ozone Park, Queens, with no energy or motivation to plunge into the work he truly loves, restoring automobiles.

He dreams of going back into business for himself. Ten years ago, he owned a machine shop that made high-performance engines. In his letter, he wrote of being "in heaven" running that business, but money got tight so he took his present job, which resulted in the closing of his auto shop. "I am 34 years old going on 70," wrote Frisch, who has since turned 35. "Every day I feel like a piece of me is wasting away."

Frisch actually thought Sher might suggest he leave his job, but no dice, she said. "You need the money and the health insurance." Her strategy, instead, was to help him get re-engaged with his passion in his off time, first by finishing work he had started on two of his own cars, a Nova and a Dart, and then by developing a side business that he eventually could switch to full time.

To do that, though, Sher needed to help him get over his inertia. First, she told him to pretend his boss said, "Everyone is now working three days a week at the same benefits and pay. Only the other four days you've got to do what you love. You can't just sit home and switch channels."

She also suggested he get rid of the Dart, which was preventing him from moving forward. "Take a loss," she said. "If you can't cut your losses, you go down with them."

That notion, says Frisch, did the trick. "I had been afraid to spend more money on the car," he says. "Whenever you build a hot rod, you do it for yourself. It's not a money making proposition…I figured either way I would lose money, so I might as well spend some and finish." Now, he is working on both cars and also researching a muffler franchise.

What has he learned going forward? When trying to reach a goal, "you don't have to use all your time. You can move an inch a day and that's still progress."

ALL IN THE DETAILS

"I have always wanted to be a writer," Jennifer Maglione, 26, of Bellerose, Queens, said in her letter. She told of writing prizes from high school and well-meaning parents who encouraged her pursue a degree that would offer her job security. She wrote that after training as a nurse and a paralegal, "I am still haunted by the knowledge that I never tried to achieve my dream."

But she felt intimidated at the thought of all the competition in the writing field, and that kept her from starting.

Sher's prescription? To stop thinking of becoming a successful writer, and envision the details of writing, the exact time, place, tools and process she would use.

"The specifics will save you," said Sher. "When you start thinking of something grand, like, 'My God, I want to be a writer,' you're thinking about the wrong stuff." When those thoughts do surface, "go back to the details."

Maglione's temporary permanent commitment: to turn out a book, not necessarily in its final form, by Dec. 31. Indeed, she has enrolled in a writers' correspondence course and completed two assignments. She's also replaced her typewriter with a computer.

She was briefly sidetracked by the notion of going into acting, but Sher helped her see that was a distraction from her commitment—the fear of missing out on something. "I learned," says Maglione, "that if you worry over which to choose, you're not putting effort out to go for anything."

Other lessons: It's never too late to listen to your inner voice and make a change. Also, after each session, she says she felt inspired, but that waned in a few days. "The world can come in on you very quickly," she says. Talking to Gary occasionally helped revive the zest. "We would cheer one another on."

STIFLED BY COMPETITION

Not everyone in the "blocked careers" group progressed at the same pace or in the same ways. Eugene Le Panto, 48, of Centerport, says the experience was fun, but he still feels like "a dormant volcano waiting to erupt." He had been a gallery visual artist; a stand-up comedian; and an aspiring writer of comedy, screenplays and essays. He now works in a well-paying technical capacity and says he has a nice house and a terrific wife. But, he says, "The job that sustains is also the job that enslaves."

He still yearns to step into a more creative role, perhaps as an actor, writer or stand-up comedian.

"At times I have confidently produced and excelled," he wrote, "despite the stresses of life and the myriad of available excuses." Still, he calls himself a "notorious procrastinator."

At the first session he talked of deep-rooted competitive feelings toward his late father, whose ambitions were not realized. Sher told of how such feelings can prevent people from moving ahead. Surpassing a parent would be destroying him or her, she said. "Children suffer more pain for their parents than the parents suffer for themselves."

Her advice for Le Panto: "Let the child inside of you weep for how sad you are that your father didn't get to make it. Let your heart break. You've been carrying this hurt heart around."

Although the sessions offered him no revelations, Le Panto said articulating the issue was helpful: "It was recognition of the father-syndrome from someone outside the confines of my cranium." He continues to write letters to film producers and advertising agencies in hopes one will bite.

A LATE START

Janis Cappiello, 42, from Franklin Square, wrote to tell of the challenge of blending career dreams with the demands of being a single mother. She told of her disappointment over a failed restaurant business and her sense of playing second fiddle to her estranged husband. Yet, she also said she was starting to realize she has talents, "degree or no degree."

She came to the first meeting determined to open a new restaurant, not as someone's assistant but running the show. So Sher discussed with her the business proposal, financial backing and locations. Her temporary permanent commitment was to find someone to help her write a proposal and have one drafted within 30 days.

Cappiello also shared the pain of wanting something so badly, but stopping herself for so long from getting it. Sher gave her an A+ for allowing emotions to surface. "There's enormous dignity in pain," she said. "You've got to be strong to cry."

Cappiello came to the next session with new perspective. Though a restaurant is still a dream, she decided for now to expand her catering side-business and allow herself time to work on her own personal development.

Sher applauded that approach. "Being good to yourself is one of the best lessons you can teach a child," she said, asking everyone in the group to imagine their own mothers saying, "No dinner tonight. I'm sitting outside and looking at the evening come down on the flowers."

"Imagine you got peanut butter sandwiches," said Sher, "and you went out there and watched your mother. Imagine that you got that instead of dinner once in a while. You'd feel a lot happier for her. We need our beds made as much as we need our mothers to write poems now and then."

Cappiello says she feels a new sense of peace, thanks to what Sher said in response to someone's comment about getting a late start: People often fritter away their first forty years. "The first forty don't count!"

By Patricia Kitchen, staff writer
From *Newsday*, Long Island, New York

CREDITS

p. 7 Excerpted from "Trees." By Joyce Kilmer. Reprinted with permission of Jerry Vogel Music Company Inc.; **p. 7** From *Happy Days* by Ogden Nash. Copyright 1932 by Ogden Nash. First appeared in *The New Yorker*. By permission of Little, Brown, and Company; **p. 7** By Jef I. Richards. Every effort has been made to contact the author of the material and to obtain permission for its use; **p. 10** Adapted from "An Overview of Advertising," by Richard F. Taflinger, Ph.D., Edward Murrow School of Communication, Washington State University. Copyright 1996; **p. 14** Art reproduced with permission from Volkswagen of America, Inc.; **p. 20** Adapted from "An Overview of Advertising," by Richard F. Taflinger, Ph.D., Edward Murrow School of Communication, Washington State University. Copyright 1996; **p. 21** *The 3rd of May 1808 in Madrid*, by Francisco de Goya, courtesy of Museo Del Prado; **p. 23** *The Scream*, by Edward Munch, courtesy of the National Gallery, Oslo, Norway; **p. 29** Adapted from "Characteristics Of Top-Scoring Advertisements in Specialized Business Magazines" by Cahners Business Information Corporate Research Department. Copyright 1991, Cahners Business Information, a division of Reed Elsevier, Inc.; **p. 41** Adapted from "Nine Steps to Great Print Advertisements," "An Even Dozen Ideas to Make Your Ads Produce More Results," and "Another Even Dozen Ideas to Make Your Ads Produce More Results," by Art Seigel, *SalesDoctors Magazine* (http://salesdoctors.com); **p. 53** Adapted from "A Short Course in Creativity," by Thomas McNamee, Results Direct.com (http://resultsdirect.com); **p. 69, p. 93,** and **p. 224** Adapted from *The Anatomy of Love: The Natural History of Monogamy, Adultery, and Divorce*, by Helen E. Fisher. Copyright 1992 by Helen E. Fisher. Reprinted by permission of W.W. Norton & Company, Inc.; **p. 74** "Strangers in the Night," words by Charles Singleton and Eddie Snyder, music by Bert Kaempfert, copyright 1966, 1994 by Champion Music Corporation and Screen Gems-EMI Music Inc. All rights for Champion Music Corporation are controlled and administered by MCA Music Publishing, a division of Universal Studios, Inc. Copyright renewed. International copyright secured. All rights reserved; **p. 98** Bailey, Beth, From *Front Porch to Back Seat*, Baltimore, Johns Hopkins University Press, 1988; **p. 103** Adapted from "The Rules: Time-Tested Secrets for Capturing the Heart of Mr. Right," by Elizabeth Gleick, *TIME*, copyright 1996; **p. 108** Reprinted and adapted from *The Psychologist's Book of Self-Tests* by Louis Janda. Copyright 1996 by Louis Janda. Permission granted by The Berkley Publishing Group, a member of Penguin Putnam Inc. All rights reserved; **p. 121** Adapted from "Thinking yourself healthy: over 12,000 readers reveal the seven mind-sets that matter most," by Cathy Perlmutter, *PREVENTION Magazine*, Vol. 48. Reprinted by permission of *PREVENTION Magazine*. Copyright 1996, Rodale Press, Inc. All rights reserved; **p. 131** Adapted from "Mind Body-Connection," by Kelsey Menehan, The Center for Mind/Body Medicine, copyright 1996; **p. 141** Adapted from "The Mental Edge," by William F. Allman, copyright August 3, 1992, *U.S. News & World Report*; **p. 147** Adapted from "The Stress Cure That's Right for You," by Daryn Eller. Copyright 1995. This article originally appeared in *Redbook*; **p. 155** Adapted from "Laughter as Therapy for Patient and Caregiver," by Patty Wooten, from *Pulmonary Rehabilitation Guidelines for Success* 2/e, edited by JE Hodgkin, Philadelphia, Lippincott-Raven Publishers, 1993; **p. 160** Adapted from "Healing Words," by Daniel Redwood, DC, copyright 1995; **p. 171** From *The Practical Guide to Practically Everything*, by Peter Bernstein and Christopher Ma, Random House, New York, 1995; **p. 173** Adapted from "From sky diving instructors to fashion consultants, some folks just love their jobs," by Meredith Kramer, *Colorado Springs Gazette Telegraph*, March 11, 1996. Reprinted with permission of Knight-Ridder/Tribune Information Services; **p. 180** Adapted from "Get Into the Flow," by Katherine Griffin. Reprinted from *Health*, copyright 1994; **p. 193, p. 196,** and **p. 204** Reprinted with permission of *Inc.* magazine, Goldhirsh Group, Inc., 38 Commercial Wharf, Boston, MA 02210: *How to Hire New Employees*, Joshua Hyatt, March 1990. *Hiring the Best*, Bruce Posner, April 1989. *What It Takes*, Browkaw, Murphy & Seglin, November 1992. (http://www.inc.com) Reproduced by permission of the publisher via Copyright Clearance Center, Inc.; **p. 200** Adapted from "The First 100 Days," by Patricia Kitchen, *Newsday*, November 26, 1995. Reprinted with permission. Copyright Newsday, Inc., 1995; **p. 210** Adapted from "Make Your Resume Do the Work," by Carla Wheeler, *The San Bernardino County Sun*. Copyright, Gannet News Service, 1995; **p. 221** "Selling to School Kids," copyright 1995 by Consumers Union of U.S., Inc., Yonkers, NY 10703-1057. Reprinted by permission from *Consumer Reports*, May 1995; **p. 224** From "Video Letter from Japan: My Family," The Asia Society, 1988. Reprinted with permission from TDK; **p. 226** Adapted from "Stressss," *MidLife Woman*, issue 1.2; **p. 229** From *Health, Healing, and the Amuse System: Humor as Survival Training* by Paul McGee. Copyright 1996, by Kendall/Hunt Publishing Company. Used with permission; **p. 230** From *Newsweek*, July 22. Copyright 1996, Newsweek, Inc. All rights reserved. Reprinted by permission; **p. 233** "Working Hard at Finding Work," by Jennifer Plantier, *The Network Journal*, April 1994.; **p. 234** "Dreams: A Work in Progress," by Patricia Kitchen, *Newsday*, May 18, 1997. Reprinted with permission. Copyright Newsday, Inc., 1997